Seeing the Big Picture

A Cinematic Approach to Understanding Cultures in America

REVISED EDITION

ELLEN SUMMERFIELD
and
SANDRA LEE

University of Michigan Press

ISBN-10: 0-472-03167-8
ISBN-13: 978-0-472-03167-2

Published in the United States of America
The University of Michigan Press

Manufactured in the United States of America

♾ Printed on acid-free paper

2009   2008   2007   2006   4   3   2   1

Contents

Acknowledgments

The authors wish to express gratitude to many groups and individuals who have lent support and assistance during the making of this book.

We owe enormous thanks to our (nocturnal) research assistant, Michele Duley, for her fearless exploration of the virtual world—many of the Internet suggestions are hers—her award-worthy annotations, her donut charts, her proofreading skills, and her terrific sense of humor, night and day. Michele's work has been exceptional.

To our friend Gloria Flower go special thanks for her generous help at a critical time. A researcher extraordinaire, Gloria's informational searches and emotional support proved invaluable.

For his splendid work on the maps and drawings, we are grateful to Steven Shoffner.

We wish to thank the wonderful library staff at Linfield College for their expertise and willing assistance, especially Jean Caspers, Sue Davis-DeHut, Carol McCulley, Frances Rasmussen, and Barbara Valentine. For technological assistance, we thank Paula Gunder.

We gratefully acknowledge the many American and international students in both our campus-based and online courses at Linfield College and Oregon State University who have thoughtfully worked with versions of the evolving manuscript. We are particularly indebted to the students who have contributed their points of view to this text.

In past years, The Oregon School for the Deaf has welcomed us and our students to its campus many times, and we have greatly appreciated the expert advice of ASL instructor Fred Farrior. We are also very thankful to student members of Fusion, the Linfield College gay/straight alliance, who have made regular visits to our classes, helping us and our students understand issues affecting gays, lesbians, and bisexuals.

Both of us extend heartfelt thanks to the generous readers of our work-in-progress: Rosario Aglialoro, Hussein Baradi, Carlos Cortés, Kate Gregory, Carlos Maeztu, Bahram Refaei, and Ann Schauber. Among the many friends, colleagues, and film lovers who have helped us along the way, we acknowledge with special appreciation David Budd, Christine Callaghan, Judy Carl-Hendrick, Toby Frank, Hyung-A Kim, Nandini Kuehn, Tammy Loveall, Candido Salinas, Sandy Soohoo-Refaei, and Cheryl Voelliger.

Sandra Lee thanks her grown children, Kate and Daniel, for their movie "reviews" and for hanging in there through a second book. Ellen Summerfield acknowledges with special affection her husband, Phillip Pirages, a gifted editor who has good naturedly reviewed the entire manuscript multiple times and who has watched more than his share of cross-cultural films.

We consider ourselves most fortunate to have worked with Kelly Sippell of the University of Michigan Press. A person who uniquely combines vision and practicality, Kelly has expertly guided us through the entire process of publication. We have thoroughly enjoyed our collaboration with her.

Grateful acknowledgment is given to the following authors, publishers, and individuals for permission to reprint their materials or previously published materials.

Erin Fleming for "Expand Your Life" signing photograph.

Nikki Giovanni for permission to reprint "The Funeral of Martin Luther King" from *Black Judgment*. Copyright © 1968 by Nikki Giovanni.

Michele Duley for three graphs.

The Joan Hawkinson Bohorfoush Memorial Foundation for permission to reprint excerpts from *Scarves of Many Colors: Muslim Women and the Veil* by Bill Bigelow, Sandra Childs, Norm Diamond, Diana Dickerson, and Jan Haaken. Copyright © 2000 by the Joan Hawkinson Bohorfoush Memorial Foundation.

Steve Kelly for "It's Time to Reclaim America" by S. Kelly, San Diego Union-Tribune. Copyright © 1994.

Library of Congress, Prints and Photographs Division, for photo of "Negro Man Entering Movie Theater by 'Colored' Entrance," LC-USF331-030577-M2, and photo of Irish immigrants.

Museum of the City of New York for the image from *The World of Suzie Wong*. Copyright © 1960.

MyFamily.com, Inc. for permission to adapt material from "Easy Steps to Writing Your Family History" by Valerie Holladay, *Ancestry* (Vol. 21, No. 4, August–July 2003).

Naomi Shihab Nye for "Muchas Gracias Por Todo" from *Fuel*. Copyright © 1998 Naomi Shihab Nye. Reprinted with permission of BOA Editions, Ltd., *www.BOAEditions.org*.

Oxford University Press for the image "White Man's Mocassins" by Lee Marmon from *Indi'n Humor: Bicultural Play in Native America* by Kenneth Lincoln. Copyright © 1993 Oxford University Press.

Syracuse Cultural Workers for permission to reprint "How to Build Global Community" artwork by Melinda Levine. Copyright © 2002 Melinda Levine/SCW Community.

Sierra Club Books for permission to adapt material from *In the Absence of the Sacred: The Failure of Technology and the Survival of the Indian Nations* by Jerry Mander. Copyright © 1991 by Jerry Mander.

Steve Shoffner for maps of "Ten Indian Culture Areas in North America," "Growth of United States by Region and Appropriation of Indian Lands," and for "Sign Language Alphabet."

We would also like to thank Pamela Bennett, Michele Duley, Fred Farrior, Erin Fleming, Fay Hurtado, Michelle Greenlee, Lorene McClure, and Yonghua Yang for giving permission to use their writing in the Point of View Sections.

Every effort has been made to contact the copyright holders for permission to reprint borrowed material. We regret any oversights that may have occurred and will rectify them in future printings of the book.

To the Students:
Developing Your Film Eyes

Some years ago, those of us working in the international office at our college sent a newly arrived Asian student to meet her host family—a welcoming, kind-hearted African American family who over the years had received students from many countries. The next day, the student came into our office in tears. She said she wanted a "real American family."

A similar thing happened in an overseas program. An Anglo American male student studying for a semester in Paris was placed with a host family of Vietnamese origin. Having barely met them, he complained that they were "not really French" and asked to be reassigned. The parents in this family were French-speaking citizens of France and long-time Parisian residents, and their children were born in France.

What is happening here? What were the two students expecting? From their point of view (p.o.v.), they may have felt they were not getting the true American or French experience. What about the p.o.v. of the two host families? Did they see themselves as somehow inauthentic?

Do you think we should have allowed the two students to move? If so, what type of new host families should we have chosen? What could we have said to the original host families by way of explanation? What if, on the other hand, we had asked the students to stay? What could we have explained to them to help them understand our p.o.v.?

Let's talk about p.o.v. Used in film, it refers in a narrow technical sense to the placement of the camera. Some scenes are shot from what seems to be no point of view at all—from a seemingly neutral or objective stance. The camera seems to function simply as a recorder, and we are like spectators looking into a scene as if it were happening before our own eyes in real life. Here the camera tries to be invisible.

Sometimes, however, we are thrust into the p.o.v. of a film character. This happens quite dramatically in point-of-view shots, when the camera is placed at the eye level of the character and gives the impression that we are looking through his or her eyes. An excellent example is the scene in *Witness* (1985) where the eight-year-old Amish boy Benjamin is wandering through the Philadelphia Amtrak station. We see and hear things as he does. The camera moves at "child's-eye level," and we walk around as Benjamin does, taking things in from his p.o.v. So, when Benjamin becomes a witness to a crime, we do, too (Bone 1997, 88).

Flashbacks of the kind you will see in *The Joy Luck Club* (1993) are also an expression of point of view. When a particular character like the Chinese mother An-Mei flashes back to a childhood experience in China, we are receiving that experience through her memory—that is, through her p.o.v.—and thus we can better understand why she behaves as she does in the present. This type of p.o.v. gives information about a character's psychological or emotional state.

Point of view in film is also used in a more general sense to refer to the particular angle or perspective from which part of the film, or the film as a whole, is being told. The movie *Smoke Signals* (1998), for example, is told from Native American points of view. We see the world through the eyes of the screenwriters, director, and main actors, all of whom are American Indians.

Everything in film—not only the camera position, but also the composition, editing, sound, and so on—influences p.o.v. This quotation from Michael Hilger's *The American Indian in Film* (1986) explains how film techniques in traditional westerns are used to bias viewers against Indians:

> The long shot, which emphasizes the setting, often stresses the landscape of the West, with either hostile Indians hiding or threatening to attack, or conquered Indians vanishing into the horizon in long processions. High angle shots, in which the audience looks down on the subject, may suggest the vulnerability of the whites about to be ambushed by Indians. Low angle shots . . . can emphasize the threat of the Indian lurking above his victims or [else] the power of the hero. (4)

Hilger further explains how editing—especially cross-cutting between pursuers and pursued (rapidly alternating the shots of the two groups)—heightens fear of the threatening Indians. **Composition,** the term for how actors and objects are placed within the camera frame, generally situates (white) heroes in positions that are higher, more central, or more in the foreground, reinforcing the idea that they are superior. Sound, such as menacing drums and rescuing bugle

calls, also sends clear messages to the audience about who the ene-
mies and the heroes are.

Though we will not be focusing in this book on the technical aspects
of filmmaking, we will ask you to look at films in new ways, becoming
aware of how certain techniques affect p.o.v. Most of you have undoubtedly grown up with movies and television, and you already possess a
rich store of experiences with visual media. But you may be used to
viewing feature films primarily as entertainment. This is not to say that
we are denying the value of entertainment. We are both great fans of the
films discussed in this book, and we hope you will enjoy them as much
as we do. But we also want you to develop a new set of film eyes and
ears. They need to be skeptical, questioning, and always alert to p.o.v.

Read and print out the two-part article (beginning and
advanced) "Film Viewing: How to Watch Movies Intelligently and
Critically" at *www.filmsite.org/filmterms.html*, and keep it available for
easy reference. It gives you great tips—such as how to use freeze-
frames to understand composition and what to look for in the final
credits of a film. As you read the article, underline and make mental
notes of terms that are new to you. Familiarize yourself now with
the basic language of cinematography (e.g., types of shots, lenses,
and camera angles) and with editing techniques (e.g., fade-ins, fade-
outs, and dissolves), and be able to describe the responsibilities of
personnel such as the director, producer, and behind-the-scenes
technicians. When you have questions later in the course, you can refer
to the excellent glossary on this site and at *http://www.imdb.com/Glossary*.
In each chapter of your textbook, the **Sneak Preview** sections will
help you build on your knowledge.

As you develop your film eyes, you should find that they enable
you to look at other forms of media differently as well. You'll begin to
see how everything we read, watch, and hear in our media-filled
world is presented from a particular point of view. Even relatively
"objective" media forms such as documentary films and *New York Times*
articles are still to be understood as interpretations. Every filmmaker
and journalist has a unique slant, a personal take on the material. One
documentary filmmaker may, for example, tell a story about the suc-
cesses deaf students experience at Gallaudet University, while another
may present a story on the failures. While both stories may be true,
they leave us with entirely different impressions. To give a second
example, if you have seen any of Michael Moore's documentaries—
like *Fahrenheit 9/11* (2004)—you know that he makes his p.o.v. quite
obvious from beginning to end. Other directors of documentaries may

not be this open about where they stand, or they may not take as extreme of a stance as Moore, but they nonetheless all have their own perspectives that are given expression in their films.

What about your p.o.v.? In each chapter of the book, you will be asked to articulate your views verbally and in writing. Please keep all of your written work in your film notebook. (We suggest that you use a three-ring binder and that you date your entries.) Many of our students have found that their film notebook has become a valuable record of the class, including in some cases poetry, sketches, and photographs. In addition to using and creating a film notebook, you'll want to write in, and "converse with" this textbook. Please get in the habit of marking up or annotating all the readings—making comments in the margins, underlining, and writing notes and questions. This will help you to become an active reader and to remember what you learn.

If you find it difficult at first to express yourself, know that you are not expected to have final opinions at this stage. You are exploring and discovering your own views and those of others. Along the way you may feel uncertain or confused, you may change your mind, or sometimes you may just wish to think silently.

As you ponder your own positions, often the best thing you can do is listen to others. In this course you will learn a great deal about American cultures and subcultures, not only by watching the films and reading the texts, but also by giving your full attention to other students' points of view. Your peers will bring to the discussions cultural backgrounds and experiences different from your own, and at times you may find yourself reacting to what they say with surprise, disbelief, or even shock.

For example, you will have the opportunity to learn and talk about different religious beliefs and practices at various points in the course. Many of us are unaccustomed to talking about religion with people whose beliefs differ from our own. Also, encountering new religions can be difficult, disorienting, and confusing. (It can also be fascinating and exhilarating.) It may help you to remember that outsiders observing your own form of worship (which seems entirely natural to you) may experience similar feelings of alienation. At the end of this section, you will find a Japanese student's initial reaction to her visit to a Roman Catholic Mass. She was clearly perplexed and even somewhat distressed. This is a normal and fine reaction. It's a first step. When she talked in class about her feelings, Catholic students were able to offer some helpful explanations. (See the guidelines in Appendix B for visits to religious services and places of worship.)

Whatever your initial reactions may be in class discussions, try to realize that differences between you and others are valuable resources for learning. It is precisely these differences that will lead to more interesting, enlightening discussions and to a clearer understanding of the films you have viewed together. To help make your discussions as productive, satisfying, and worthwhile as possible, we suggest some guidelines as outlined in the **Respect Agreement** in Appendix A. These guidelines will allow you to express yourself more freely and be confident that your peers will treat your comments with respect and interest, regardless of their own perspectives.

Depending on the topic or exercise, your instructor will ask you to work with a partner, in groups, or with the entire class. If you find it difficult to speak in front of groups, you might make a conscious effort to try one or more of the specific discussion roles that follow. These roles can allow you to contribute to a discussion without feeling pressured to make a brilliant remark, have special oral skills, or be an expert on the topic at hand. Gradually, as you grow more comfortable in the group and more familiar with the topics, you can begin to drop the roles. Also remember that in any discussion you may adopt multiple roles.

The roles are also useful for those who may already be confident and experienced in group discussions but who tend to play the same roles all the time.

1. **Rebooter**—you help to get the discussion restarted or recharged whenever it begins to lag.
2. **Affirmer**—you provide encouragement to others by nodding, agreeing, and so on.
3. **Includer**—if you become aware that a group member is being left out, you can verbally or nonverbally encourage that person to join in. You might express your interest in hearing the person's point of view.
4. **Tension reliever**—if a discussion becomes heated, you may be able to inject a lighter note or make the group laugh without trivializing the topic.
5. **Questioner and clarifier**—you ask questions to gain information, provoke thought, clear up misunderstandings, and stimulate further discussion. This role is often underutilized.
6. **Navigator**—if you become aware that the conversation is going

off course or that your group is running out of time, you politely help to keep the discussion on track or bring it to a close.

7. **Recorder**—you jot down the main points your group has made. You may be called upon at some point to provide a summary.

Please feel free to add other roles to the list. In your film notebook, identify two roles: one you feel you can play easily and another that you feel less confident about but would like to try.

We'd like to reemphasize the idea that no one develops a well-informed p.o.v. in isolation. Only by listening to others and taking their views into careful consideration can we begin to get a sufficient sense of the bigger picture necessary to define our own position intelligently. An ancient Chinese proverb tells us *Two good talkers . . . not worth one good listener.* A more modern take on the same idea is the saying that *God gave us only one mouth to speak but two ears to listen.*

Why is it sometimes so hard to listen to each other? In our teaching experience, we've observed two main barriers to listening. The first is a values barrier. Just how many pro-choice people and anti-abortionists are really able to LISTEN to each other? When deeply held values are concerned, all of us tend to shut down.

The second barrier is power. If we are a member of the power group, we don't really have to listen to the minority or take interest in less powerful individuals or groups. We may not even realize how important it is to keep listening. If, on the other hand, we're in the minority, we may, out of sheer frustration and even anger, stop listening to what the more powerful have to say.

Your job in this course is to find ways to cross these barriers. Please try to take every opportunity to learn about values, points of view, and ways of life that may be very different from those you have grown up with or have come to cherish. The multicultural golden rule is: *The greater the differences, the more important it is to explore them.* Don't be surprised if you find yourself feeling defensive or annoyed in the process of opening up and exchanging views. Looking beyond (or outside) the beliefs one identifies with is never easy.

Native Americans knew this. Their saying that you should not judge others before walking a mile in their moccasins is a well-known expression used in many contexts. Try to take not just a few steps but to walk for a while in the p.o.v. of others before dismissing it or them. This is the only way we will begin to close some of the gaps that divide us; heal some of the wounds we all feel; and begin to create a more sane, more peaceful future.

Student's P.O.V.

I went to St. James this morning. First, I was very surprised that on a pole there was a place with some water, and they brought their finger to their forehead. I was like "What!!!?" I felt very nervous because I wasn't used to it, so I didn't do as they did. When they prayed, and said *amen*, they moved their hands from their forehead to their stomach, and from their left chest and right chest. I thought "What are they doing!!!" Before the priest read the Bible, the priest held the Bible and walked around the stage with two little girls on both sides of him. . . . ???? When someone wanted to say something on the stage, they had to bow, and they could go up to the stage. I thought this is the rule for this church. At the end of the ceremony, we had to line in front of the priest. The priest held something to eat in his right hand, and he gave the food to just certain people. When I went to the front of the priest, he touched my head with his left hand. In Indonesia to touch another person's head means an insult, and also the left hand is regarded as a dirty hand. If the priest did the same thing in Indonesia, people who don't believe in this religion will be very mad.

—Marisa Haruta, exchange student from Japan

Explanatory Note: At the entrance of Catholic churches are fonts, or bowls, filled with holy water. When Catholics enter the church, they dip one or two fingers into the water and bless themselves by making the sign of the cross. Crossing oneself is done by touching one's forehead, center of the chest, left shoulder, and right shoulder while saying, "In the name of the Father, and of the Son, and of the Holy Ghost. Amen." The stage Marisa refers to is the altar from which the priest leads the service. In Catholic tradition, altar boys assist the priest with the ceremony, so this church is quite progressive in having altar girls. Marisa observed that when members approach the altar, they bow. Near the end of the service (called Mass), members receive Holy Communion from the priest. They line up and receive a "host," or wafer, of consecrated bread. According to Catholic doctrine, the host is the actual body of Christ, the bread having been changed during the Mass through the miracle called transubstantiation. Formerly the priest placed the host on the tongue of each member, but now some priests simply place the wafer in each member's outstretched hand. Why did the priest touch Marisa on the head? In the past only Catholics would line up to receive Communion, but today sometimes non-Catholics line up simply to receive the priest's blessing, or touch. Having an Indonesian mother and being familiar with customs in that country, Marisa was taken aback by the fact that the priest used his left hand and touched the top of her head.

To the Instructor: Behind the Scenes

Our Goals

In writing *Seeing the Big Picture,* our primary goal has been to broaden students' awareness, understanding, and appreciation of the many cultures and subcultures in the United States today. We believe film is a splendid tool for this purpose, as it provides insights into the ways in which cultures are both similar and different—in their values, histories, and verbal and nonverbal modes of communication. Film also facilitates discussion of topics related to ethnicity, religion, and sexual orientation that might otherwise seem too controversial or too sensitive.

In the process of using and experimenting with different parts of this text, we have seen both American and international students benefit enormously from an exposure to the breadth of diversity in America. Despite an increasing emphasis on multicultural education in our schools, most of our students seemed to know only a smattering about the various cultures we discussed, and they appreciated the opportunity to learn more.

In learning about others, students will, of course, reflect on their own culture, language, and worldview and use these as benchmarks for comparison. They are often surprised to discover that they suddenly want to know a lot more about their own cultural background.

We also try to help students learn to analyze and evaluate more critically what they see on film and, by extension, in the media generally. Whereas at the beginning of the course students might be tempted to believe what a film tells them about a culture they do not know, by the end, they will know how to ask probing questions. Bombarded daily by media images as we are, this skill seems indispensable to us.

Finally, we also aim to help both native and non-native speakers of English develop and refine their language abilities. The course is designed to provide students with tools to become more attentive listeners and readers, more thoughtful and articulate discussants, and better writers.

Our Audience

Seeing the Big Picture can be used in a wide range of educational settings. We have used the materials with excellent results in different kinds of classes focusing on topics of multiculturalism and diversity—required freshmen writing courses with native and non-native speakers of English (called Inquiry Seminars at our college), ESL courses at intermediate and advanced levels, and online courses offered through the department of adult education. The titles of our courses are "Exploring American Cultures on Film" and "Diversity in American Cinema."

We also believe the text is suitable for introductory college classes in areas such as American studies, English composition, film, communications, history, anthropology, and ethnic studies. We can envisage its use as a training tool for diversity workshops in the workplace. And we hope that instructors of English or other subjects in countries abroad might find it useful and interesting.

Getting Started

To prepare your students for the cultural and cinematic journey on which they are about to embark, we advise first reviewing with them the introductory chapter **To the Students.** Here students are asked to think about what it means to be American. To what extent does American still mean white American, both in the minds of people who live within our borders and those who view us from the outside?

Students are also introduced to the concept of point of view (p.o.v.), which is a unifying theme throughout this text. In a country as diverse as the United States, we all need to gain increased understanding of how others view the world, and we need to learn how to talk with each other across lines of difference. The process is often a bumpy one, and emotions can run high. To facilitate communication, we recommend establishing a **Respect Agreement** at the outset of the course (see Appendix A). The principle underlying this agreement is a willingness to listen respectfully to each other's views, regardless of differences of opinion. We advise introducing the Respect Agreement in the first class meeting, asking students to make changes or additions to it if they wish, and requesting that they sign on to it. They should know that it is a working document that can be reviewed and revised at any time.

Additionally, we encourage conscious use of **Discussion Roles** (see pages xiii–xiv). These show students that they do not have to make a profound remark or be an expert on the subject at hand in order to join a discussion. Rather, they can simply ask a question or request clarification. We are not suggesting that you formally assign these roles to specific students but that you draw attention to them. You can encourage your students at various times during the course to assess the discussion roles they use most frequently and try new ones. We've actually had our best success advising students on an individual basis; one very articulate young man, for example, was great at expressing his own views but rarely showed interest in others, so we encouraged him to try being more of a questioner.

Sequencing the Films and Allotting Time

We usually follow the sequence of films as it is presented in the text. Of course, you can change this order or select only certain films to meet your course objectives. However, we advise handling the more sensitive material, such as the chapter on gay culture, later in the course. By then, students have become better acquainted with each other and have built trust with you and one another. Also, **Creating Community** is intended to be, and probably works best as, the concluding chapter.

We have designed this text for use in either a quarter or semester term of ten to fifteen weeks, meeting at least three hours per week. If you spend one or two class periods discussing **To the Students,** you can devote two to three weeks to each feature film and spend one final class session on the **Flashback/Flashforward** closure activity. In this way, you should be able to study four or five feature films per quarter or semester. In a year-long course, students can immerse themselves in all the films and cultures.

We realize that there are more chapters, with more material within each chapter, than you will probably use. We have never tried to use in one course all the chapters or all the exercises in any of the chapters; they are there simply to provide options for you.

One idea we have used very successfully is to give (in addition to assignments done by the entire class) one "Assignment of Choice" in each chapter. The students can choose from **Your P.O.V.** or any of the other sections, or they may follow up on a question or website from **History Flashback.** Students seem to appreciate being able to choose, and they like to share their results.

Using the Film Notebook

We ask students to collect all their writing, from the roughest notes to the more formal, polished entries, in a three-ring binder. As the course progresses, the film notebook becomes a valuable resource, providing ideas for future essays, research papers, and oral reports, depending on your course requirements. Students should be encouraged to use their film notebooks not only for the written exercises in the text, but also as a place to jot down thoughts while watching the films or listening to class discussions.

We collect selections of work from the film notebooks at regular intervals. We do not promise to read every word; rather, we skim through, commenting in the margins and annotating with a check-mark (✔), plus (+), or minus (–) to indicate the degree to which thought and energy are being applied to the task at hand. Of course, you may wish to assign formal grades to the more polished pieces of writing. More than the grades, however, students seem to appreciate receiving our notes and comments.

The film notebooks are an important source of information for us as instructors. We are able to track the students' academic progress and also to gain insight into their struggles with the emotional content of the material. Again and again, we read in the notebooks of problems and questions that simply do not surface in class discussion. Depending on the student and the issue, we can then decide how best to respond.

When we see particularly creative, interesting, well-written work—especially the sections expressing p.o.v.—we ask students to share their writings in class. This is when some of the most careful listening skills and attention to others' p.o.v.s can be developed. Also, students are often astonished by the capabilities of classmates and are inspired to do better themselves.

Viewing the Film

We recommend that students view the films directly after they have read and discussed the **Sneak Preview** and before they read the **History Flashback.** In our experience, students are eager to watch the films, so we don't like to delay too long. Having seen a film, they approach the accompanying history section with more curiosity and focus. Also, the historical background makes more sense to them when they can relate it to the film.

What about the logistics involved? We have had no difficulties asking students to view the films outside of class as part of their homework. If your school or university has a media center, you can buy or rent the film and put it on reserve for students to borrow. Some students appreciate this, but others choose to share the rental cost of a video or DVD and watch with their peers in their home or residence hall. With just a few exceptions, the DVDs should be easily accessible in local video stores. Be sure to tell students in your syllabus about convenient, relatively inexpensive mail services (see suggestions on pages xxix–xxx); some students may decide to become members for the period of the course to avoid having to search for films.

Whenever possible, we try to make film-watching a weekend assignment so that students can more easily fit it into their schedules. Getting together on their own to watch the films gives them the opportunity to clarify questions and share their initial reactions immediately after viewing. This kind of informal activity outside the classroom also helps to reinforce trust and foster positive group dynamics. We've been pleased to see that many adult students watch and discuss the films with their families. In online courses, students have used the film assignment as a chance to get together.

Guidelines for Using the Exercises

Most instructions are embedded within the exercises; however, some additional guidelines are offered here. We have made every effort to formulate exercises that you and your students will find interesting and instructive. They are designed to help students practice the different skills of reading, writing, listening, speaking, thinking critically, developing media literacy, and empathizing. (This last skill is developed as students become more adept at seeing different points of view.) Please be aware that not every exercise is included in every chapter; you can, however, find them all in the chapter on *Smoke Signals*.

Setting the Scene: Freewriting and Discussion

This exercise is intended to break the ice, capture students' attention, and elicit their initial p.o.v.s. Freewriting can be done in or out of class. We try to make **Setting the Scene** a fairly quick exercise, perhaps five minutes of writing and ten minutes of exchanging ideas with a partner or group.

Sneak Preview: About the Film, the Filmmakers, and the Actors

This section provides background information to help students to focus their "film eyes"; attune their "film ears"; and begin asking new questions about a film's credibility, importance, and p.o.v. For example, does the film break new ground in its depiction of a culture? What are the director's credentials for making a particular film? Are the actors credible representatives of the culture? Are the setting and props authentic? What do insiders and reviewers say? This section gives the students some of the tools, information, and vocabulary necessary to increase their film literacy.

As you see in the section **To the Students,** we encourage class members to mark up this book with questions, underlining, and marginal notes. Occasionally, you might want to remind students to read with pen in hand and interact with the text. If after some weeks their pages are looking too blank, you can give them prompts, asking them, for example, to write responses in the margins—as they read—to questions like: *What surprised you? What did you agree with or find questionable? Did anything make you angry or upset? What did you find confusing? What would you like to know more about? What would you like to talk about in class?* We specifically like to ask them to note what it is about **Sneak Preview** that entices them to watch the film or dissuades them.

Who's Who in the Film

We include this section so that students can become more sophisticated in their discussions and presentations, referring to filmmakers and characters by their exact names. Especially when foreign names are involved, the students can make good use of the **Who's Who** boxes.

Terms to Know

We have provided lists of selected terms relevant to each culture. While these lists are far from exhaustive, we hope that you and your students will find them useful. You will probably want to spend extra time on the terms in the sections on gay and Muslim Americans, since many of these are unfamiliar or commonly misunderstood. Students in your classes who belong to the cultures featured in the text may be able to provide further explanations and clarifications on the terms and their usage.

History Flashback

This section makes the statement that cultures simply cannot be understood without history. We trust that you can help your students realize that if they are to undertake the hard and important work of understanding people different from themselves, they must be willing to study the past.

In our experience, the students have very much enjoyed and benefited from these reading sections. We always worried that they were too long but that never seemed to be the case. Students seem especially pleased when parts of the films that were unclear to them all of a sudden make sense. In hindsight, they begin to pick up all kinds of small details that they missed before. Familiarity with the historical background helps them enjoy and appreciate the film more. For example, the film *Far and Away* (1992) becomes much richer when one is informed about Irish immigration. Even students who already are quite knowledgeable about certain aspects of U.S. history have been glad to refresh their memories.

Notwithstanding the students' positive responses, we strongly suggest giving them short reading tasks or activities as incentives to study the **Sneak Preview, History Flashback,** and **Spotlight** sections carefully and become actively engaged. Rather than putting these instructions into the text, however, we prefer to leave it to you as to what works best for your group.

One easy, reliable task is simply to ask students to select one website from the **History Flashback** section, explore it, and write a paragraph in their film notebooks about why they chose it and what they learned from it. Another effective, simple task is to ask students to find a relevant website we didn't include and recommend it to others. A third possibility is to ask students to respond to one or more of the questions we pose within the readings. For example, in the chapter on Chinese Americans, we ask if director Wayne Wang portrays the male characters in *The Joy Luck Club* (1993) in stereotypical ways.

Additionally, generic reading tasks like these two have worked well:

1. Based on the reading, create a quiz of three to five factual or opinion-related questions for your peers to answer verbally in pairs or small groups. Be sure to make a note of the answers for yourself.

2. Respond in a focused freewrite in your film notebook to these cues: Before reading this text, I had assumed that. . . . After reading this text, I learned that. . . . The authors provoked my curiosity about. . . .*

Points of View: Director's, Insider's, Student's, and Poet's

These p.o.v.s run throughout the text. They are intended to give the students thought-provoking perspectives that they might not otherwise encounter and to help them realize how broad the panorama of perspectives on a given topic can be.

....

*This exercise is adapted from a similar one described in John C. Bean's *Engaging Ideas* (San Francisco: Jossey Bass, 1996), 142.

Cultural Backpacking: Real and Virtual

This exercise has proven extremely rewarding as students discover an aspect of the culture they are studying, write about it in their film notebooks, and give a presentation on their findings. Although we allow students to do virtual exploring, we see this more as a backup than a first option, and we hope you will encourage your students to experience a new culture firsthand.

We recall how one of our students from Hong Kong was reluctant to embark on his cultural backpacking assignment to discover Mexican America, especially when he spoke absolutely no Spanish. Taking his American roommate with him for moral support, he ventured to a Mexican bakery in our small town and came back elated. Not only did he try his first Mexican dessert, but he also returned with a stack of photos. The welcoming Mexican proprietor had made him feel at home and thereby helped break down the student's stereotypes. The student returned to class with a fresh p.o.v.

We have been using the cultural backpacking exercise regularly with students of different language abilities, nationalities, and ages, and they all seem to find pleasure and meaning in it. It gives them an extra little push to venture out (and you might want to emphasize that they'll need to leave their comfort zones). For some students, that might mean using chopsticks for the first time, and for others it might be more like joining the Chinese or Asian student organization on campus. You'll find that some of the ideas students come up with are surprising and ingenious. One student, for example, toured a Chinese garden, another attended a performance of a gay men's chorus, and another took a class in belly dancing.

Our adult students often take their families along on their cultural backpacking trips, so everyone explores and learns. Occasionally, but rarely, a student has an unpleasant experience. (One Anglo student who went to a Mexican party felt she was being hit on by the men, for example, but she later realized in class discussion that they were probably just being friendly.) Students are often impressed and moved by the warm and welcoming reception they receive as "tourists." So, in addition to the many other rewards, we see this as a valuable community-building effort. Please encourage and remind your students to thank verbally and in writing anyone who has been especially helpful to them in their backpacking explorations. Of course, you may decide to organize one or more class field trips rather than having students choose their own destinations.

Diversity Detective

This activity is similar to **Cultural Backpacking** in that its success depends on students' ingenuity and resourcefulness. Most students seem to welcome the challenge of tracking things down, especially on the Internet, and, in the process of searching, they learn lots of things related to their topic.

Spotlight

The **Spotlight** exercise presents a single theme from the respective film and culture that we want to highlight in order to raise students' awareness. Racial profiling, body image, and language/dialect prejudice are a few of the key topics. In several of these exercises, we ask students to select and show clips from the film to illustrate the point under discussion, which can make for lively classroom discussion. Whenever students show clips—in response to **Spotlight** or other assignments—you can take the opportunity to ask about, or point out, film techniques.

What's Cooking?

This light, enjoyable exercise is an excellent way of bringing your students together for an in-class cooking session or a trip to a local restaurant. You may be able to combine **Cultural Backpacking** with **What's Cooking?**; for example, we mention in the text that if you visit a Chinatown, you can make time for a meal. We realize that finances can be a problem, and a few times we've been able to receive modest amounts of money from institutional funds. In some of our classes, we've brought samples of different ethnic snacks to pass around during breaks, and inevitably students will begin to bring snack foods from their respective cultures to share.

Many students also seem to like trying out recipes on their own—from beverages like chai (Arabic tea) and laban (a yoghurt drink) to tortilla soup and fry bread. One student reported that her fry bread was delicious, but another said hers came out a bit dense, like coasters or Frisbees, on which her children smeared peanut butter and jelly. An adventuresome student made an entire Irish dinner for her family, with steak and Guinness pie for the main course and barm brack for dessert, which she said was a big hit.

When we asked students to reflect on what they learned from the **What's Cooking?** exercises, their responses reinforced for us the unique role of food in promoting cross-cultural learning. One student said cooking allows her to journey to a new place. Another discussed the research she did to understand recipes, such as looking up the meaning of "shin of beef," "knob of butter," and "double cream" for Irish dishes, research that gave her insights into the culture. Several students talked about how food opens up conversation with people from other countries and ethnic groups—in obvious ways such as sharing recipes and meals, and in less apparent ways like interacting with knowledgeable people in ethnic restaurants and grocery stores. Finally, one student wrote: "Most other cultures aren't as hung up on time and busy-ness as we are. Their food is often labor intensive and time consuming to make. Food is so much a part of culture that cooking it is sharing in the culture, even if only in a small way."**

Lights! Camera! ACTION!

Our goal in this section is to provide students with ways to translate their knowledge into action, perhaps even resulting in their long-term involvement with something they find worthwhile. Although this is an optional exercise, we hope you'll do some brainstorming with students and help them think of new ideas for taking action. Please add your own suggestions to ours and encourage the students to add theirs.

Your P.O.V.

The final exercises of each chapter provide students with an imaginative outlet for their learning. Depending on the talents and learning styles of your students, **Your P.O.V.** can allow for lots of creativity. Wherever possible, you can help students do real-life writing that other people read. Writing and submitting film reviews to Internet sites such as Amazon *(www.amazon.com)* and The Internet Movie Database *(www.imdb.com)* is a simple and often exhilarating way for students to be "published." Of course, they can submit reviews and other writing to their student or local newspaper. One first-year student, for example, who had attended a campus performance of Latin

....

**Our appreciation to Charlotte Allen, Crisha Galbraith, Jami Krietzman, and Gail Wood for their contributions to this discussion.

folkloric dance, was thrilled to see her review appear in the student paper. You can also remind students to submit excellent drawings, photography, or other creative work to a student literary magazine.

Toward the end of the term, we usually ask each student to contribute one favorite piece of writing or creative work to a class album that is photocopied and distributed at the final session. (We might ask for a modest contribution from each student to cover photocopying.) This works beautifully in online courses as well by simply creating a new file for the album and having students cut and paste their entries and then print out the final product on their own.

Students gain important practice for real-life writing by sharing their written and other work with each other in class. While they may at first feel shy or embarrassed, they soon come to understand how wonderful it can be to be heard by others.

In each chapter, the final question of **Your P.O.V.** asks students to imagine that they are making a film on one of the suggested topics and to create their plan. Since this can be a relatively time-consuming group project, you might use it as a capstone assignment. Alternatively, the partial assignments suggested in Appendix D can be completed relatively quickly by individuals or small groups. Should you wish to assign research papers in this course, the topics suggested here are intended to provide ideas for you and your students.

And Our Book Awards Go To . . .
And Our Film Awards Go To . . .

We have selected and annotated books and films that we feel are truly exceptional. They are our personal favorites. We provide them so that your students can keep learning more about the cultures they've encountered. Most of the films we've chosen are fairly accessible, though we note in the annotations cases of a few, like *El Norte* (1983), that may unfortunately take some effort to find (but that are really worth the effort). All other things being equal, we tried to list films that your students may not know. We chose the books not only because of their importance and merit, but because we believe students will be drawn to them. They are all great reads, and most of them are relatively inexpensive.

Flashback/Flashforward

Students like and appreciate this exercise as a way of bringing closure to the course. It helps them reinforce what they have learned as well as look to the future. Please have students complete both parts of the assignment at home prior to the final class meeting.

Some Commonly Asked Questions

I am neither a historian nor a film expert. How can I teach this course?

Neither are we! But one of the most rewarding aspects of teaching these materials is that we continue to learn more with each new class of students. A lack of historical or film expertise should definitely not deter you from using this text. We explain to our students at the beginning of each course that this is a cooperative learning experience about cultures and about the cinema—a learning experience for all of us. Depending on your academic background, you might want to consider team teaching the course with someone whose areas of expertise supplement your own.

An indispensable reference work containing well-written historical surveys as well as charts, timelines, annotated bibliographies, and pedagogical approaches is James A. Banks's *Teaching Strategies for Ethnic Studies* (2003). We also recommend the splendid Library of Congress Internet site on immigration at *http://memory.loc.gov/learn/features/immig/introduction.html*.

How do I find film information and reviews?

These days the best way to find reviews and movie information is to go online, beginning with the Internet Movie Database and Amazon. Also, Google® or other search engines can be used to research specific films (by title), directors, actors, and film festivals. You and your students can also consult the Internet sites provided in Appendix E.

How can I purchase or rent videos and DVDs?

For rentals, services like Netflix *(www.netflix.com)*, DVD Avenue *(www.dvdavenue.com)*, and Café DVD *(www.cafedvd.com)* are available. Café DVD allows rentals of single films. For purchase, there are a number of options, including Amazon *(www.amazon.com)*, Best Buy *(www.bestbuy.com)*, and Sam Goody *(www.samgoody.com)*. There are also legal downloads at ifilm *(www.ifilm.com)*, Movieflix *(www.movieflix.com)*, and Movielink *(www.movielink.com)*.

You'll also want to check out the extraordinary offerings of Facets Multimedia Center *(www.facets.com)*. You can sign up online to receive regular free e-newsletters and specialty catalogs. Their huge, inexpensive catalog listing thousands of videos, accompanied by short blurbs, that are offered for rental or purchase is a must-have.

Other important distributors include:

1. California Newsreel *www.newsreel.org*
2. Filmakers Library *www.filmakers.com*
3. Home Box Office *www.hbo.com*
4. National Geographic *http://shop.nationalgeographic.com*
5. NAATA/Crosscurrent Media *www.naatanet.org*
6. PBS Video *www.shoppbs.org*
7. Third World Newsreel *www.twn.org*
8. Women Make Movies (WMM) *www.wmm.com*

Will the language of the films be too difficult for my ESL students?

Certainly the culturally rich words, phrases, and expressions will be challenging but no more so than the language your students encounter every day outside the classroom—on the street, on the radio, or on television. So far our ESL students and our native speakers alike have enjoyed the linguistic challenges of the films. Sometimes, our international students are assisted by native-speaking culture partners in order to tackle unfamiliar phrases and idioms. Although it is not our intention in this text to provide traditional language exercises, you could select specific film clips for the purpose of focusing on those grammatical structures, vocabulary words, or idioms that you wish to highlight for your students.

All students tend to work hard on their own to understand the films. We have witnessed, for example, non-native English speakers repeatedly replaying and transcribing parts of films or film clips, sometimes with the assistance of native-speaking friends or culture partners, in order to hear, and come to grips with, unfamiliar phrases and idioms. In this sense, film viewing offers practice similar to a language lab. Native speakers also come to understand the value of repeated viewings of certain scenes or entire films. The unfortunately rapidly vanishing VHS tape is much better for the purpose of rewinding and replaying than DVDs.

What are culture partners?

Culture partners participate in our ESL classes to facilitate small-group discussions and contribute to cross-cultural exchanges. They are usually native speakers of English—students or volunteers from the community. Some Culture Partners receive regular or internship credit for the course.

What are cultural informants?

We often invite guests or speakers as cultural informants. For example, our students have been greatly moved by student visitors from The Oregon School for the Deaf, and some have gone on to take classes in American Sign Language as a result. Cultural informants do not need to be experts or specialists. Clearly, students in your class will be able to serve as informants about their own cultures, but they should not automatically be expected to do so. Some students may not feel that they know enough about a specific topic to act as a resource person, and some may have personal reasons for declining this role (such as a gay student not wanting to come out). Students of color and international students in particular are often placed in the role of representative, or ambassador, and they may not (at least initially) feel comfortable with this extra responsibility and expectation; they may even resent being asked. On the other hand, students who enroll in this type of course usually welcome the opportunity to share knowledge and experiences from their own cultural backgrounds. If approached with tact and respect, those who are at first hesitant or reluctant will generally become more open, especially once trust has been established in the group.

What if my students have already seen a film?

Many of our students have already seen one or more of the films, but they do not seem reluctant to watch them a second time. We explain that our viewing goals in this class are very different from watching films for entertainment. In fact, most of our students comment on how the readings, exercises, and discussions help them to look at the films from a new viewpoint. They learn to develop their film eyes and ears and focus on aspects of culture and communication they might otherwise have overlooked.

How does the chapter on Muslim American culture differ from the other chapters?

It provides a change of pace for both you and your students. Instead of analyzing one feature film in its entirety, students in pairs or small groups can choose a film from among the selection of six, and then each group can present a meaningful clip to the class. (Or, if you wish, you can ask that all students view the same film.)

However you choose to proceed, please be aware that *House of Sand and Fog* and *The War Within* need to be debriefed carefully. In both cases, we recommend asking students to write or talk about their emotional responses before they begin any type of intellectual analysis. Because most students are likely to find these two movies upsetting or depressing, it's important that they have a chance to express their feelings.

When we moved to in-depth discussions of *House of Sand and Fog*, we found that students wanted to focus on who was to blame. We asked them to try to put the question of blame aside in an attempt to understand and empathize with each person's p.o.v. We also found it useful to ask them to identify points in the film when certain actions or decisions could have led to reconciliation rather than to destruction. And we found it important to ask them to identify characters' prejudicial statements or discriminatory actions.

The DVD extra feature should be useful to you in preparing your debrief of *The War Within*.

What do you do if students become angry, upset, or argumentative? What if conflicts arise in the class?

The subject matter and nature of this class are such that emotions can run high. We are reminded frequently that, for the most part, the current generation of students has not experienced the struggles of the civil rights movement except in abstract ways, perhaps in high school history books. Because the medium of film brings this history alive for them, Anglo American students can feel shock and dismay—or sometimes defensiveness and denial—and U.S. students of color or international students can become upset or angry. Some international students feel they are fulfilling a dream by coming to the United States, and then all of a sudden this class seems to burst their bubble: America is not what they thought it was. Other students from abroad can see their worst fears about the United States confirmed. Depending on their age and educational background, adult students, too, often struggle with the material and can find themselves becoming angry, hurt, or defensive.

While this generation of American students may not be fully informed of the issues treated in the text, they do have the experience of September 11, 2001, and its aftermath, as part of their emotional life, and this is a powerful point of reference. International students inevitably have their own sets of harsh realities on which to draw as they explore in some depth the painful aspects of the American past and present.

As instructors, we make every effort to keep students working together in a constructive environment. When you review the Respect Agreement in Appendix A at the outset of the course, spend some time preparing your students for the possibility of anger, hurt, or disagreements with others. They need to know that this is normal. But they also need to know that their challenge is to remain respectful of others at all times. You might want to alert students to the fact that they need to be prepared to apologize if they offend or hurt someone, or if they violate the Respect Agreement.

Unfortunately, the atmosphere of political correctness that has pervaded American life for the past twenty years has worked against opportunities to talk with each other in authentic ways across ethnic, cultural, and religious lines. We simply have not learned how to do so, and we have few opportunities to practice.

For us, this course offers a wonderful opportunity to practice intercultural and interracial communication in a relatively safe environment. As we tell our students, what better place to make mistakes than in a classroom? At the same time, we make it very clear that grades do not depend on saying the supposedly right thing. We use the phrase *authentic and sensitive* throughout the course to remind students that the objective here is to express authentic views, ideas, and questions, even if they are not popular, in a way that shows as much sensitivity as possible. If each student does that, we will create an extraordinary learning environment.

Because of the nature of the material, we find it important to balance hot topics with lighter ones. The cooking exercises in each chapter, for example, offer a perfect way to build rapport and ease tension, as do many of the **Cultural Backpacking** ventures. Chapter 9, which centers on the delightful film *What's Cooking?* has proved to be an uplifting way of concluding the course.

How does Chapter 9 differ from the other chapters?

This is a shorter chapter that is intended to be a wrap-up. Of the five main cultures portrayed in *What's Cooking?*, we have already given histories of three (Mexican American, African American, and gay) in previous chapters. Rather than providing two additional histories here

(Vietnamese and Jewish American), we leave it to you and your students to research the information and supply what is desired.

Do you ever use the Extra Features on DVDs?

Certainly! Some of the extra features, especially the commentaries provided by directors, were extremely valuable in the preparation of this text. A great assignment is to ask students to select and show clips that illustrate aspects of the filmmaking process as explained in the extra features.

What should I do if a website becomes defunct?

We specifically tried to include reliable websites sponsored by organizations that will be likely to last. But not all websites are forever, and sometimes web addresses change. If a website fails, we suggest first trying to search from the website's root menu (i.e., *www.[website].com*) for the specific topic discussed, and, if this yields no results, simply consulting a search engine (like Google®) to locate another site. Your students will likely enjoy finding good replacements.

How should I use the demographic donut charts?

Our students have found these charts invaluable in visualizing the changing face of multicultural America. We have used them to give both an overview of current demographics and to complement specific information provided in the **History Flashback** sections. For example, you can refer your students to Appendix F (Race and Ethnicity in the United States) when discussing the current Native American population in Indians Today or the browning of America in Mexican Americans Today. You can direct your students to Appendix G (Latino Population by Place of Origin) and Appendix H (Asian American Population by Place of Origin) to help students understand the diversity within each broader group. Additionally, in mock competition, we have quizzed students on U.S. demographics early in the course. They have enjoyed using the donut charts to check their answers—and have often been surprised by their findings. Other students have commented on the usefulness of the charts for in-depth research projects. The statisitcs have been compiled from multiple sources, including the U.S. Census Bureau, and reflect survey information gathered as recently as 2004.

1

Native American Culture:
Smoke Signals

Setting the Scene:
Freewriting and Discussion

This photograph is from the book *Indi'n Humor* (1993) by Kenneth Lincoln. Taken by Lee Marmon from the Laguna Pueblo tribe in New Mexico, it is called "White Man's Moccasins." What thoughts and feelings does it evoke for you? Think about the setting, the mood, and the point of view. Consider the following questions: How do you think this man feels about his clothing and footwear (sneakers)? Why do you suppose he is not wearing traditional moccasins? Does wearing white man's shoes make him more assimilated? Freewrite in your film notebook, and then turn to a classmate and share ideas.

Sneak Preview

About the Film

Smoke Signals (1998) is a film about Indians,[1] but it may not be what you expect, especially since the title suggests that it could be just another standard Western so popular in cinematic history. If you've seen even a few of the more than 2,000 Westerns made since the early 1900s, you know that Indians are usually depicted in stereotypical fashion—as bloodthirsty renegades, stoic warriors, noble savages, or buckskin-clad princesses. Except for historical figures such as Geronimo and Cochise, Indians in western films rarely have names or individual personalities; they speak neither English nor any other language (though they do grunt and whoop), and they spend a lot of time ambushing whites. In the typical cowboy-and-Indian scenario, handsome, rugged heroes like John Wayne play the parts of men charged with bringing civilization to the Wild West and protecting women and children settlers from the warriors' arrows and tomahawks.

But *Smoke Signals* is not about warriors, nor is it set on the 19th-century Western frontier. It distinguishes itself as a full-length feature film written, directed, coproduced, and acted (in all major roles) by Native Americans. Based loosely on Sherman Alexie's short novel entitled *The Lone Ranger and Tonto Fistfight in Heaven* (1994), it won two awards at the Sundance Film Festival. By all measures it is a landmark film that, in Alexie's words, "challenges the cinematic history of Indians" (Summa 1998). It does so by bringing new Indian characters to the screen who, as Alexie says, are not the silent, stoic types we're used to, nor are they depressed victims. In real life, Alexie tells us, "Indians are the most joyous people in the world" (D4).

In fact, notice when you watch the film how humor plays a central role. As early as 1969, Native legal scholar Vine Deloria, Jr., tried to correct misconceptions about stone-faced Indians in his book *Custer Died for Your Sins* (1969). He begins his chapter on "Indian Humor" by stating that "One of the best ways to understand a people is to know what makes them laugh" (148). Not only is the popular image of Indians all wrong, he says, but even experts on Indian affairs have failed to mention how humor pervades Indian life.

··········

1. As is often common practice, we use *Indians* and *Native Americans* interchangeably. See **Terms to Know** for further explanation.

In his fascinating *Indi'n Humor,* author Kenneth Lincoln says that Indians respond to life with "sharp humor, a good dose of sarcasm, resigned laughter, and a flurry of ironic 'rez' (reservation) jokes" (5). For many Native people, humor is a way of enjoying life and also a means of psychological survival. Lincoln provides a quote from John (Fire) Lame Deer of the Lakota Sioux to help clarify what Indian humor is about: "For a people who are as poor as us, who have lost everything, who had to endure so much death and sadness, laughter is a precious gift . . . We Indians like to laugh" (58).

When you watch the film, you'll see how real, ordinary people living in the present time go about their daily lives with humor and dignity. As you get to know the characters, you may wonder why it took so long for this unromanticized, demythologized presentation of Indians to come to the big screen. The main reason is that feature films are expensive to make and thus have been produced, directed, and written by those with sufficient means to do so—which has usually meant white men. For more than a century, directors like John Ford (of Irish-American descent) were the ones making decisions about how to present Indians to primarily white audiences.

Furthermore, because authenticity has been less important than drawing big crowds to movie theaters, the more important, more glamorous Indian roles of the past have commonly been played by heavily made-up non–Native American actors familiar to the moviegoing public. Rock Hudson, Elvis Presley, Raquel Welch, and Audrey Hepburn are a few of the Hollywood stars who have been cast as Indians. You can imagine that from an Indian p.o.v., it can be insulting (not to mention rather ridiculous) to see made-up white actors playing major Indian roles.

This is not to say that enlightened filmmakers never deviated from the old patterns prior to *Smoke Signals.* A few early movies are sympathetic to Indians, such as *Broken Arrow* (1950) and *Little Big Man* (1970); in addition, the more recent *Dances with Wolves* (1990) and *House Made of Dawn* (1987) break new ground (as do the movies recommended at the end of the chapter). But the p.o.v. of Indians themselves has been found almost exclusively in documentaries. Created by a large number of active, dedicated Indian filmmakers such as Alanis Obomsawin (of the Abenaki tribe) and Victor Masayesva (of the Hopi tribe), these splendid, usually low-budget works are evidence of a richness that as yet has not reached a wide audience. Since it can be difficult to find the documentaries, you might keep an eye out for Native American film festivals.

Check the website at *www.imaginenative.org* to see what kinds of exciting things are going on.

About the Filmmakers and Actors of *Smoke Signals*

One of six siblings, Sherman Alexie (born 1966) grew up in poverty on the Spokane Indian Reservation in Wellpinit, Washington. His mother is part Spokane, and his father is full-blooded Coeur d'Alene. Both of his parents were alcoholics, but his mother was able to break her addiction when her son was seven years old, and she subsequently became a tribal drug and alcohol abuse counselor.

A frail and sickly child, Alexie realized early that humor was an effective way to stave off bullies.

> People like to laugh, and when you make them laugh, they listen to you. That's how I get people to listen to me now. . . . I'm saying things people don't like for me to say. I'm saying very aggressive, controversial things, I suppose, about race and gender and sexuality. I'm way left [in my viewpoints], but if you say it funny, people listen. If you don't make 'em laugh, they'll walk away. (Blewster 1999, 26–27)

Alexie also avoided being picked on by spending a lot of time in the reservation school library. He later attended junior high and high school off the reservation in the nearby predominately white town of Reardon, where, he recalls with humor, he and the school mascot were the only Indians. Successful as a high school basketball player, honor society member, class president, and debater, he received a scholarship to Gonzaga University in Spokane.

After two years at Gonzaga, where he struggled with a drinking problem, he discontinued his studies, finishing later at Washington State University in Pullman. He credits Alex Kuo, his professor in a poetry class, with helping him discover his talent as a writer. Several poems written for Kuo's class were published in his first book, *The Business of Fancydancing* (1991). While still living in Pullman, Alexie, now sober, became a popular figure at local poetry readings.

Since 1991, Alexie's literary career has been remarkable. Though he considers himself primarily a poet and has published more than ten volumes of poetry, his widespread popularity has come from his fiction and screenplays. His frequent readings and literary presentations are well attended and hugely successful. Quick-witted and a natural comic, he does not simply read from his works but engages the audience in a freewheeling style that keeps people captivated and laughing throughout. He has a large and loyal following among Indians and non-Indians alike.

You can find interesting information about Alexie, including his schedule of upcoming presentations, on his website *http://fallsapart.com*. Don't miss the opportunity to hear him speak.

Director Chris Eyre (born 1969) is of Cheyenne/Arapaho descent. He was adopted by a white family and grew up in Klamath Falls, Oregon, later attending school in Portland. Since receiving his master's degree in filmmaking at New York University, he has directed an impressive number of films. You might visit his website *www.chriseyre.org*.

The cast of experienced and accomplished Native American actors includes Gary Farmer, who won a loyal following for his role as Philbert Bono in *Powwow Highway* (1989); Tantoo Cardinal, who has played dozens of fine roles, including that of Black Shawl in *Dances with Wolves* (1990); Adam Beach, who speaks to native youth throughout the United States and Canada; Evan Adams, who plays the lead role in Sherman Alexie's directorial debut, *The Business of Fancydancing* (2002), and who is an obstetrician in Vancouver, British Columbia; Irene Bedard, who was the physical model for, and the voice of, the Disney character Pocahontas; and John Trudell *(www.johntrudell.com)*, who is a poet, musician, and political activist known especially for his leadership of AIM (American Indian Movement) and his participation in the takeover of Alcatraz Island (see pages 15–16). For further information on the actors, check *www.imdb.com*.

Who's Who in the Film

Victor Joseph (Adam Beach)—young man abandoned by his father

Thomas Builds-the-Fire (Evan Adams)—Victor's storyteller companion

Arnold Joseph (Gary Farmer)—Victor's father who leaves for Phoenix

Arlene Joseph (Tantoo Cardinal)—Victor's mother

Grandma Builds-the-Fire (Monique Mojica)—relative who raises Thomas

Randy Peone (John Trudell)—K-Rez announcer

Suzy Song (Irene Bedard)—woman who befriends Arnold Joseph in Phoenix

Director—Chris Eyre

Screenwriter—Sherman Alexie

Ten Indian Culture Areas in North America

Terms to Know

aboriginal peoples—Used primarily to refer to the original inhabitants of Australia, but sometimes also used in reference to other Native peoples.

Alaska Natives—Used to refer to the **indigenous peoples** of Alaska, such as Aleuts and Inuits (Eskimos).

American Indian—Similar to **Indian;** often used in everyday speech and in legal documents.

First Nations—Used in Canada to refer to sovereign Native people. **Native Canadian** and **Native people** are also used in Canada.

Hawaiian Natives, Native Hawaiians, Hawaiians—**Indigenous people** of Hawaii.

Indian—Widely used to refer to the many different **indigenous peoples** who inhabited this country before the European conquest and to their descendants. The word itself is attributed to Christopher Columbus, who, falsely believing he had landed in India, used the Spanish word *indios* to refer to the people he encountered. **Indian** is not used with relation to the original inhabitants of Alaska or Hawaii.

indigenous people—Often used by anthropologists and others to refer to groups native to a region; avoids the word **native,** which sometimes has pejorative associations with the idea of being primitive.

nation—Similar to *tribe* and suggesting political independence. (In the legal terms of the dominant white society, not all tribes are actually nations.)

Native American—First came into widespread use in the 1960s in the Bureau of Indian Affairs. Devised as a respectful way of referring to Indians, it is used more by others than by Indians themselves.

Native people—Has gained international acceptance as a way of referring to **indigenous people.**

powwow—Probably derived from an Algonquian word for a healer or spiritual leader who could see the future in dreams. The term is commonly used to refer to a talk or meeting ("Let's powwow . . ."), but to Native Americans, powwows are opportunities to express and celebrate their heritage. Often open to the public, powwows are occasions for socializing, singing, dancing, and feasting.

red man—Reference to the skin color of Native Americans, which is not really red. Though generally considered dated and offensive, the term is sometimes used neutrally in phrases like, *I don't care if his skin is black, white, red, or purple.* **Red Power** was a slogan used by Indian activists during the Civil Rights Movement.

redskin, squaw, injun—Highly derogatory terms.

res or rez—Short for *reservation;* may seem disrespectful if used by non-Indians.

reservation—Fixed areas of land in the western part of the United States where Indians were forced to settle and reside beginning in the mid-1800s.

tribe—Group of Indians sharing a common heritage.

History Flashback

Victor, Thomas, and most of the other Indians we meet in *Smoke Signals* are living on the Coeur d'Alene Reservation in Washington State, one of approximately 300 reservations in 29 states. According to the 2000 U.S. Census, about 538,000 Indians, or one-fifth of the total Indian population, are living on reservations. Refer to the map.

How did reservations come about? Who created them, and when and why did they come into existence? What are they like, and what do they offer to modern-day Native Americans?

American Indian Reservations

MAP KEY
- Federal American Indian Reservations
- State American Indian Reservations

Indians as Original Inhabitants

To answer these questions, let's flash back more than 500 years to the time of Columbus's landing in the New World in 1492, when Indians were the sole inhabitants of the hemisphere. At that time hundreds of tribes occupied a vast stretch of territory equivalent to one-fourth of the earth's habitable land, extending from northern Alaska to Cape Horn. There is no way to know the size of the population at the time of Columbus; among scholars much controversy surrounds the figure, with estimates ranging from two to twelve million indigenous people living in North America (north of present-day Mexico).

The landing of Columbus marks the beginning of a brutal takeover of the continent by the European powers of Spain, England, and France, as well as by Russia and the Netherlands. During the following centuries, as colonizers waged their campaigns for land, religious converts, and riches, Indians were almost always the losers. Though many Europeans were originally received with hospitality, and notwithstanding some good relations and intermittent periods of relative peace, contact with the newcomers overwhelmingly demonstrated to Indians that the white man's presence ultimately meant betrayal, destruction, and death. You may recall that in *Smoke Signals,* Columbus is still a presence in everyday conversation and a source of ironic humor. For example, Thomas says, "I wish we were this organized when Columbus landed."

Generation after generation, Indian individuals and groups tried to oppose the white man's attempts to convert, assimilate, deceive, subjugate, and dispossess them. They fought ongoing skirmishes, battles, and wars. To learn more about the power of the invaders on the one hand, and the resistance of the indigenous peoples on the other, consider looking at three episodes of terrible destruction that took place in successive centuries: the Pueblo Revolt (1680), Little Turtle's War (1790–95), and the Wounded Knee Massacre (1890).

Ultimately, the Indians could not win. They were outnumbered, deceived countless times, and unable to match the advanced weaponry of their foes. By the late 18th century, European-borne disease and continuous warfare had decimated or in some cases completely wiped out entire groups of Indians. In the movie, when an angry Thomas wants to prove to Victor that his father won't return, he has examples quick at hand, like the Mohicans and the Winnebago. Even as a young boy, Thomas has learned that "when Indians go away, they don't come back." (For the sake of historical accuracy, neither tribe is extinct today, although James Fenimore Cooper's famous 1826 novel *The Last of the Mohicans* certainly created that false impression about the Mohicans, and the Winnebago were once reduced from 25,000 to only 150 people.)

As Indians struggled to avoid extinction, a new nation of primarily white Americans was being constituted on their lands. This new nation was "born" when it declared its independence from England on July 4, 1776, a day enshrined in U.S. history and celebrated annually with displays of patriotism. For many non-Indians, it may come as a shock to hear in *Smoke Signals* that not everyone feels the same way about the holiday that Arnold Joseph irreverently calls "White Man's Independence Day." Does it make sense to you that the tragic event of the film is set on July 4, 1976—the very day when elaborate, jubilant bicentennial celebrations took place across America?

Of course, simply declaring independence in 1776 did not mean that the rebellious European Americans' claims to the new land were recognized by the mother country of England. It took a great conflict, the Revolutionary War of 1776 to 1783, to end British rule over the entire territory (excluding Florida) that extended from the eastern seaboard to the Mississippi River (see map on page 11) and to legitimize the right of the Americans—at least from their point of view—to own and govern their new country.

Indians "Removed"

But what about the fact that Indians with prior rights were still living on the land? Though greatly reduced in territory and numbers, most eastern Indian nations still occupied portions of their original homelands—until President Andrew Jackson forcibly relocated them west of the Mississippi. In 1830 Jackson, whom historian Howard Zinn (2005) calls "the most aggressive enemy of the Indians in early American history," pressed Congress to pass the infamous Indian Removal Act (127).

Under this act, more than 50 tribes (approximately 80,000 Indians) were driven from their homelands in an attempt to remove them entirely from the country as it existed at the time. The stories are heartbreaking. For example, on their forced 1,000-mile trek from Georgia to Oklahoma in 1838–39, one of every four Cherokees perished from hunger, cold, and exhaustion. Read more about the period that Cherokees call The Trail of Tears at *www.*

Growth of the United States by Region and Appropriation of Indian Lands (1776–1867)

powersource.com/cherokee/history.html. Another amazing story you might investigate is that of the Florida Seminoles, who refused to leave and who fought a brilliant and prolonged war against the United States from the swamps and marshes of the Everglades (see the excellent website at *www.seminoletribe.com*).

Jackson's government assured the exiled Indian nations that in return for being relocated, they would receive an "ample district west of the Mississippi . . . to be guaranteed to the Indian tribes, as long as they shall occupy it" (Richardson 1896, 458). But this promise of a permanent solution ("as long as they shall occupy it") was broken almost immediately. What happened? Why did the government fail to uphold its legal and moral commitments?

Insight can be gained from President Jackson's second annual message to Congress on December 6, 1830. He said:

> What good man would prefer a country covered with forests and ranged by a few thousand savages to our extensive Republic, studded with cities, towns, and prosperous farms, embellished with all the improvements which art can devise or industry execute, occupied by more than 12,000,000 happy people, and filled with all the blessings of liberty, civilization, and religion? (521)

This idea of a noble, civilizing mission is often referred to as Manifest Destiny, a term coined later that decade by a journalist named John L. O'Sullivan. It expresses the belief held by most whites that they were entitled to the land by virtue of their innate superiority and religious mission. They believed it was their God-given right, and their sacred obligation, to expand the nation westward to its furthermost borders and to rule over it. As O'Sullivan writes: "We are the nation of human progress, and who will, what can, set limits to our onward march?" *(www.mtholyoke.edu/acad/intrel/osulliva.htm).*

In light of this unquestioned destiny, promises made to Indians were simply not that important. Between 1778 and 1871, the federal government signed 371 legal documents, or treaties, with Indian nations, every one of which was violated or abrogated. Today, non-Indians tend to look at treaties as relics of the past, as mere pieces of paper signed so far back in history that it would be absurd, not to mention highly impractical, to think of resurrecting them.

Many Indians feel differently. As Deloria (1969) explains, "It is this blatant violation of treaties that causes such frustration among the Indian people. Many wonder exactly what their rights are, for no matter where they turn, treaties are disregarded and laws are used to deprive them of what little land remains to them" (38). From an Indian point of view, the issue of broken treaties has not been resolved, and battles are still being fought in the courts. You may recall from the film that treaties are a source of ironic humor.

If you look again at the map on page 11, you can see how quickly the U.S. government acted to fulfill its "destiny" by appropriating tribal land. This history of expansion through theft, deceit, and war is not what non-Indian Americans think of when they recall with pride the history of western settlement. As the map shows, in 1803 the new country purchased the huge Louisiana Territory from France, and in 1819 it acquired Florida from Spain. By mid-century, the missing pieces in America's continental building scheme were all obtained, most notably by annexing Texas from Mexico in 1845 and by virtually stealing from Mexico one-third of its country in the Mexican American War of 1846–48 (see pages 77–78). Thus, in fewer than 100 years after breaking away from England, the Americans had acquired sole "possession" of a nation that reached from coast to coast and included Alaska.

Still, the far West might have remained remote, inhospitable, and uninteresting to white settlers if gold had not been discovered in

California in 1848. That event decided the fate of Western Indians forever. Whereas trappers, traders, and missionaries had long roamed the distant territories, and some wagon trains of settlers had been rolling westward on the Oregon Trail across Indian lands since the early 1840s, suddenly tens of thousands of fortune hunters moved west through territories Native people held—either as original inhabitants or by treaty. This relentless migration and the accompanying growth of railroad and communication lines severely disrupted native hunting and fishing practices, destroyed food-gathering grounds, depleted natural resources, and spread white men's diseases.

The Reservation System

I have heard that you intend to settle us on a reservation near the mountains. I don't want to settle. I love to roam over the prairies. There I feel free and happy, but when we settle down we grow pale and die.

—Chief Satana (Kiowa)

When the Indians could no longer be "removed" any further west to unwanted lands, they posed a tough problem. In the mid-1800s, sentiment began to grow among U.S. government policymakers that Native Americans should be gathered together and forced to reside on permanent, fixed areas of land known as reservations. This plan had three important goals: to concentrate Indian populations, to isolate them from whites, and to train them in agriculture as a means of moving them toward assimilation.

The reservation plan was clearly illegal, immoral, and unworkable. It ignored and violated treaties signed by the U.S. government and various Indian nations detailing precise conditions by which Indians would be guaranteed ownership of certain lands. It set out to enclose and, in effect, imprison people on lands they had not agreed to occupy and turn them into farmers against their will. (Even if the Indians had been willing to undertake farming, it would have been a useless enterprise, since the specific lands reserved for agricultural purposes were for the most part barren wastelands that were not tillable.) And, finally, the reservation plan was corrupted by its administrators, who were mostly political appointees lacking qualifications and integrity.

The latter half of the 19th century is marked by major battles fought by whites to claim "their" new Western lands and by Indians to oppose being dispossessed and forced onto reservations. In popular culture, this is known as the era of the Wild West, the frontier, the cowboys and Indians. It has given rise to enduring and cherished national myths about the heroism of white settlers who "tamed" the West.

Though much less is widely known or acknowledged about heroism on the part of Indians in general, the powerful Sioux have long captured the imagination of non-Indians. In fact, many of the cultural features now associated (often mistakenly) with all Indians are characteristic of the former Sioux way of life: teepees, war bonnets and eagle feathers, buffalo hunting, and superior horsemanship. The great Sioux leaders—Little Crow, Red Cloud, Sitting Bull, Black Elk, Crazy Horse, and Spotted Tail—have achieved legendary status in American history.

Not until recently, however, has the mainstream society begun to see the decisive Sioux victory over George Armstrong Custer at the Battle of the Little Bighorn (1876) in a way that places the cavalry commander in a critical light (see *www.hanksville.org/daniel/misc/Custer.html*). Although widely celebrated as a hero for more than a century, he was, in fact, known to Indians for his extreme brutality. At the Little Bighorn, Custer miscalculated and was killed, along with his entire 7th cavalry, by the Sioux and their Cheyenne and Arapaho allies. After his death, he was elevated to the status of a tragic figure who sacrificed his life for his country, and the battle was viewed as evidence of Indian treachery and barbarism. Indians, by contrast, have never had a doubt about who Custer was, and his ruthless reputation lives on. In the film, characters refer to him mockingly, and they keep the famous battle alive in clever ways. For example, playing on the fact that Crazy Horse was said to have uttered the famous Sioux battle cry "Hoka Hey" ("Today is a good day to die") as he led the attack, the K-Rez announcer tells his listeners that "it's a good day to be indigenous," and Thomas says, "It's a good day to eat breakfast."

Indian Nations within the United States

Having had little choice but to try to survive for decades in desperate conditions on reservations, Indians are now using their outsider status to achieve new goals. Still largely unwilling to assimilate—which to them means losing their cultures and heritage and buying into a white system they do not respect—they are determined to maintain their independence, or so-called sovereignty. In 1886, Chief Pound Maker (Cree) expressed this idea prophetically: "Our old way of life is gone but that does not mean we should sit back and become imitation white men" (Wearne 1996, 15).

Sovereignty (also called self-determination or self-governance) is the most significant issue facing Indians today. Even if you have not heard the word itself, you have most likely encountered struggles over sovereignty in the form of rights to hunting, fishing, or casino gambling. Or, if you have visited an Indian reservation, you may have been greeted at the entrance by a sign welcoming visitors to that particular Indian *nation*.

The words *nation* and *sovereignty* refer to monumental changes that have been taking place in recent decades in the status of Indian territories and the definition of Indian rights. Significantly, many non–Native Americans do not realize that approximately 150 sovereign, or separate, Indian nations are now legally established within the United States. Why have we not learned more about this in school and the media? Without knowing about sovereignty, we cannot understand one of the most profound developments in our nation's history. Most Indians, of course, are fully aware of sovereignty. In the film, when Lucy and Velma give their two friends a ride, they joke about passports and vaccinations being necessary to leave the reservation and enter a "foreign country." Though Thomas and Victor don't need passports, they actually are going to a different nation when they leave the reservation.

How did Native Americans begin to reclaim their rights and power? Inspired by the civil rights and Black Power movements, in 1968 a group of activists led by Chippewa Indians Dennis Banks and George Mitchell founded AIM (American Indian Movement), whose slogan "Red Power" expressed their political goal of self-determination. The following year, a small group of Indians sympathetic to AIM occupied Alcatraz Island in San Francisco Bay, claiming it for Indian use. Why Alcatraz, the site of a former federal prison? As Deloria (1992) explains in *God Is Red: A Native View of Religion,* the militants "compared Alcatraz to most Indian reservations: no water, no good housing, land unfit for cultivation, no employment; in short, a prison" (9).

During the year and a half occupation of Alcatraz, the Indians' cause gained nationwide publicity. This particular protest ended when federal marshals invaded the island and arrested the occupants, but the Alcatraz occupation sparked further acts of resistance throughout the country, including a number of spectacular events planned to raise public awareness of Indian grievances. To learn more about these, search the Internet for information on the occupation of Mount Rushmore (1971), the Trail of Broken Treaties Caravan to Washington, DC (1972), and the protest at Wounded Knee (1973).

While the reasons for choosing Mount Rushmore and the nation's capital are fairly evident, not everyone is aware of the significance of Wounded Knee. It was here, at Wounded Knee Creek in South Dakota, that a dreadful massacre by U.S. soldiers of nearly 300 unarmed Sioux men, women, and children took place on December 29, 1890. The massacre was not forgotten by future generations of Indians. In 1973, demonstrators decided to return to this site to stage a peaceful protest. But warfare broke out between a small group of protesters (including women and children) and hundreds of federal agents armed with the most sophisticated weaponry. The armed siege, which lasted more than two months, brought national and international attention to Wounded Knee II, as it came to be called.

Eventually, the pressure applied by activists both in public protests and in the courts bore fruit. The major turning point came in 1975 under President Richard Nixon's administration with the passage of the Indian Self-Determination and Education Assistance Act. As the concept of self-government continued to evolve, other landmark pieces of legislation promoting and elucidating Indian sovereignty were passed, including, for example, the Indian Child Welfare Act (1978), the American Indian Religious Freedom Act (1978), and the Indian Gaming Regulatory Act (1988).

But what does it really mean for an Indian tribe to be a sovereign nation within the United States? The issues are highly complex, and there is no simple answer. Moreover, the concept is undergoing constant change. In truth, all Americans—Native and non-Native alike— are involved in an experiment that is reshaping our understanding of the United States and its government. What does it mean to have semiautonomous units within the borders of a larger nation—in effect, nations within a nation? Where do federal laws and tribal laws collide? What about the relationship between individual states and the nations within them? Can they coexist peacefully and prosperously? Finally, will the dominant society hold to its new legislation or overturn recent laws promoting Indian sovereignty as it has broken so many treaties in the past?

Insiders' Points of View on Sovereignty

We have our own governments. Sovereignty means the right to define the present and the future as a people. I do not feel included in the U.S. founding documents.

> —Faith Smith, Ojibway educator

Sovereignty is a state of mind, or should I say, a state of heart. . . . [It] means the ability to say who you are and what you are and to think for yourself. It means the ability to run your own schools and to move about in the world with dignity, as your own nation.

> —Joy Harjo, Creek/Cherokee poet and musician

Many people don't understand the word sovereignty. Sovereignty is the ability to carry out your own direction. If you think sovereign, you can be sovereign. . . . Part of sovereignty is being able to see the things you know are right and fight for them.

> —Audrey Shenandoah, Onondaga Clan Mother

> From *Every Day Is a Good Day: Reflections by Contemporary Indigenous Women*

Indians Today

For many Native Americans, this is an exciting time of renewal and hope. Whereas in 1900 the census counted what may have been an historic low of 237,196 Native Americans, the 2000 census revealed more than a four-fold growth—with 2.47 million people declaring American Indian or Alaska Native as their only race, and an additional 1.9 million stating they were part Indian, for a total of 4.3 million.

Drawing on a seemingly inexhaustible spirit and on a history of strength and resilience, Native people nationwide are dedicating themselves to protecting the environment, to preserving their languages and heritage (see *www.ewebtribe.com/NACulture/lang.htm* and *www.indians.org/welker/americas.htm*), and to educating themselves in their own tribal colleges. Simultaneously, Indian lawyers and advocates are working to regain and safeguard Native rights. On reservations and in urban areas, Indians are finding their own solutions to endemic problems of poverty, crime, despair, and alcoholism. While the difficulties cannot be minimized, neither should they overshadow the tremendous optimism that many Native people express for their future.

This optimism can be seen, for example, in the arts. Indigenous artists (traditional and modern), writers, museum curators, and film-makers are experiencing a renaissance, bringing renewed pride to their communities and changing the public perception of who Native people are. The recently dedicated National Museum of the American Indian at the Smithsonian Institution in Washington, DC, is a symbol to some of a dynamic and more positive landscape *(www.nmai.si.edu)*.

Director's P.O.V.

Well, we call ourselves "Indians," because it's not a bad term. I understand respecting people, but it's like people say, what do you want to be called? I say, how about Chris, you know? And if you want to know what my tribe is, I'm Cheyenne and Arapaho. So it's not really that big an issue. "Indian" is what we call ourselves, and it's not a derogatory term. And I guess everybody else will have to figure out what they want to call you, if they don't want to use your first name.

—Chris Eyre

www.minireviews.com/interviews/eyre.htm

Insider's P.O.V.

I enjoyed *Smoke Signals* because it was the first time I saw things in a movie that I might see at home. Some of the scenes that people saw as comedy actually show what we see and live with on a daily basis. Remember the girls with the car that only drove backwards? Their transmission was out. We see that here and think nothing about it, because our laws are such that we have young people driving without licenses and people driving with no windshields or forward gears in their cars. Those are the rez cars. The car never leaves the rez but it allows people to get around within our small community.

—Fay Hurtado, member of the Confederated Tribes living on
the Warm Springs Reservation, Oregon

Cultural Backpacking: Native America

To find Native America, you have to glimpse the world of Native American people, their history and traditions, thoughts and beliefs, visions and realities. You have to give a piece of yourself over to the insistent beat of a powwow camp; surrender to the prayerful rhythms of a kachina dance; experience the beauty of Pueblo pottery or Shoshone beadwork; grasp the subtle wisdom of a Navajo coyote story; feel the timeless presence of ancient cliff-dwellings, temple mounds, historic battlefields and massacre sites; hike the grasslands, canyons, deserts, and forests of Indian country; and try to understand a people who regard the earth as their mother and the sky as their father. (Gattuso 1993, 24)

In this spirit, put on your "backpack" to discover a part of Native America that is meaningful to you. Wherever you choose to travel, try to "give a piece of yourself" over to the experience. You may, for example, visit a reservation, museum, memorial, or historic site, or you could attend a powwow or other similar event. Alternatively, you may choose to do your backpacking in the library or at your computer. In this case, your task is to find one place you would like to visit or one event you would like to attend. Whether your backpacking is real or virtual, be sure to choose something that gives you new insight into, and appreciation for, Native people and cultures.

When you have completed your backpacking, write a page to describe what you chose and why. What was your experience like, both emotionally and intellectually? What gave you a glimpse into Native culture?

If you're struggling to come up with an idea, you can consult guidebooks (such as the *Insight Guide* described at the end of the chapter) or sites such as *www.powwows.com* and *www.500nations.com/500_Powwows.asp*. You may be surprised to learn how many places and events of interest are nearby, regardless of where you live.

A word of caution: In your write-up, be sure to narrow your focus. For example, if you visit a museum in real life or on the Internet, zoom in on one painting or basket that seems of special interest to you. If you attend a powwow, select one dance or costume. Try to attach a picture or photograph to your essay. If you choose a website, book, or magazine, include the relevant URL or other information.

Before undertaking your backpacking, especially to powwows or reservations, check guidebooks and websites for recommendations on etiquette.

Diversity Detective: Who Are Well-Known Native People Today?

Your detective firm has been given a major assignment to investigate modern Indians in an attempt to move beyond the image of Indians "frozen in time" in the era of the Wild West, replacing it with a more realistic, accurate view of contemporary Native people and life. Use your ingenuity to crack the case, tracking down leads from print or electronic media, consulting knowledgeable people, or sleuthing in any other legal way. You may work individually, with partners, or in small groups.

Indian heroes, leaders, and legends of earlier times include names like Geronimo, Sitting Bull, Black Elk, Pocahontas, and Sacagawea. But how many present-day Indians are known to the general public? Locate one man and one woman who are alive today and who, in your opinion, deserve more widespread recognition. They may be from any walk of life, such as politics, the arts, sports, media, or education. Introduce your two people to the class, explaining why you have chosen them, and include information on the sources you used. If possible, show relevant pictures as part of your presentation.

Spotlight: Indians Are Not "Just Like Us"

Values differ, sometimes radically, from culture to culture. Worldwide, we see again and again the tragic results of conflicts that arise when one national, ethnic, or religious group attempts to force another to accept its values. In its current position of economic and military dominance, the United States is seen by many peoples in the world as imposing its values beyond its borders, as refusing to learn the lesson that different ways of life are as legitimate and sacred to others as our ways are to us.

In truth, Americans do not have to look overseas for this lesson.

Here within our own borders, Native people have been telling the dominant society for 500 years that they have a way of life different from that of the mainstream society and that they do not want to change, join up, or assimilate. The message could not be clearer. Even at the high price they have paid—and are still paying—many Native people today retain their right to hold their own values and beliefs, as summarized in the chart on page 22.

As you study the chart, try not to be disturbed about the fact that it is vastly oversimplified. There are *obviously* many exceptions and gradations, and parts of the Native American side of the chart are perhaps more descriptive of the past than of today. The chart serves only as a rough guide and a stimulus to further study.

Your task is to find a scene in the movie that illustrates one of the differences between the values of the dominant society and of Native peoples as shown on the chart. Once you have written a paragraph or two in your film notebook explaining your choice, present it to the class. Time permitting, you might show the scene.

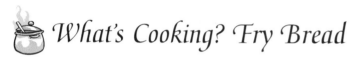 *What's Cooking? Fry Bread*

"Making fry bread is simple. But making good fry bread is an art," reporter Barbara Durbin concludes after interviewing Native American experts. Few people realize that fry bread comes from hard times. Fry-bread specialist Tanya Sanchez (Shoshone/Bannock/Ute tribes) explains that when Native Americans were confined to reservations, they received white flour, lard, and baking powder from the U.S. government so that they wouldn't starve. These unfamiliar ingredients did not resemble the Native peoples' healthy natural foods. As Sanchez relates, "They handed it to us and said 'Figure out what to do with it.' So we figured out what to do" (Starke 2001, FD1).

There are only four or five basic ingredients for fry bread, but it's not easy to find an exact recipe. Everyone makes it a little differently, and there are many variations, somewhat like muffins.

Mix 3 cups flour, 1 tablespoon baking powder, and 1 teaspoon salt. Add 1 cup warm water and knead until dough is soft but not sticky. (Sanchez advises not to play or fight with the dough and to make sure there are no dry spots in it.) Tear off a small piece, stretch and pat dough until thin, and poke a hole through the middle. Carefully drop

U.S. Mainstream, Dominant Society	Native Peoples (Mainland, Alaska, Hawaii)
Fundamental belief in private ownership of land and resources	Fundamental belief in impossibility of private ownership of land or other resources
Materialistic	Nonmaterialistic
Leadership often by command or authority; "top-down"	Leadership by example and consensus
Written tradition important	Oral tradition important
Immediate (nuclear) families	Extended families and clans
Reverence for the young	Reverence for the old
Earth viewed as "dead," inanimate object; mastery over nature	Earth viewed as living; harmony with nature
Humans seen as superior to other life forms	Humans viewed as equal and integral part of web of life
The dead seen as gone	The dead seen as present
Saving and acquiring emphasized	Sharing and giving emphasized
High-impact technology	Low-impact technology
Futuristic/linear concept of time	Circular, flexible concept of time
Speaking valued	Silence and listening valued
Confident and assertive	Modest and noninterfering
As much as possible desired	As little as possible desired
Principle of independence	Principle of interdependence
Competition valued	Cooperation valued
Impatient	Patient
Skeptical	Mystical
Seeking converts to own religion	Respecting others' religions
Separation of church and state; religion a part of life	Spirituality embodied everywhere and at all times; religion a way of life

*Adapted in part from Jerry Mander's *In the Absence of the Sacred: The Failure of Technology and the Survival of the Indian Nations* (San Francisco: Sierra Club Books, 1992), 214–21.

into sizzling hot corn oil (an electric fry pan can work in a classroom).
Cook 3–5 minutes, turning only once. Brown on both sides. Remove
from oil with tongs or a slotted spoon. Drain on paper towels.

Serve while still warm. Fry bread can be eaten with stew or chili.
With jam, powdered sugar, cinnamon sugar, or honey, it's a sweet treat.

See other Native recipes at *http://nativetech.nativeweb.org/food/index.php*
or *www.kstrom.net/isk/food/recipes.html.*

Lights! Camera! ACTION!

The knowledge and skills you are gaining from this course will enable
you to take action in your life, perhaps even resulting in your long-
term involvement with something you find worthwhile. The suggestions given here and in the **Lights! Camera! ACTION!** sections of
other chapters are optional. Please pursue them if you are so motivated, or feel free to propose your own ideas for taking action and to
brainstorm others with your class.

Go to the website for NARF (Native American Rights Fund) at
www.narf.org, AIM at *www.aimovement.org*, or the International Indian
Treaty Council at *www.treatycouncil.org/home.htm*, and identify a cause
you might like to support.

Your P.O.V.

The **Your P.O.V.** exercises here and at the end of each chapter are intended to stimulate your imagination and provide you with exciting ways to expand your learning. Choose an assignment that allows you to express your point of view in a creative way—e.g., by writing a poem, essay, or film review; by drawing or sketching; or by designing a poster, button, or bumper sticker. Whatever you do, consider gaining a wider audience by submitting your work to your campus newspaper or literary magazine, or by posting a film review on the Internet. Information on the filmmaking assignments proposed at the end of each **Your P.O.V.** section is provided in Appendix D.

1. Some bumper stickers you might see on vehicles driven by Indians are:

    - Of course you can trust the government! Just ask any Indian!
    - Proud to be Native American
    - I brake for powwows
    - America: love it or give it back
    - I was Indian before being Indian was cool
    - We don't want a bigger piece of the pie—we want a different pie (Winona LaDuke)

    Design a bumper sticker that expresses something you have learned from this chapter.

2. Write a review of *Smoke Signals* and post it on Amazon at *www.amazon.com* or the Internet Movie Database at *www.imdb.com*.

3. Flash forward to ten years in the future, and imagine that Victor and Thomas (or Victor and Suzy) meet. Under what circumstances do you think they might meet? What would they discuss? Write a script of their dialogue. Or write an outline of a plot for a sequel to *Smoke Signals*.

4. Imagine that as a reporter for the newspaper *Indian Country Today* you are writing an investigative article to see how enlightened your school or university is about Indian peoples and issues. What would you include in your article and whom

would you interview? Time permitting, write the article and submit it to your campus or local newspaper.

5. Assume the p.o.v. of an elder in your nation and the last speaker of your language. Write a letter to your grandchildren describing your thoughts and emotions as you face the loss of your language.

6. Imagine that you and your crew are making a film on present-day Native American life. Consult the guidelines in Appendix D for further information. Here are some potential topics for consideration:

   a. the role of basketball on reservations

   b. the survival of Native American languages

   c. Winona LaDuke and other environmental activists

   d. the good and bad of reservation casinos

   e. the role of powwows today

   f. the story of Leonard Peltier

 And Our Native American Book Awards Go To . . .

Every Day Is a Good Day: Reflections by Contemporary Indigenous Women by Wilma Mankiller (Golden, CO: Fulcrum Publishing, 2004). A "rare opportunity for outsiders to sit in on the candid conversations of indigenous women as they speak about love, life, their families, and their communities" (xxv–xxvi). Mankiller's innovative book has the power to change lives. In her splendid introduction, Gloria Steinem says this "could be the most important [book] of this new century if it were to get the mindfulness it deserves" (xiii).

Insight Guides: Native America (2nd ed.), edited by John Gattuso (Boston: Houghton Mifflin, 1998). A comprehensive guide including helpful cultural information, great illustrations and maps, and valuable etiquette tips. This book takes us to Indian country—to "communities, ceremonies, powwows, historic places, trading posts, art shows, archaeological sites, and special events" (24).

The Native Americans: An Illustrated History, edited by Betty and Ian Ballantine (Atlanta: Turner Publishing, 1993). Our favorite introduction to Native American history. Within the covers of this one volume, containing 449 captivating illustrations, mostly in color, the reader gains an overview of Indian history and culture. This is a book you can turn to again and again.

Prison Writings: My Life Is My Sun Dance by Leonard Peltier (New York: St. Martin's Press, 1999). The p.o.v. of an extraordinary man seen by many as a Native American equivalent of Nelson Mandela. Believed by millions of supporters to have been wrongfully imprisoned by the U.S. government three decades ago, Peltier has become a symbol of the oppression and injustices experienced by indigenous peoples worldwide. His passion for his people and remarkable forgiveness and compassion for all—including his captors—shine through.

And Our Native American Film Awards Go To . . .

Powwow Highway (1989)—The offbeat tale of two Indian friends on the road to New Mexico in a dilapidated Buick. Based on David Seals's novel of the same title and directed by Jonathan Wacks, this film has achieved cult status among many Native Americans.

Thunderheart (1992)—A thriller that gives insight into the situation of Native American environmental activists and reveals the injustices perpetrated against Leonard Peltier. Inspired by true events that took place on Indian reservations in the 1970s, the film is directed by Michael Apted, who also directed the fine documentary *Incident at Oglala* (1992) that examines the same events.

Where the Spirit Lives (1989)—A painful story of a brother and sister kidnapped from their homes by the government. Directed by Bruce Pittman, this film brings to life the suffering caused by removal of Indian children to boarding schools.

2

African American Culture:
The Long Walk Home

Setting the Scene:
Freewriting and Discussion

This photograph shows a common sight from the period prior to the civil rights movement of the 1950s and 1960s. At this Mississippi movie theater, "colored" patrons paid their admission of 10 cents, but they could not mix with whites, so they had to enter by the segregated stairway and sit in the balcony. Though not totally visible, the door at the bottom left is marked "White Men Only." Study the photo and freewrite your immediate reactions in your film notebook. How would you describe the mood of the photograph? How do you suppose the man pictured here feels? Discuss what you wrote with a partner or small group.

Sneak Preview

About the Film

The Long Walk Home (1990) provides insight into the lives of two families (one black, one white) during the historical 1955–56 bus boycott in Montgomery, Alabama. The film takes a close look at the hardships people endured and the often difficult choices they had to make. Whoopi Goldberg (as Odessa, the black maid) and Sissy Spacek (as her employer Miriam) give brilliant performances in the two leading roles.

The Long Walk Home belongs to the genre of historical films: As you watch the film, you'll be seeing actual history come alive. While an historical film is not a documentary, it also is not fiction. So what expectations should we have as viewers? To what extent should "Hollywood history" be accurate? How much license should the filmmakers be given to change or modify the facts?

First, remember that there's a strong temptation to believe whatever we see on the screen. Visual images are powerful, and they seem real. Moreover, for many of us, Hollywood history might be all we know about a particular era. So we may forever associate Ben Kingsley with the loin-clothed Mahatma Gandhi sitting at his spinning wheel in his ashram, and we may link Tom Hanks landing on the beaches of Normandy with the World War II D-Day invasion. Is there anything wrong with this?

A fascinating book called *Past Imperfect: History According to the Movies* (1996) helps us reflect on the above questions. Editor Mark C. Carnes explains:

> Like drama and fiction, movies inspire and entertain. They often teach important truths about the human condition. They do not provide a substitute for history that has been painstak-

ingly assembled from the best available evidence and analysis. But sometimes filmmakers, wholly smitten by their creations, proclaim them to be historically 'accurate' or 'truthful,' and many viewers presume them to be so. Viewers should neither accept such claims nor dismiss them out of hand, but regard them as an invitation for further exploration. (9–10)

This is precisely how we will look at historical films, as "an invitation for further exploration." Using *The Long Walk Home* as our example, where might you begin this exploration? A good place to start is with reviews, always keeping p.o.v. in mind. When you finish reading this section, search the Internet for a review of the film that you find helpful. One place to begin is the Internet Movie Database at *www.imdb.com.*

One especially important review, written by Martin Luther King Jr.'s widow, Coretta Scott King, praises *The Long Walk Home* for being a "true look at [the] past." Having lived through the Montgomery bus boycott at her husband's side, Mrs. King clearly had an invaluable insider's p.o.v. This, however, does not mean that she was neutral. As an African American woman and a civil rights leader herself, she had her own agenda. And she judged the film from the perspective of a woman deeply committed to the ideals for which her husband lived and gave his life. She wrote:

> Although Hollywood has rarely done justice to the black freedom struggle, the last two years have brought some impressive exceptions, including *Glory,* the television movie *Murder in Mississippi,* and now, *The Long Walk Home.* . . . The film . . . captures the feel of the segregated south of the 1950s. (King 1991, A12)

She liked the fact that the film focuses on average citizens rather than on her husband, Rosa Parks, or any of the other well-known leaders of the boycott; in this way, it "better portrays the experience of the community." She also said that the decision to feature a domestic worker was "on-target" since, according to a survey she mentions, more than half of black women in Montgomery, Alabama, at the time—an astonishing 63 percent to be exact—were maids. Although she found some minor inaccuracies and exaggerations, Mrs. King said that *The Long Walk Home* is "faithful to the spirit and history of the Montgomery story. It reveals the quiet courage and dignity of the people of Montgomery and the revolutionary power of disciplined nonviolence" (A12).

Another valuable perspective can be gained by looking at the film from a historian's point of view. Jacqueline Jones, Professor of American Civilization, writes in *Past Imperfect:* "At last—a Hollywood film that gets pretty nearly right a small but compelling piece of southern history" (Carnes 1996, 262). She points out the accuracy of various details, such as the scene when Miriam drives alone past Dr. King's house after hearing reports of damage from a firebombing. In fact, on the night of January 30, 1956, a bomb was thrown onto the porch of the King home, causing substantial damage although no injuries.

Professor Jones says that in many respects the film, which was shot on location, "aims for historical accuracy," noting that in some parts it even resembles a documentary (265). The very first scene showing the bus, for example, was shot in black-and-white in a documentary style, reflecting perhaps the fact that the events depicted were originally viewed on black-and-white TV screens. Adding to the authentic feel is the fact that original recordings of several of Dr. King's speeches are featured, including his address to the Holt Street mass meeting on December 5, 1955, which Odessa and her family hear from outside the church.

About the Director and Actors of *The Long Walk Home*

Trained as a cinematographer, director Richard Pearce began his career with a group of filmmakers who were producing documentaries on social themes. Notable from his early period are the Oscar-winning *Woodstock* (1970) and two explorations of controversies surrounding the Vietnam War: *Interviews with My Lai Veterans* (1971), which also won an Oscar, and *Hearts and Minds* (1974). Pearce debuted as a feature film director in 1979 with *Heartland,* followed by *Country* in 1984. He later returned to the documentary form with *The Blues: The Road to Memphis* (2003), which focuses on blues legend B.B. King and pays tribute to the city that gave rise to a new style of blues.

Comedienne, producer, writer, and actress Whoopi Goldberg has been active in the entertainment industry for much of her life. Among her many memorable performances are the roles of Celie in *The Color*

Purple (1985), Sister Mary Clarence in *Sister Act* (1992), Mary Masembuko in *Sarafina!* (1992), and Myrlie Evers in *Ghosts of Mississippi* (1996). Sissy Spacek has also had a long and illustrious career in film and television. She originally studied acting at the Lee Strasberg Theatre Institute and won a Best Actress Oscar for *Coal Miner's Daughter* (1980). Irving "Ving" Rhames, born and raised in Harlem, studied drama at the New York High School of Performing Arts and then at the Julliard School of Drama. He has performed in Shakespeare in the Park productions in Manhattan and may be best known for his roles in *Pulp Fiction* (1994) and the *Mission: Impossible* movies.

Who's Who in the Film

Odessa ("Dessie") Cotter (Whoopi Goldberg)—African American maid and boycotter

Herbert Cotter (Ving Rhames)—Odessa's husband

Selma Cotter (Erika Alexander)—daughter of Odessa and Herbert

Theodore Cotter (Richard Habersham)—older son

Franklin Cotter (Jason Weaver)—younger son

Miriam Thompson (Sissy Spacek)—Southern wife and mother in household employing Odessa

Norman Thompson (Dwight Schultz)—Miriam's husband

Mary Catherine Thompson (Lexi Randall)—seven-year-old daughter ("Boo Boo") and adult narrator (voice of Mary Steenburgen)

Sara Thompson (Crystal Robbins)—older daughter

Tunker Thompson (Dylan Baker)—Norman's brother

Claudia (Cherene Snow)—black maid and friend of Odessa

Director—Richard Pearce

Screenwriters—John Cork and Randy Meyer

Terms to Know

African American—Widely accepted term that places emphasis on the origins of most American blacks; replaces the outdated term **Afro American**.

Afrocentrism—Ideology that places greater emphasis (than does the prevalent "Eurocentric" approach) on African cultures as they have affected American and world history.

black—Also a widely accepted term, often interchangeable with **African American,** that arose in the civil rights era as an affirmation of one's skin color (e.g., black pride, black power, "black is beautiful" slogan).

colored—Term dating from the earliest days of slavery; unacceptable today except in certain historical contexts and titles (e.g., National Association for the Advancement of Colored People [NAACP]).

the enslaved, enslaved persons—Preferred by some African Americans to **slaves,** which does not convey the reality of oppression but rather suggests a permanent status or condition.

Negro—Term originating with the Spanish and Portuguese colonists, from the word *negro,* meaning *black.* Widely used in the period between the two World Wars, it replaced the outdated term **colored** but is now outdated itself.

nigger—Highly derogatory term when used by nonblacks but is sometimes used by blacks to refer to themselves. Some call it the *N-word* to avoid saying it.

people of color—Term that gained popularity in the 1980s to refer to nonwhites, especially African, Native, Hispanic, and Asian Americans, and to emphasize their solidarity.

History Flashback

The Montgomery Bus Boycott

The 1955–56 Montgomery, Alabama bus boycott, which is the subject of *The Long Walk Home,* was described by Dr. Martin Luther King, Jr., as a "movement that was to alter Montgomery forever and to have repercussions throughout the world" (King 1958, 24). This boycott can be seen as both a beginning and an end. What was coming to an end was almost a century of struggle by African Americans to overthrow a rigid system of segregation. Given that the United States was founded on the principles of democracy and equality, does it not seem almost unimaginable that segregation was legal, as well as accepted and practiced by many, until so recently? Well into the 20th century, blacks were set apart, denied the basic opportunities of American society, and persecuted in the most violent ways.

When the South lost the Civil War (1861–65) and two centuries of slavery came to an end, an estimated four million blacks dared to believe that a new life was possible for them. The situation for African Americans did, in fact, quickly improve, and impressive initial strides were made. But the progress achieved during what was known as the Reconstruction period was brief. A backlash of momentous proportions on the part of primarily southern whites, marked by whippings, rapes, mutilations, lynchings, and massacres, acted to replace slavery not with long-awaited equality and freedom but with a new form of subjugation—a system of segregation called Jim Crow.

Perhaps derived from the saying "black as a crow" or from the name of a black enslaved man, James Crow, the term *Jim Crow* referred in the 19th century to a common song-and-dance act in minstrel shows that was performed by whites in blackface (they applied charcoal paste or burnt cork to their faces so they looked black). These entertainers sang and danced in mockery of the supposed clownish and inferior ways of Negroes. It's unclear how the meaning of the term evolved, but by the turn of the century it was used to refer to the entire system of laws and customs that enforced racial segregation and white supremacy in much of the nation, especially in the South. Today we speak of the period from the late 19th century to the 1960s as the *Jim Crow era*. See the fascinating interactive website "The Rise and Fall of Jim Crow," where you can listen to first-hand Jim Crow stories and podcasts *(www.pbs.org/wnet/jimcrow)*, and a second fine resource at *www.jimcrowhistory.org*.

While this system of apartheid was more visible and virulent in the South, other states also segregated the races to varying degrees. Hundreds of laws, decrees, and customs kept whites and blacks apart by requiring separate rest rooms, restaurants, hotels, parks, movie theaters, drinking fountains, railroad cars, and schools. Blacks were to be born in Negro hospitals and buried in Negro cemeteries. In South Carolina, black and white cotton-mill workers were not allowed to look out the same window; in Oklahoma there were separate telephone booths; and in Birmingham, Alabama, blacks and whites were forbidden to play chess together.

Again, from today's perspective, it seems unthinkable that Jim Crow was allowed to prevail for a century after slavery. The first major attempt to overthrow it failed. In 1896 the Jim Crow doctrine came before the U.S. Supreme Court in the infamous case *Plessy v. Ferguson*, which contested the constitutionality of segregated railroads in Louisiana. The outcome of this case represented a devastating blow to the cause of civil rights. The decision revolved around the Supreme Court's interpretation of the Fourteenth Amendment to the U.S. Constitution, which guarantees all citizens equal protection under the law. In this test case, the Supreme Court upheld the states' rights to enforce segregation under the guise that facilities could be "separate but equal." In other words, according to the Court, segregation alone was not sufficient to violate the equal protection clause.

Throughout subsequent years of Jim Crow, opposition was strong and creative from such distinguished black leaders as W.E.B. Du Bois, Ida B. Wells, Mary McLeod Bethune, Marcus Garvey, Asa Philip Randolph, Adam Clayton Powell, Jr., Ralph J. Bunche, Reverend Ralph D. Abernathy, Charles H. Houston, and Thurgood Marshall. These men and women, along with many others, devised strategies to keep the dream of equality alive despite fierce obstacles and the constant threat of violence by members of the Ku Klux Klan and similar white militant groups. Moreover, countless unknown individuals stood up for their rights and helped promote the cause, knowingly risking, and sometimes sacrificing, their lives. Blacks worked through national organizations, labor unions, the military, the media, and the courts to gain their proper place in American life.

Thus, by the time of the bus boycott in Montgomery, a tradition of protest was well established in black America. What was now to take place, however, was unprecedented in American history. Deeply influenced by the teachings of Jesus and Mahatma Gandhi, Reverend Martin Luther King, Jr., a little-known and recently hired 26-year-old pastor at the Dexter Avenue Baptist Church in Montgomery, led common people, professionals, workers, students, and children in a masterfully orchestrated plan of great daring that inspired a national civil rights movement.

As King writes in *Stride toward Freedom: The Montgomery Story* (1958), "I had begun to see early that the Christian doctrine of love operating through the Gandhian method of nonviolence was one of the most potent weapons available to the Negro in his struggle for freedom" (85). King was likewise guided by Henry Thoreau's essay *On the Duty of Civil Disobedience* (1849). He understood from Thoreau the power and righteousness of "refusing to cooperate with an evil system" (91).

King also knew that nonviolent resistance is never passive or safe. Realizing that many people falsely believe it to be a "do-nothing method," he explained that "nothing is further from the truth"; it requires great courage as well as imagination and determination to stand up to power (102). The boycotters were instructed in advance how to behave when taunted, threatened, attacked, or arrested. We see clear examples of this in the film—when, for example, young Franklin Cotter clenches his fists to defend himself against attack by the white boys from the bus and then unclenches them in his commitment to nonviolence.

The historical bus boycott was sparked by Rosa Parks, a 43-year-old seamstress and NAACP (National Association for the Advancement of Colored People) member, who was arrested for refusing to yield her seat on a bus to a white man. At that time, although black patrons accounted for more than three-fourths of all riders in Montgomery, they were forced to sit in the back of the buses—the first five front rows were reserved for whites—and to give up a seat in the back section to any white person who would otherwise have to stand. The opening scene of the film shows an example of how the system worked.

While Rosa Parks deserves enormous credit for her strength and courage, her story is often simplified and romanticized; she is falsely portrayed as a simple seamstress who, exhausted after her day of work, decided at that moment not to yield her seat. To find out the truth, you can read her autobiography, *Quiet Strength* (2000), read accounts written by biographers and historians, or check the website at *www. rosaparks.org*. Questions you might investigate include: Was she the first to defy bus segregation? How had she prepared herself for this act of civil disobedience? What were the roles of other women activists such as Jo Ann Robinson, of whom Martin Luther King, Jr., later wrote, "Apparently indefatigable, she, perhaps more than any other person, was active on every level of the protest" (King 1958, 78).

Rosa Parks's arrest prompted a massive protest in the black community that was planned at first to last for a day but continued for more than a year: from December 5, 1955, to December 20, 1956. As seen in *The Long Walk Home,* organized carpools were critical to the success of the ongoing effort; the sponsors of the boycott provided up to 20,000 rides daily. The film focuses primarily on the first stage of the boycott. If you're interested, you can check into the remarkable details of the year-long effort. Find out:

- Who were the organizers and leaders?
- How was the day-to-day operation financed?
- How was the momentum maintained?
- How did the carpools work?
- What were the dangers?
- What was the White Citizens' Council?
- What was the Montgomery Improvement Association?
- What nonviolent philosophies and tactics were employed?

The historic boycott ended successfully after the U.S. Supreme Court ruled that state and local laws requiring bus segregation were unconstitutional. On December 21, African Americans began riding the buses again—this time taking seats wherever they wished.

After the Boycott

The period immediately following the end of the boycott was a time of unprecedented citizen revolt and social change. Inspired by the success of the Montgomery action and by similar acts of resistance, rebellion by African Americans continued for a decade in a civil rights movement that swept the nation and captured the imagination of people around the world. Newly founded organizations— such as the Congress of Racial Equality (CORE), the Student Non-Violent Coordinating Committee (SNCC), and the Southern Christian Leadership Conference (SCLC)—trained their members, many of whom were students, in the philosophy and tactics of nonviolence and civil disobedience. Sit-ins, kneel-ins, and jail-ins, freedom rides and boycotts, voter registration campaigns and court battles, and marches and mass demonstrations culminated in the 1963 March on Washington for Freedom and Jobs, when more than 250,000 participants converged on the Capitol and Dr. King delivered his "I Have a Dream" speech. Take the opportunity to listen to an excerpt from this historic address as well as to other speeches and sermons often requested by the public at the extraordinary site *www.stanford.edu/group/King/popular_requests*. To learn more about Dr. King and his legacy, visit the King Center website at *http:// thekingcenter.org*.

The beauty of the movement lay not only in its inspiring leadership but also in the determined participation of masses of ordinary people. As described by Lerone Bennett, Jr., in his book *Before the Mayflower: A History of Black America* (1993):

> Blacks hurled themselves in larger and larger numbers against the unyielding bars of the cage of caste. They surged through the streets in waves of indignation. They faced police dogs and armored police tanks. They were clubbed, bombed, stoned, murdered. (386–87)

Though it is hard to describe the phenomenal level of activism on the part of African American citizens nationwide, consider that in one year alone—the 100th anniversary in 1963 of Abraham Lincoln's Emancipation Proclamation that officially freed southern slaves— more than 10,000 racial demonstrations (including sit-ins, lie-ins, sleep-ins, pray-ins, stall-ins) took place and approximately 5,000 black Americans were arrested for political activities (387). (See *www.answers.com/topic/sit-in* for an explanation of sit-in and other related nonviolent forms of protest.)

The first major breakthrough was the ruling of the U.S. Supreme Court in *Brown v. Board of Education* (1954), which effectively overturned *Plessy v. Ferguson* (see page 34) by determining that separate educational facilities were inherently unequal. Think about this for a moment: Whereas the Court had previously ruled that races could be separated as long as facilities were equal, the new ruling stated that "in the field of public education the doctrine of 'separate but equal' has no place." The Court was persuaded by the brilliant arguments of Thurgood Marshall, chief counsel for the NAACP, that there can be no such thing as separate educational facilities for black children that are "equal" to those of whites; given the socio-economic realities, separation inevitably results in inferior schools, causing lasting harm to black children. Although dealing only with segregation in public schools, this case laid the groundwork for the wholesale dismantling of Jim Crow through the Civil Rights Act of 1964—which was the most comprehensive civil rights bill in American history—followed by the Economic Opportunity Act (1964) and the Voting Rights Bill (1965).

While unquestionably constituting enormous victories, the legislation of the period could not alone cut through the "unyielding bars of the cage of caste." In some ways the new laws initially exacerbated the tensions even as they were intended to provide a solution. For many African Americans now disillusioned with what they saw as inadequate results of nonviolent protest, an emerging vision of radical black activism, eloquently articulated by the outspoken orator and writer Malcolm X, began to take hold.

Although assassinated in 1965, Malcolm X gave inspiration and hope to large segments of the African American community. By that year the civil rights movement was losing momentum, and the concepts of black power and black nationalism were gaining credence. The subsequent assassination of Martin Luther King, Jr., in 1968 was experienced nationally and worldwide as a profound blow and loss, and it left the African American community and the civil rights cause in temporary disarray.

Despite the dreams of the 1960s for an integrated society, despite the end of Jim Crow, and despite the gains of the civil rights movement, racial segregation continues to flourish 50 years later in ways that often seem impossible to eradicate. An obvious example is residential segregation. The phenomenon of white flight became widespread in the 1970s, when white city dwellers moved in droves to the suburbs to escape the influx of black neighbors. Today, a fast-growing trend across the country is the establishment of "gated communities," which are generally built for whites and closed to all but residents and their guests.

As 2004, the year of the 50th anniversary of *Brown v. Board of Education,* approached, many reports, articles, and studies appeared in an attempt to evaluate the nation's progress in terms of school integration and racial harmony. Most analysts were forced to conclude that the society had fallen seriously short of the dream to integrate its schools as a means of ensuring equal opportunities for all and also of allowing young children of all races to meet and learn to accept each other. In an article on "The Lost Promise of School Segregation," for example, *The New York Times* reported that "black students became increasingly isolated in the 1990s," with fully one-third of black students attending schools where only one in ten classmates was white (Rosen 2000, 5).

In the years since the civil rights era, many African Americans themselves have come to reject or abandon the hope of genuine integration, preferring instead to live in their own communities and attend their own schools. This voluntary separation is reminiscent of more radical approaches calling for total or near-total separation, approaches advocated by figures like Marcus Garvey, who championed a "return to Africa" in the 1920s, and Elijah Muhammad (see pages 123). For more on this topic, see *Integration or Separation: A Strategy for Racial Equality* by legal scholar Roy L. Brooks (1996), who puts forth a powerful argument for "limited separation" (199).

Notwithstanding undeniable progress since the era depicted in *The Long Walk Home,* Americans cannot yet claim with any degree of satisfaction that the realities of the 21st century live up to the professed ideals of a democratic society. Whether and how Americans of all ethnic backgrounds are able to keep moving toward the type of society envisioned by Martin Luther King, Jr., Malcolm X, and other champions of the civil rights era remains an open question.

Student's P.O.V.

I am curious as to why the story had to be told by Miriam's daughter, a white person, and not by Odessa's daughter . . . or why did it need to be told from someone else's perspective at all? Perhaps the movie industry thinks that an ethnic story is more palatable to a mainstream audience if a white person has the lead role, as in *Shogun* (Richard Chamberlain), *Hawaii* (Julie Andrews), *The Last Samurai* (Tom Cruise), and *Driving Miss* Daisy (Jessica Tandy).

—Pamela Bennett, Adult Degree Student, Ethnicity Japanese/ Portuguese, born and raised in Hawaii

---

Poet's P.O.V.

The Funeral of Martin Luther King, Jr.
Nikki Giovanni

His headstone said
FREE AT LAST, FREE AT LAST
But death is a slave's freedom
We seek the freedom of free men
And the construction of a world
Where Martin Luther King could have lived and
preached non-violence.

Cultural Backpacking:
African American Historical Sites

African American cultural travel has been flourishing over the past few decades as millions of black Americans are discovering and reinterpreting their heritage. Rather than seeing the historical experiences of enslavement and forced segregation as a source of shame, African Americans are taking pride in the ability of their ancestors to resist and survive, to endure the most dehumanizing conditions with dignity and creativity.

Many African Americans are researching their family trees and tracing their roots back as far as possible, whether to Africa, the Caribbean, or other places. The television miniseries *Roots* (1977) played a key role in changing the consciousness of black and other Americans with regard to understanding and honoring their past.

The burgeoning African American tourism industry focuses on sites relevant to the history of slavery, the civil rights movement, black literary achievement, and jazz and other musical innovations. There are various guidebooks that describe, for example, tours of the historic black South, black Washington, DC, and black New York City. Websites you might consult include an interactive site, primarily for children, which allows one to travel the Underground Railroad *(www.nationalgeographic.com/railroad/j1.html)*, and a fascinating heritage guide to Harlem at *www.harlemheritage.com*. (If you visit the National

Geographic Underground Railroad site, see whether you think it's a good idea to place people in the role of an escaping slave, as is done here.)

In the spirit of discovering and redefining the past, put on your backpacks to explore a part of African America that is meaningful to you. Wherever you choose to travel, try to be fully open to the new experience. You may visit a museum, memorial, church, or historic site, or you may attend a meeting or cultural event. You can probably find out about interesting possibilities from your campus multicultural office or Black Students Association. Alternatively, you may choose to do your backpacking in the library or at your computer. Whatever the case, your task is to explore something that gives you new insight into, and appreciation for, African American people and cultures.

When you have completed your backpacking, write a page to describe what you chose and why. What did you experience, both emotionally and intellectually? What gave you a meaningful glimpse into African American culture?

A reminder: Be sure to limit your choices. For example, if you visit a museum in real life or on the Internet, "zoom in" on one painting, sculpture, or other object. If you attend a musical performance, choose one musical piece. If possible, include a picture or photo of what you chose in your write-up, and be sure to include the relevant URL or other source information.

If you are African American, you may wish to revisit a place that is meaningful to you and that you would like to share with others. Or you may decide to explore and find something new.

Diversity Detective: A Better History Textbook

Your detective firm has been charged with tracking down perspectives on the African American past that are not widely known. These points of view will be used in the development of a new American history textbook to be distributed nationwide. After reading this section, search the Internet or other sources to find one particular fact, person, tradition, custom, or perspective you personally want to see included in the textbook. See *www.africanaonline.com* and be sure to track down at least one other interesting website. Write a page to explain what you wish to include in the history book and why, and provide the source of your information.

African American history and culture have long been given too little attention in U.S. schools and universities. An example of a nation-wide attempt to rectify the situation is Black History Month. Many African Americans and others are working to add missing parts to the story as well as to rewrite American history in its entirety from new perspectives. As historians reexamine and revise standard accounts of the past (thus the term *revisionist* history), new questions arise. Whose history—whose p.o.v.—matters? That of conquerors, presidents, and military leaders? That of people like us? That of women, children, workers, and enslaved persons? And who is entitled to tell history?

The question of who controls history—and of how the criteria for historical validity are established—is illustrated by the ongoing debate over Afrocentrism. Simply defined, Afrocentrism is "the study of Africa and its history from a non-European perspective" (Appiah and Gates 1999, 45). The term was coined in 1976 by revisionist scholar and professor Molefi Keti Asante. According to Afrocentric ideology, ancient Egypt —which is viewed as a black society—is regarded as the source of Western civilization rather than ancient Greece. An Afrocentric curriculum in the schools would allow students to learn more about the central role of Africa, Africans, and African Americans than has traditionally been the case. Critics of Afrocentrism, such as classical scholar Mary Lefkowitz (*Not Out of Africa: How Afrocentrism Became an Excuse to Teach Myth as History*, 1996) vigorously oppose it as a distorted or inaccurate way of viewing history. For further information, see *www.swagga.com*.

Probably the most influential, and highly regarded, comprehensive revisionist work is Howard Zinn's *A People's History of the United States* (2005). Other landmark volumes include Ronald Takaki's *A Different Mirror: A History of Multicultural America* (1993) and Dee Brown's *Bury My Heart at Wounded Knee: An Indian History of the American West* (1970).

Spotlight: Freedom Songs of the Civil Rights Movement

From the earliest days of enslavement, music was the African American's primary source of self-expression, offering some measure of solace, diversion, and inspiration in times of desperation. Through their music, enslaved people could maintain traces of their former cultures, they could yearn for freedom and better lives, and they could communicate their protest and hopes to each other in masked language. A rich oral tradition of black music evolved, including such forms as spirituals, field hollers, and work songs.

Drawing on this tradition, protesters in Montgomery and throughout the civil rights movement again turned to music to galvanize the people, reinforce their communal bonds, and lift their spirits. Their music was sung everywhere—in the streets, on buses, at mass meetings and rallies, in churches, in police stations, in jails, and in cemeteries. It has been described as some of the most powerful music in human history.

While some of the old songs were revived with virtually no changes, others were recast and updated—and words were changed to fit the times. The anthem of the movement, *We Shall Overcome*, has since been adopted by people struggling for their rights worldwide. You might be interested in trying to locate recordings, sheet music, and information about such songs as *O Freedom*, *Ain't Gonna Let Nobody Turn Me 'Round*, *Free at Last*, *I'm Travelin' to Mississippi on the Greyhound Bus Line*, *No More Jailhouse over Me*, and *Keep Your Eyes on the Prize*. Listen again to *We're Marching to Zion* and *Going through Jesus*, both of which are sung in *The Long Walk Home*. (An excellent resource for information and audio recordings is *www.negrospirituals.com*.)

 ## What's Cooking? Soul Food

What picture does the term "soul food" conjure up in your mind? Possibly a table laden with delicious and hearty homemade foods such as Southern fried chicken and biscuits, gumbo, cornbread, and sweet potato pie? These are but a few of the foods that have become a beloved part of African American cuisine. Did you know that historically these flavorful dishes resulted from the ingenuity of enslaved peoples who brought knowledge and skills from Africa and then had to make do with whatever leftovers they received from the plantation houses? Today, soul food (the familiar name for African American cuisine) encompasses everything from yams, greens, and okra to spicy sauces to incredible desserts like fudge pie. To learn more, consult *www.foxhome.com/soulfood/htmls/soulfood.html*, *www.soulfoodcookbook.com*, or *www.soulfoodonline.net/index.php*. Work with other students to choose a recipe and try it. Write a page about the experience in your film notebook.

Lights! Camera! ACTION!

Take a look at the inspiring Civil Rights Memorial *(www.splcenter. org/crm/memorial.jsp)* designed by Maya Lin (the Chinese American architect of the Vietnam Veterans Memorial) for the Southern Poverty Law Center (SPLC). Under the leadership of founder Morris Dees, the SPLC has long been involved in combating discrimination. Also, consult the Tolerance pages of the SPLC website for ideas about how you might become involved in anti-bias efforts *(www.splcenter.org/center/torg/toler.jsp)*.

Your P.O.V.

1. Flash forward ten years, and imagine a meeting between Odessa and Miriam. Under what circumstances do you think they might meet? What would they discuss? Write a script of their dialogue. Or write an outline of a plot for a sequel to the film.

2. You are interested in how power affects communication in the film. Find a scene that illustrates a point you would like to make, and analyze the scene in a page or so. Be sure to consider both verbal and nonverbal communication in your write-up.

3. Take the p.o.v. of a passenger (either black, white, or some-one from another ethnic background or nationality) riding on the bus on December 1 when Rosa Parks refused to move. Write an account of what you witnessed and describe your thoughts and feelings.

4. Imagine you were to be denied your most important form of transportation (whether it be a car, bus, subway, or other form) for a year. What impact would this have on you? How would you cope? How would you feel?

5. Imagine what the next day after the ending of the film might be like. What happens on this day? What is the mood? What types of conversations take place?

6. Have you ever taken an action you would consider to be a form of civil disobedience? If so, what did you do and why? How did you feel? What were the results?

7. Imagine that you and your crew are making a film on African American life, history, and culture. Consult the guidelines in Appendix D for further information. Here are some potential topics for consideration:

   a. gated communities

   b. Spike Lee's contributions to filmmaking

   c. Black English as a distinct language

   d. the role and value of historically black colleges and universities (HBCUs) today

   e. the women behind the scenes of the civil rights movement

   f. the latest in hip-hop culture

And Our African American Book Awards Go To . . .

The African-American Century: How Black Americans Have Shaped Our Country by Henry Louis Gates, Jr., and Cornel West (New York: Simon and Schuster, 2000). An intriguing and highly readable collection of short biographies (including photos) of 100 of the past century's leading black figures. Scholars Gates and West explain that one fundamental truth informs the book: "American life is inconceivable without its black presence" (xv). From intellectual W.E.B. Du Bois to jazz diva Sara Vaughan and golf superstar Tiger Woods, these individuals had the courage to "embody and live their respective truths in the face of overwhelming obstacles" (xiii–xiv).

American Negro Poetry, edited by Arna Bontemps (New York: Hill and Wang, 2000). A small volume that has sold more than 200,000 copies since it first appeared in 1963. Even if you don't normally read poetry, you'll find treasures here. A new 2000 edition offers, for just $12, the great African American voices past and present, many renowned and others lesser known.

Before the Mayflower: History of Black America (6th ed.) by Lerone Bennett, Jr. (New York: Penguin Books, 1993). A classic history book that is wonderful to read. African American historian Bennett set out to bring this story alive for a large audience of readers and to capture its drama and humanity. He succeeded. If you read only one history book about African Americans, this is the one.

Fight the Power: Rap, Race and Reality by Chuck D with Yusuf Jah (New York: Dell Publishing, 1998). An insider's view of hip-hop culture by the controversial lead singer of the rap group Public Enemy. A long-time community activist, Chuck D helps us understand the phenomenon of hip hop within the context of larger social, racial, and artistic issues. You might read his book together with *Hip Hop America* by Nelson George (New York: Penguin, 1998) to gain an understanding of hip hop as, what George calls, "a music, a style, a business, a myth, and a moral force."

And Our African American Film Awards Go To . . .

Do the Right Thing (1989)—A masterful film that is intriguing, entertaining, disturbing, and thought-provoking. Director Spike Lee brings African Americans, Italian Americans, Korean Americans, and Puerto Ricans together inside Sal's Pizzeria and outside on the street of one block in Brooklyn to make a powerful statement on racial tension and violence.

Glory (1989)—An unforgettable epic film about the little-known Massachusetts 54th Colored Infantry, an all-black unit that served heroically during the Civil War. Directed by Edward Zwick.

Mississippi Burning (1988)—Based on the true story of the FBI investigation of the disappearance of three civil rights workers in Mississippi during the summer of 1964. Some critics fault the film for giving undue attention to the role of whites in the civil rights movement and also for exaggerating the concern shown by the FBI, but the film remains a classic indictment of racism. Directed by Alan Parker.

Something the Lord Made (2004)—Based on the true story of the pioneering work in heart surgery by Alfred Blalock and Vivien Thomas. Working as a team at Johns Hopkins University for more than 30 years, Blalock and Thomas made medical history, but as an African American, Thomas was long denied recognition. This painful, inspiring film is a little-known gem. Directed by Joseph Sargent.

3

Chinese American Culture:
The Joy Luck Club

Setting the Scene:
Freewriting and Discussion

This photograph is taken from the film *The World of Suzie Wong* (1960). Look at it carefully, and freewrite your thoughts in your film notebook. You might consider: Is this the image that comes to mind when you think of Asian women? Why or why not? If you were an Asian American woman, what would you think of this portrayal? Why do you suppose these women are depicted as sensual and exotic? Discuss what you wrote with a partner or small group.

Sneak Preview

About the Film

The Joy Luck Club (1993), based on Amy Tan's 1989 best-selling novel of the same name, was a landmark in Asian American cinema. A spectacular success, it has the distinction of being one of the first feature films to bring Asian American family life and identity issues before the general public. While Asian martial arts and action films have long been popular throughout the world, Asian Americans as real, ordinary people have had little place on the big screen. (For information on outstanding documentaries on Asians and Asian Americans, check *www.asianamericanmedia.org* and *www.aems.uiuc.edu/index.las.*)

In the film you will be drawn into the lives of eight women—four mothers born during the harsh times of early 20th-century imperial China and their four daughters born into privilege and prosperity in America. It is a classic story of the conflicts—and bonds—that exist between first- and second-generation immigrants.

The film begins with a voice-over Chinese fable that encapsulates the hopes and "good intentions" of the four mothers—Suyuan, Lindo, Ying Ying, and An-Mei—for their respective daughters June, Waverly, Lena, and Rose. June narrates the fable that, as we later learn, was told to her by her mother Suyuan:

> In America, I will have a daughter just like me, but over there nobody will say her worth is measured by the loudness of her husband's belch. Over there, nobody will look down on her because I will make her speak only perfect American English. And over there, she will always be too full to swallow any sorrow.

In China, the mothers led lives of struggle and pain; they had to "eat bitterness," as the Chinese expression goes. At this time in Chinese history, women were subordinate to men and restricted to narrow, prescribed roles in life. Brought up to desire nothing for themselves, they were to spend their lives serving others, not only the men in their lives, but also their husbands' parents. Bearing a son was all-important, whereas a daughter was considered a burden. According to a Chinese proverb, *Eighteen gifted daughters are not equal to one lame son.*

But Suyuan, Lindo, Ying Ying, and An-Mei dare to dream of joy and luck, if not for themselves, then one day for their daughters. They see departure from their homeland as a chance to break free from the oppression and misery of a culture that devalues women and to find a place where "nobody will look down on" their daughters. Contrary to all their hopes and efforts, however, they ultimately see the same destructive patterns repeating themselves in their daughters' lives. Instead of being "too full to swallow any sorrow," their Chinese American daughters are plagued with doubts about who they are and how they should behave. Even with all the freedoms and opportunities of America, these young women have not yet become strong and self-confident.

As you get to know the eight women in the film, keep in mind that throughout decades of American cinema, leading roles depicting Asian women have often been offered to Caucasian actresses. It is astonishing to see the lengths that Hollywood has gone to over the years to "orientalize" white actresses—with cosmetologists applying heavy makeup to their faces and taping their eyes to achieve the desired effect. Consider Katherine Hepburn playing the role of Jade, a heroic young Chinese woman, in *Dragon Seed* (1944), and you get the idea. In general, the few screen roles available to Asian American actresses have been superficial and demeaning. As Filipina author and screenwriter Jessica Hagedorn explains in her article "Asian Women in Film: No Joy, No Luck" (1994):

> Most Hollywood movies either trivialize or exoticize us as people of color and as women. Our intelligence is underestimated, our humanity overlooked, and our diverse cultures treated as interchangeable. If we are 'good,' we are childlike, submissive, silent, and eager for sex. . . . And if we are not silent, suffering doormats, we are demonized dragon ladies—cunning, deceitful, sexual provocateurs. (74)

In *The Joy Luck Club,* the filmmakers were determined to show Asian Americans who, as Tan puts it, "are not emperors, not martial artists, not servants in rich houses" (Corliss 1993, 70). Certainly, they succeeded in achieving their goal with all eight women. Ironically, however, the film has been criticized for perpetuating negative stereotypes of Asian males, who are often portrayed in the cinema as weak, sexless, and conniving. The response to the critics from director Wayne

Wang is straight to the point: "If the Asian men want to have a movie that's deeper and more complex about the men, well, let them write a great book about it, and I'll make a movie of it" (Xing 1998, 187). As you watch the film, see what you think of the Chinese and Chinese American male characters. Are they negative and superficial?

About the Filmmakers and Actors of *The Joy Luck Club*

Amy (An-mei) Tan was born in Oakland, California, in 1952 as the daughter of Chinese immigrants John and Daisy Tan. She and her mother had a stormy relationship, partly because of her mother's expectations that her only daughter become a concert pianist or brain surgeon. Among other ways, Tan rebelled by leaving the college of her mother's choosing and following her future husband to San Jose, where she completed her undergraduate studies and earned a master's degree in linguistics at San Jose State University.

Tan's novel hit the bestseller lists within the first two weeks of its appearance, and she was instantly approached by movie and television producers. She says, "I met with dozens of people who wanted to make the book into a movie. Five actually made offers, but I never took them. I wasn't entirely convinced that it *should* be a movie." She explains her hesitations: "What if the movie was made and it was a terrible depiction of Asian Americans? What if the movie showed women wearing coolie hats and tight dresses slit up their thighs?" (Tan 2003a, 180–81) It wasn't until she met Wang that she decided to go ahead. Tan says she and the director "ended up having such a wonderful conversation" about their own past experiences that she knew she "wanted him on the project" (Xing 1998, 35).

Like Amy Tan, Wayne Wang is familiar with both the Chinese and American worlds, having been born in Hong Kong in 1949 and raised in a bilingual home. After graduating from a Jesuit high school in Hong Kong, he moved to California, where he earned a bachelor's degree in painting and a master's degree in film and television. His first commercially successful film, the low-budget *Chan Is Missing* (1982), deals in a humorous way with the search for a missing man in San Francisco's Chinatown. While remaining dedicated to Chinese and Chinese American themes in subsequent films such as *Dim Sum* (1985), *Eat a Bowl of Tea* (1989), and *Chinese Box* (1997), Wang did not want to restrict himself to a single genre, as evidenced by films such as

Slamdance (1987), *Smoke* (1995), *Anywhere But Here* (1999), and *The Center of the World* (2001).

Wang tells his own story of how he became involved with the filming of Tan's novel:

> I read *The Joy Luck Club* as a book, and I loved it, and I said, "There's a movie here." Amy Tan happens to live in San Francisco, so I somehow got her phone number, asked her out for a meeting, and just basically begged her to let me make this movie. Then the two of us hooked up with Ron Bass, and we wrote the script for it. Nobody wanted to make the movie, because everybody said, "Well, this is a movie about eight Chinese women? Who's going to go see it? You can't even find enough good actresses to play them." *(http://filmforce.ign.com)*

Eventually Disney agreed that Wang could make the film (and that he and Tan could have creative control) but allowed him very little money. Operating on a minimal budget of $10.5 million, Wang and his crew succeeded.

The eight lead actresses won their roles in auditions with 400 Asian competitors. Though not necessarily recognizable to American audiences, the mothers or "aunties" all have distinguished careers. Kieu Chinh (Suyuan) and Tsai Chin (Lindo) are celebrated actresses in Vietnam and China, respectively. In addition to acting, Chin has written an autobiography called *Daughter of Shanghai* (1994), directed theater internationally, and taught at Tufts University. Lisa Lu (An-Mei) has published a translation of Chinese plays and is a respected journalist. France Nuyen (Ying Ying) debuted in the movie of the musical *South Pacific* (1958), played the title role in the Broadway production of *The World of Suzie Wong,* and has had a long career with many TV and movie appearances. She is also a professional therapist for abused women and children.

Among the daughters, you might know Rosalind Chao (Rose) from her lead role in *Thousand Pieces of Gold* (1991) and Tamlyn Tomita (Waverly) from her lead roles in *Come See the Paradise* (1990) and *Picture Bride* (1994). Lauren Tom (Lena) is popular with science fiction fans for her long career in the television series *Star Trek: The Next Generation* and *Star Trek: Deep Space Nine*. She has also appeared in Broadway musicals. Ming-Na Wen (June) is the voice of Mulan in the animated film *Mulan* (1998) and is known to fans of the television series *ER* as Dr. Jing-Mei Chen.

In a 1993 interview, the actresses explained that their own lives were similar to their roles in the film, often in painful ways. Rosalind Chao laughingly recalls how playing piano was "a big thing" for practically every child: "Walk up to any Asian American and you'll find a pianist." Ming-Na Wen relates to June's lack of self-confidence, recalling her own move from China to the United States at the age of four and the difficulties of being the only Asian child in her school. "There were these incredible insecurities," she says, such as "not being able to speak English, not really fitting in, not knowing the Pledge of Allegiance." And Kieu Chinh draws a parallel between her character Suyuan's decision to leave her infant twins on the roadside and her own experiences of being separated first as a young girl from her family in Vietnam, and later from her own two children, whom she sent to safety in Canada before being able to flee Saigon herself in 1975. "Mother and children separated, evacuation, refugees—this is what my own life is about," she says (Simpson 1993, 45–46).

A ninth "actress" is Amy Tan, who has a walk-on role as a guest coming into the farewell party just as the film begins.

Who's Who in the Film

Jing-Mei **"June"** Woo (Ming-Na Wen)

Suyuan Woo (Kieu Chinh)—June's mother

Waverly Jong (Tamlyn Tomita)

Lindo Jong (Tsai Chin)—Waverly's mother

Lena St. Clair (Lauren Tom)

Ying Ying St. Clair (France Nuyen)—Lena's mother

Rose Hsu Jordon (Rosalind Chao)

An-Mei Hsu (Lisa Lu)—Rose's mother

Rich (Christopher Rich)—Waverly's husband

Ted Jordan (Andrew McCarthy)—Rose's husband

Harold (Michael Paul Chan)—Lena's husband

Director—Wayne Wang

Screenwriters—Amy Tan and Ronald Bass

On a first viewing, it can be difficult to keep the characters apart. The frequent flashbacks can be confusing, and some characters are played by multiple actors, such as An-Mei at age 4, at age 9, and as a grown woman. We suggest that you fill in this chart with some hints to help you remember who the characters are. We've put in some examples.

Mother/daughter	Something about her past life that helps you remember who she is	Something about her present life that helps you remember who she is
Auntie Suyuan	Had twin babies in China	
Daughter June		Takes her mother's place at the mah-jong table
Auntie Lindo		Goes to beauty parlor with Waverly
Daughter Waverly	Was Chinatown chess champion	
Auntie Ying Ying	At age four watched her mother sent away in disgrace	
Daughter Lena		Hates ice cream
Auntie An-Mei	Mother was raped and then became a concubine	
Daughter Rose	Had a fellowship in fine arts	

Terms to Know

ABC—Slang for *American-born Chinese.*

Asian American—Broad label used to refer to Americans from more than twenty Asian nations. Many Asian Americans prefer more specific categories, such as Filipino/a, Hmong, or Korean American.

Chink, chinaman, slanteye—Disparaging terms for Chinese.

coolie—Meaning an unfree or a slave laborer, used in an insulting way to apply to any Chinese worker. Historically, many Chinese immigrants came voluntarily to the United States, so they were not coolies.

FOB—Slang, usually disrespectful, for newly arrived Asians who are "fresh off the boat."

Oriental—Once used neutrally to refer to Asian Americans but now widely rejected as having negative connotations associated with exoticism. Today the term is used to refer to carpets or other objects but generally not to people.

yellow—Derogatory term referring to people of Asian descent. The skin color of most Asians and Asian Americans is actually more tan or brown than yellow. The term is universally rejected as having associations with cowardice. *Yellow menace* and *yellow peril* have been used to incite fear that America will be overrun by people from Asia.

History Flashback

Set in the present day, *The Joy Luck Club* tells the tale of four Chinese immigrants and their four American-born daughters. The lives of these eight women are part of a history of Asian immigration that reaches back to the late 1840s. To understand the historical background of the film, we must examine two distinct strands of Chinese immigration, one of men and one of women.

When Anglo Americans express pride in this country as a land of immigrants, they do not typically think to include newcomers from Asia. What Anglos understand by the term *immigration* is usually limited to the influx, since colonial days, of millions of Europeans. The two renowned landmarks of this immigration, the Statue of Liberty and Ellis Island—where new arrivals were detained before they were admitted or sent back—are both on the Atlantic coast.

Asians who made the journey across the Pacific Ocean and landed on the West Coast—after detainment at places such as Angel Island in San Francisco Bay—have been for the most part quietly overlooked. But contemporary scholars like Ronald Takaki (1989) have uncovered and recorded accounts of those who came with the same dreams as the Europeans but were afforded little opportunity to realize them. Of the immigrants from more that twenty "different shores" who landed on the West Coast, the Chinese were the first to come in large numbers. (See *www.angelisland.org/immigr02.html.*)

These early Chinese venturers were almost exclusively men. Yearning to escape poverty as well as political and social upheaval, tens of thousands of peasants, mostly young married men from the southeastern province of Guangdong, left to seek their fortunes in Hawaii and in the gold fields of California (a place the Chinese called *gam saan,* or "Gold Mountain"). They generally expected to stay only a few years—long enough to pay back their passage and save enough to return home to their families as wealthy, respected men.

Gradually, most of the men came to realize that they were trapped on Gold Mountain with no way to pay for their family's passage over or even for their own return trip. Their story is one of determination, ingenuity, and hard work in a place that initially counted on them as cheap, reliable labor but then turned against them. In California and nearby states, Chinese men were a vital part of the workforce in mid-century, originally playing a valuable role in the mining industry. When mining became less lucrative, they moved into other areas, establishing restaurants and laundries and working in construction and factories. Their key role in building the nation's transcontinental and western railroad networks is well documented, and you can read accounts of their skill and daring at *www.cprr.org/Museum/Chinese.html.*

As experienced farmers, they also helped to develop California's agriculture. They reclaimed farmland from swamps, became skilled fruit packers, developed the shrimp industry in the San Francisco Bay area, worked in vineyards, and became tenant farmers and truck gardeners. Their innovations in agriculture extended well beyond California. In Oregon, for example, Ah Bing bred the famous Bing cherry, and plant genius Lue Gim Gong developed the frost-resistant orange so vital to Florida's citrus industry.

In the final decades of the century, however, the economic and political landscape changed. A nation where land and opportunities had always seemed limitless was now faced with a new situation of economic depression and unemployment. In a cruel twist of fate, the Chinese workers' reputation for dedication, speed, and reliability on the job worked to their detriment, triggering anti-Chinese sentiment on the part of whites who complained about unfair competition from "heathens" and "barbarians." Outright racism was condoned, including mob violence, attacks by the press, and discriminatory legislation. Scholar Elaine Kim summarizes the various ways in which the Chinese were persecuted by the law:

> [There were] ordinances against laundries, laws against long hair, laws requiring a certain amount of cubic feet of air per Chinese person, a tax on being Chinese, laws against getting business licenses, laws against attending schools with whites or testifying against whites in court, laws against intermarriages, laws prohibiting Chinese from owning land, and, of course, laws against Chinese immigration or naturalization. (Hagedorn 2004, viii–ix)

The most severe of the "laws against Chinese immigration or naturalization" was the infamous Chinese Exclusion Act (1882), which prohibited Chinese (except for merchants) from entering the country and made it illegal for those already here to become citizens or bring their wives. Belonging to a culture in which family was all important, most of the men living on Gold Mountain were destined to live out their lives alone.

Ironically, the fears that led to the Exclusion Act—that hordes of Chinese were entering the country and threatening the American way of life—were unfounded in terms of actual population statistics. At the time, only two in every one thousand people in the United States were Chinese. But the anxieties and hostilities persisted. The original 1882 exclusion legislation was later renewed and broadened, remaining in effect until 1943. Even then, the number of legal entrants from China was limited to a token annual quota of 105. Though this history is not widely known to the general population, the period of more than 60 years of exclusion lives as a painful memory in the minds of many Chinese Americans.

Even in the early years when U.S. immigration was still relatively open, few Chinese women traveled to Gold Mountain. There were many obstacles. The two-month journey by ship was considered too arduous, as were the living conditions in mining and frontier towns. Men who were still paying off their own passage could not afford to bring their wives. And cultural restrictions on women in Chinese society kept them from leaving.

These cultural restrictions are depicted in memorable detail in the film, but we need to remember that, unlike documentaries and some historical films, *The Joy Luck Club* does not strive to give a completely true or accurate picture of China. Tan clearly sees herself as an artist rather than a historian or ethnic scholar: "I know from reactions to my fiction that there are people who believe that the raison-d'être of any story with an ethnic angle is to provide an educational lesson on culture. I find that attitude about art restrictive" (Tan 2003a, 191).

With this caution in mind, we can nonetheless gain from the mothers' stories some insight into Chinese women's situations in the 19th and early 20th centuries. At that time China was a feudal, patriarchal society in which women's roles were predetermined and highly traditional. Following the Confucian social order, women were destined to assume roles subservient to men. The Confucian three obediences prescribed a lifetime of servitude, first to the father, then to the husband, and finally to the eldest son. Girls were usually betrothed at a young age by matchmakers and had to leave their homes to serve their husbands and in-laws. Their worth depended primarily on their ability to manage the household and produce male heirs. While men could divorce, remarry, commit adultery, and keep concubines and mistresses, female adulterers were punished, and widowed women were not supposed to remarry. In *The Joy Luck Club*, you will witness Lindo, at age four, being introduced to matchmakers and then groomed over the next ten years for marriage to a man she has never met. Also at age four, An-Mei experiences the injustice done to her mother, a widow whose parents reject her, turning her onto the street in disgrace after she is raped by a wealthy man. And you will see lovely young Ying Ying's mistreatment at the hands of her husband, a cruel philanderer.

The story of Lindo shows the inescapable misery of a peasant mother and daughter, whose poverty leaves them with virtually no options and no hope. But it also becomes evident from the other stories that wealth and status do not spare women from mistreatment, suffering, and entrapment. (In fact—though we do not see examples in the film—historically the practice of foot-binding was more commonly found among more well-to-do families who could afford the luxury of keeping women relatively inactive and immobile.)

How, we might wonder, did Chinese women view lives in which they were the property of men? While millions of women undoubtedly knew nothing other than to accept their fate, there was, in fact, a tradition of bold defiance shown by those who refused to submit to their prescribed lot in life. Can you recall scenes in the film that show women making extraordinary attempts to change their situations?

Among those who defied the odds are women who escaped to America. Until recently, little was known about their lives. Groundbreaking research by scholars such as Judy Yung in *Unbound Feet: A Social History of Chinese Women in San Francisco* (1995) and Huping Ling in *Surviving on the Gold Mountain: A History of Chinese American Women and Their Lives* (1998) provides a fascinating view into a part of history that to date is rarely found in textbooks.

In her introduction to *Unbound Feet*, Yung poses a central, and unsettling, question: "Did immigration, work, and family life in America oppress Chinese women or liberate them?" (5) Unfortunately, as she and others show, the promise of a better life in America was, at least for the first generation of immigrants, an illusion. For the most part, these women faced severe forms of oppression in America, not only from gender and class, but additionally from being a racial minority.

The least fortunate of the first-generation women were those who were stolen, bought, traded, or deceived by traffickers who imported them and forced them into prostitution or domestic slavery. For these destitute, illiterate women and girls, Gold Mountain offered no more freedom or equality than had their lives in China.

The women who came as higher-class wives of merchants were kept protected indoors, but as virtual prisoners. Since many of them had bound feet, they could not walk or stand for long, let alone venture out on their own.

Lower-class women who were married to laborers would have toiled beside them—laundering, mining, fishing, and performing other strenuous work in addition to their household duties. Those who lived in rural areas were often viewed as curiosities and given generic names like China Mary by Anglos. Though most of their stories remain unknown, a few have survived, providing fascinating glimpses into these women's strength and adaptability.

One such story with a relatively happy outcome is that of Polly Bemis, who was born into poverty in northern China and sold by her father to bandits for two bags of seed. Resold for $2,500 into prostitution in America, she was freed, as the story goes, by Charlie Bemis, who won her in a poker game. The truth seems to be that another Chinese woman called Molly was won in a different poker game, but Polly did marry Charlie Bemis and was able to thrive as a successful Idaho farmer beloved in her small community (see *www.mccunn.com/PollyBemis.html*).

During the period between the Exclusion Act and World War II, women desiring to join their husbands or immigrate for other reasons often entered the United States with false papers or were brought in by smugglers. Women finally achieved some hope of legal entry with the War Brides Act of 1946, an important step in reversing decades of discriminatory immigration policies against Asians. (A film that gives a sense of the importance of the War Brides Act in personal terms is the classic *Sayonara* [1957] starring Marlon Brando.)

This new legislation permitted Asian wives and children of all U.S. servicemen to enter as non-quota immigrants (meaning they were not subject to the restriction of 105 legal entrants each year), making possible the arrival of nearly 8,000 Chinese women between 1946 and 1950. The four Chinese mothers in *The Joy Luck Club* immigrated during this post-war period, but the exact circumstances are not made clear in the movie.

Entry restrictions were dramatically relaxed when Congress reformed immigration law in 1965. With the passing of the landmark Immigration and Nationality Act of 1965, U.S. government policy that had long favored northern and western Europeans began to allow immigrants from other parts of the world to compete on a more equal basis. This legislation was so important in immigration history that it can be seen as the basis for what we know today as our multicultural society, truly made up of people from all of the world. See *www.cis.org/articles/1995/back395.html* for interesting information on this act and its legacy. After the 1965 law went into effect, the number of Chinese immigrants from Taiwan and Hong Kong, including many students, increased substantially. The normalization of relations between the United States and mainland China in the late 1970s, coupled with the liberalization of China's emigration policy, led to a large growth in immigrants from the mainland.

Since 1965 a new class of Chinese Americans has emerged, as upwardly mobile second- and third-generation professionals have been joined by many highly educated immigrants entering the ranks of white-collar employment. In recent decades the phenomenal success of Chinese Americans and Japanese Americans in achieving the American Dream has led to the stereotype of Asian Americans as the model minority: hardworking, uncomplaining, brilliant in school, and highly accomplished in their professions. Think about how this stereotype might apply to the four daughters in the film and how, although it is positive, it can nonetheless be harmful. If you are interested in learning more about it, check the website at *http://modelminority.com.*

Insider's P.O.V.

I know some of the scenes of the movie can be so absurd to people who don't understand Chinese culture. To me, the stories told in the movie are very true. I think many people will be shocked when An-Mei's mother cuts the flesh of her arm and cooks it in a soup for her mother to eat. None of my acquaintances have done this, but in China there is a proverb *to cut the leg to cure the parents.* This goes back to the tradition in imperial China when parents were ill, and some children would cut the flesh of their leg and use it as medication to treat their sick parents and show their filial piety. For centuries in China, the most important virtue of a person was to be loyal to the Emperor and to one's parents. Though in modern China, people no longer follow this tradition of cutting their flesh, children are still expected to be obedient to their parents and to live up to what their parents expect of them.

—Yonghua Yang, Lecturer in English, Wenzhou University,
People's Republic of China

Cultural Backpacking: Chinatowns

San Francisco, where the four mothers of *The Joy Luck Club* lived and raised their daughters, is the home of the oldest large-scale Chinese neighborhood, or Chinatown, in the United States. Having received the label Chinatown from the press in 1853, the San Francisco neighborhood grew in the next 30 years to comprise twelve blocks populated by 26,000 people, then fell to a low of 11,000 by 1920. Along with Chinatowns in many other large U.S. cities, it survives today as an intriguing combination of old and new.

How did the old Chinatowns like the one in San Francisco come to be? Why and how have they changed? What role do they play in the lives of Chinese Americans today? What draws tourists from all over the world to Chinatowns? What do tourists see and what remains hidden to them?

Purposes served by Chinatowns have changed with the times. Originally, men who spoke little English, faced frequent insults and prejudice, and planned to stay for only a limited time lived together in largely self-contained Chinese neighborhoods. Here they could receive needed support in the form of religious, political, and social organizations, but as men without families, they nonetheless faced hard years of loneliness and desperation, turning to gambling parlors, opium dens, and houses of prostitution for solace and recreation. During the exclusionary period, populations in Chinatowns shrank, and some of the original ones are no longer in existence.

But a new era began with the 1965 reform in immigration law (see page 59); since then, many old Chinatowns across the country have been revitalized by immigrants from Hong Kong, Taiwan, and mainland China. For example, the original six-block perimeter of Chinatown in Manhattan has flourished over the past 25 years and now encompasses a 30-block area.

Due to overcrowding in the inner cities, so-called suburban or satellite Chinatowns have sprung up in places such as Edison, New Jersey, and Alhambra, California, near Los Angeles. All too often, these are places where unacceptable working conditions for newly arrived immigrants prevail:

Whether in New York, California, or elsewhere in the country, late-20th century Chinatowns have something in common: they provide low wage employment in industries that would have left the United States long ago if not for the cheap labor of new immigrants. In the garment industry, sweatshop conditions are a rule. (Mišcevic and Kwong 2000, 188)

If you live close to a Chinatown, obtain a map as well as relevant historical information before you make your visit. If your backpacking is virtual, choose a Chinatown anywhere in the United States for your exploration. Your task in either case is to zoom in on two aspects of your Chinatown: one that is oriented toward tourists and one that is more hidden to tourists and is part of the fabric of life in this particular neighborhood. Write a page on each aspect, and try to find or take photos to illustrate your work. (The class as a whole might prepare a PowerPoint or other visual presentation.) Members of the class who are of Chinese descent or who speak Mandarin or Cantonese can be of assistance in helping to discover and interpret the hidden side of Chinatown. You might try to arrange an interview with a store or restaurant owner, resident, social worker, or member of the clergy. See the guidelines for intercultural interviews in Appendix C.

The Wikipedia website *(http://en.wikipedia.org/wiki/Chinatown)* provides information on Chinatowns in film, television, and the arts and also supplies external links to Chinatowns worldwide. Check the terrific site on Honolulu's Chinatown at *www.chinatownhi.com.*

On whatever aspect of Chinatown you decide to focus, be sure to leave time for a dim sum lunch.

Spotlight: Many Englishes

The Joy Luck Club contains wonderful examples of how English is used by non-native speakers, in this case by four Chinese women who all learned the language as adults. Thinking back, how would you describe their English? Is it broken or fractured? Is it limited? Amy Tan doesn't like to think of it that way. In her essay "Mother Tongue" (2003b), she explains that although she used to be ashamed of her own mother's English, she later came to appreciate and enjoy it. But she never knows how to describe it to others: "It has always bothered me that I can think of no way to describe it other than 'broken,' as if it were damaged and needed to be fixed" (274). Using her mother's language as a model, Tan gives us four film narrators who speak with accents and whose mastery of grammar and vocabulary is imperfect. Nonetheless, their English is fluid, vivid, and colorful. They use the language in creative ways and are able to express their ideas and personalities.

Because language is inextricably linked to culture, the mothers speak English in ways that reflect their Chinese ways of thinking. For example, as mothers Lindo and Suyuan sit in the audience at the music recital early in the film, they compare their young daughters' respective talents in chess and piano. Lindo says about her daughter Waverly: "I ask my daughter help me carry grocery. She think this too much ask. All day long she play chess. Appreciate me—no. I dust off all her trophy. All day she play chess. You lucky you don't have the same problem." Suyuan responds: "My problem worser than yours. If we tell June time to wash dish she hear nothing but music." Typical of Chinese ways of communicating, the mothers are, of course, bragging, but they do so in a disguised or indirect way, as if they're actually complaining about their daughters.

The same thing happens, you may recall, at the dinner table when Auntie Lindo brings in her best dish with an "apology": "This dish not salty enough. No flavor. It's too bad to eat." Taking her words literally, Rich proceeds to add flavor. But everyone else knows to listen to the culture rather than the words. Chinese must be modest, and this is Lindo's way of expressing pride.

Tan says she hears her mother's English not only as "perfectly clear, perfectly natural" but also as "vivid, direct, [and] full of observation and imagery" (273). So she is somewhat taken aback when some of her friends tell her they only understand half of what her mother says: "Some say they understand eighty to ninety percent. Some say they understand none of it, as if she were speaking pure Chinese" (273). Why do you think some friends do not understand Daisy Tan? Even if they do understand, what might they think of her? Do they, like Amy, find her English "vivid, direct, [and] full of observation and imagery" (273)? Do they admire and respect her for learning a second language? Do they make an extra effort to understand and communicate with her?

In "Mother Tongue," Tan says that when she was growing up, she observed how badly her mother was treated in banks, stores, and restaurants. People "did not take her seriously, did not give her good service, pretended not to understand her, or even acted as if they did not hear her" (274). So teenage Amy would make phone calls in her own "perfect" English, pretending to be Mrs. Tan (275). Amusing incidents from Tan's widely read essay can be found in *The Opposite of Fate: A Book of Musings* (2003a).

Your task is to choose one of the mothers and find a scene in the film illustrating something you like about the way she expresses herself. Write a page in your film notebook to explain what you chose and why. Then present your choice to the class.

If you have studied or learned more than one language yourself, or if your own parents (or someone else you know) have immigrated to a country where they have had to learn to speak a new language, you might add something about your personal experiences or insights into the phenomenon of second language learning. Amy Tan has done something unusual and valuable in bringing this topic to our attention, beginning, of course, with a film title—*The Joy Luck Club*—that defies easy English translation.

What's Cooking? Dim Sum

If you ever visit a Chinatown during a busy lunch hour, don't miss the opportunity to step into a restaurant serving delicious Cantonese treats known as dim sum—meaning *touch your heart*. You will undoubtedly see busy waiters and waitresses weaving between the typical round tables with trolleys of delicacies—each served from small steaming bamboo baskets. A selection will be brought to your table, and you can choose from among savory and sweet. Steamed scallop dumplings, sticky rice in lotus leaf, and mango pudding are but a few of the choices.

Because you are sometimes charged per delicacy, you might want to go with family or friends so that you can share. One mistake beginners often make is to accept everything first offered from the trolleys and leave no room for later! Some restaurants serve as many as one hundred different items at one meal. You can check *www.ethnicfoodsco.com/China/RegionalChineseCuisine.htm*, which separates Chinese cuisine by province; *http://asiarecipe.com/china.html*, which offers lots of cultural information; and the very interesting *www.inu.org/meiwah*, which tells a charming personal story about "learning to be an aware eater" of Chinese foods.

Lights! Camera! ACTION!

Are you interested in learning a way to reduce stress, relieve chronic pain, lose weight, build energy, quit smoking, and improve and maintain your health into old age? The Chinese have brought thousands of years of wisdom in the healing arts to American society, including the highly popular physical exercises *t'ai chi* and *qigong*. T'ai chi is a system of slow, flowing movements. Qigong is a classic set of exercises designed to balance and strengthen one's qi, or life force, and has been used by the Chinese for centuries to maintain a healthy body.

Take a class to gain insight into these long-practiced and historically revered Chinese medicine self-healing techniques. You might see if classes are offered by your college or university, a local community college, or a nearby acupuncture school. A good Internet resource that offers both information and practice exercises is *www.everyday-taichi.com*. To learn about acupuncture and Chinese medicine in general, see *www.acupuncture.com*.

Student's P.O.V.

Like so many others, I was highly skeptical when I first tried acupuncture. *Will it hurt? How can sticking a bunch of needles in someone possibly work? I don't really like needles, anyway.* . . . I had always considered myself to be a scientist and had a hard time believing in anything that couldn't be proven scientifically.

Despite my reluctance, I figured it couldn't hurt to give it a try. I had a chronic ankle problem that had caused me a lot of pain for years, and nothing (and I mean *nothing*) in Western medicine worked. Even the acupuncturist warned me that such chronic problems often required multiple treatments. *Oh, great,* I thought, *so this is how they make all their money.*

Much to my amazement and delight, the positive effects from that one treatment were both drastic and immediate. My ankle problems cleared up; I was no longer in frequent pain. And, despite what I had feared, it wasn't painful or weird. In fact, I liked it so much and was so pleased with the results that I kept going back for more treatments—allergies, pain management, digestive problems, and chronic insomnia were now all treatable. And in the process of being a patient and learning about the treatments, I fell in love with the philosophy of Chinese medicine, so much so that I enrolled in a program several years later to become an acupuncturist.

I heartily recommend Chinese medicine to anyone who cares about their own health or the health of their loved ones. As skeptical as I still am (to this day!) of things that I don't fully comprehend or can't explain, I have to admit that this medical paradigm just works. I have faith in this holistic, all-inclusive approach to treating the whole person instead of just the ailment. Balance in one's body, as well as within one's world, is essential in these times of uncertainty and stress, and I, for one, have found my path.

—Michele Duley

Your P.O.V.

1. Imagine that you are taking a friend from a different cultural and linguistic background to your home for dinner, just as Waverly took Rich to her mother's home. First determine your friend's culture, and then describe how you would prepare both your friend and your family for any differences they might encounter.

2. Imagine that you could have tea or dim sum with one of the mother-daughter pairs in the film. Which two characters would you like to meet and why? What specific aspects of their stories would you like to learn more about?

3. If there is a Chinese or Chinese American organization on your campus or in your community, find out if you can attend a meeting or event. Then write up your experience for the class.

4. Read Amy Tan's novel *The Joy Luck Club* (1989), and compare it with the film. You might choose a chapter such as "Without Wood," which describes the relationship between An-Mei and her daughter Rose. What differences do you find between the

prose and the cinematic versions of the relationship? Be specific. Do you like the way the novel was adapted for the screen?

5. Look at Tan's children's books, and watch an episode of her television cartoon series about Sagwa, the Chinese Siamese cat. Would you want your children to read the books and watch the cartoon series or videos? Explain in a page or two.

6. Imagine that you and your crew can make a film about Chinese American life, history, and culture. Consult the guidelines in Appendix D for further information. Here are some potential topics for consideration:

   a. the relatively unknown story of Angel Island

   b. the growth and popularity of Buddhism in the United States today

   c. the early immigration of a Chinese woman to the United States

   d. the status of Chinese language study in schools and universities

And Our Chinese American Book Awards Go To . . .

The Accidental Asian: Notes of a Native Speaker by Eric Liu (New York: Vintage, 1998). An absorbing memoir. Liu's thoughtful, intelligent essays on being a second-generation Chinese American are a great read. See especially the chapter entitled "The Chinatown Idea."

The Chinese in America by Iris Chang (New York: Viking, 2003). A beautifully written, meticulously researched tale of why the Chinese left their homeland and what happened to them once they arrived here. Chang opens her book with the simple but profound statement that "The story of the Chinese in America is the story of a journey, from one of the world's oldest civilizations to one of its newest" (vii). She understands this journey and makes it possible for the reader to understand it as well. Her book is the best combination of fine scholarship and popular history.

The Rice Room: Growing Up Chinese American—From Number Two Son to Rock 'N' Roll by Ben Fong-Torres (New York: Plume, 1994). A fresh and lively look at the emergence of bicultural identity. This memoir of the author's Chinese roots and American upbringing examines the confusion, difficulty, and struggles of immigrants who look to embrace their future without forgetting the past. Fong-Torres, a celebrated journalist for *Rolling Stone* magazine (and a former radio rock DJ), grew up in the two disparate worlds of San Francisco's Chinatown and the counterculture of the 1960s. He tells his story of identity crises and family tribulations with candor and unassuming charm. *Rice Room* speaks to the dilemmas that immigrants face everywhere.

Strangers from a Different Shore: A History of Asian Americans by Ronald Takaki (Boston: Little, Brown, and Co., 1998). A pioneering book by one of the nation's leading multiculturalists. The grandson of Japanese immigrant plantation laborers in Hawaii, Takaki fulfilled the American Dream by becoming professor of ethnic studies at the University of California, Berkeley, and a researcher and lecturer of international renown. Deeply humanistic in his approach, he has created a new history by giving voice to the unknown and unrecognized Asians who came from "other" shores. Takaki uncovered many of their stories himself in oral interviews and original documents such as letters, telegrams, songs, and poems. He has made a lasting contribution to our understanding of who these many "strangers" really were.

And Our Chinese American Film Awards Go To . . .

Dragon: The Bruce Lee Story (1993)—A thoroughly entertaining and moving biography of Bruce Lee, the greatest icon of martial arts cinema. The inside story of Lee's short life goes beyond his artistry to include perspectives on his rise to fame as a Hong-Kong born American, including his struggle against prejudice. The fight scenes are spectacular, and Jason Scott Lee (no relation) delivers a compelling performance as Bruce Lee. Directed by Rob Cohen.

A Great Wall (1986)—The light-hearted story of a Chinese American family's first trip to visit relatives in the People's Republic of China.

Though the film is dated, the examples of culture clash are amusing and relevant. Directed by Peter Wang.

Thousand Pieces of Gold (1991)—The story of a young Chinese woman (played by Rosalind Chao) who is trapped in the harsh life of a prostitute in a small frontier mining town. It is based on the true story of Polly Bemis. Directed by Nancy Kelly.

Mexican American Culture:

Real Women Have Curves

Setting the Scene:
Freewriting and Discussion

Study this cartoon, and freewrite your interpretation and reactions. Then share ideas with another student or small group. Look at the placement of the figures in the cartoon; what does this say to you? How do you interpret the clothing and body language? What is the white man assuming, and what does he want? What is the Indian expressing in a few words? What are the Latinos thinking? Do you think the cartoon is humorous? Explain.

Sneak Preview

About the Film

Real Women Have Curves (2002) is one of the best among a number of recent films that focus on the conflicts between first-generation immigrants and their Americanized[1] children. The main character, Ana, is a Mexican American teenager living in the predominately Latino section of East Los Angeles. An excellent student, she passionately wants to attend college, but her mother insists that she work at her older sister's dressmaking factory. Ana's struggle to assert herself and yet remain true to her family is depicted in a realistic and tender way.

The main actors, director, and co-screenwriter are all Latinas themselves. In U.S. cinematic history, Mexican Americans have all too often suffered the same Hollywood fate as other minority groups— being reduced to unflattering stereotypes. The men are usually untrustworthy and unsavory, depicted as greasers, villains, and *bandidos*. (The famous Latin lover role has generally been reserved for lighter-skinned men from Spain and Italy.) Though Mexican American women have fared a bit better, they often appear as spicy, alluring seductresses and frequently as prostitutes.

Yet alongside movies that show Mexican Americans in negative, stereotypical ways, a tradition of progressive Chicano cinema— produced independently and, to some extent, in Hollywood—has also flourished. An early classic is the independent film *Salt of the Earth* (1954), and other noteworthy independents include *The Ballad of*

----

1. For reasons of economy and convenience, we have elected to use *America* and *Americans* in this chapter—and in the book as a whole—to refer to the United States and the citizens thereof, though we realize that the word belongs to other countries in the hemisphere as well and that Latin Americans, for example, generally refer to us as *norteamericanos*, or *North Americans*.

Gregorio Cortez (1982), and *El Mariachi* (1992). Perhaps the best-known film in this group is *Selena* (1997), a biography of the tejana singer Selena (played by Jennifer Lopez), who was wildly popular among Latinos in the Southwest and was poised to achieve crossover success when she was murdered at age 23.

Among early Chicano films produced in Hollywood are three that are based on true stories: *Zoot Suit* (1981), based on the murder of a young boy in Los Angeles in 1942; *La Bamba* (1987), based on the life of rock-and-roll singer Richie Valens; and *Stand and Deliver* (1988), based on the experiences of a high school teacher from an East Los Angeles barrio whose students surprised everyone by scoring among the highest in the nation on the Advanced Placement calculus test. More recent films include the long (spanning three generations) but interesting *Mi Familia/My Family* (1995) and the exaggerated, sometimes silly, but thought-provoking *A Day without a Mexican* (2004). For an excellent discussion of Mexicans and Mexican Americans in cinema, see the chapter entitled "Cinema" in *Chicano Popular Culture* (listed at the end of this chapter).

About the Filmmakers and Actors of *Real Women Have Curves*

Director Patricia Cardoso came to the United States from her native Colombia in 1987. Originally an archaeologist, she was drawn to film and received a graduate degree in fine arts from the University of California, Los Angeles, in 1994. In *Real Women Have Curves*, her first full-length film, she brings to the screen the real-life experience of her Mexican-born screenwriter, Josefina López. As a young woman, López worked illegally in an East Los Angeles sewing factory. "My mother was a seamstress and my older sister sewed [too]," she says. "Another sister used a settlement from an automobile accident to buy a small factory, and that is where I worked," according to the website that promoted the movie.

Having entered the United States with her family at the age of five, López lived undocumented in Los Angeles for almost thirteen years before receiving legal residency status in 1987 through the Immigration Reform and Control Act (see page 78). She originally wrote *Real Women Have Curves* as a stage play, which debuted in San Francisco in 1990 and was an instant hit. The movie premiered at the Sundance Film Festival in 2002 to strong praise; it received the Dramatic Audience Award, and its two stars, America Ferrera and Lupe Ontiveros, were jointly awarded the festival's Special Jury Prize for Acting.

In the leading role of Ana García, the talented and spirited eighteen-year-old America Ferrera makes her film debut. The youngest of six children born in California to Honduran parents, she is the only one of the lead actresses who does not speak fluent Spanish (a fact that is cleverly disguised in the film). Though not really bilingual, she does relate to the difficulty of growing up in two cultures. With regard to her film role as Ana, she says, "I was immediately drawn to the character because I've been experiencing similar things in my own life." She says that she constantly feels like a "cultural rubber band"—with the "American side stretching one way and the Latina side stretching the other." She's always questioning whether she is Latina or American and, having attended American schools all her life, she sometimes feels that that she's "not Hispanic enough" *(www.splicedonline.com)*.

Born in El Paso, Texas, Lupe Ontiveros is a veteran actress who was cast in small parts for twenty years, including the TV show *Desperate Housewives*, and playing, by her own count, more than 150 maids. "I'm proud to represent those hands that labor in this country," she says. "I've given every maid . . . soul and heart," according to the website that promoted the movie. Educated as a social worker, she has long combined her love for acting with community activism. For example, she produced an award-winning film in Spanish focusing on breast cancer awareness for Latinas. As a founding member of the Los Angeles Latino Theater Company, she has helped to further the situation of Latinos in the arts.

If you were struck by the rich speaking voice of Ingrid Oliu (Estela), you might be interested to know that she has extensive experience in Spanish-speaking commercials and voice-overs. As the voice of Sears for three years in Los Angeles, she is credited with winning many loyal customers for the company. The daughter of Nicaraguan parents, she was born in East Los Angeles.

Producer and co-screenwriter George LaVoo decided to produce the film the day after he saw the play. He says, "At the theater, I sat on folding chairs with a mostly Latino audience and got caught up in those women's lives just like they did." He especially identified with the issue of body weight, having been heavy as a child. "I went through high school understanding what that prejudice is all about," LaVoo says on a website that promoted the movie.

Who's Who in the Film

Ana García (America Ferrera)—Mexican American high school senior

Carmen García (Lupe Ontiveros)—Ana's mother

Raúl García (Jorge Cervera, Jr.)—Ana's father

Estela García (Ingrid Oliu)—Ana's sister

Mr. Guzman (George López)—Ana's teacher

Jimmy (Brian Sites)—Ana's Anglo boyfriend

Grandfather (Felipe de Alba)—Ana's beloved grandfather

Patricia Cardoso—director

Josefina López—co-screenwriter

George LaVoo—producer, co-screenwriter

Terms to Know

barrio—From the Spanish word meaning *neighborhood,* used to refer either to mainly Spanish-speaking neighborhoods in the United States or to urban sectors within Latin American cities. *Barrios* are often tight-knit, cohesive communities. Perhaps the most famous example in the United States is Manhattan's *El Barrio,* better known as Spanish Harlem.

brown people—Sometimes considered offensive, but can also be used neutrally. "Brown power" was a slogan popularized during the civil rights movement. Today, social scientists talk about the "browning of America" to indicate that people of color are expected to outnumber whites by mid-century.

Chicano/a—Used by Mexican American activists in the late 1960s as a label of pride and rebellion. The word itself probably derives from the Spanish *mexicano* (Mexican), in which the *x* is pronounced as *sh* in some regional dialects. Today **Chicano/a** is accepted by some as a generic term for Mexican Americans but is scorned by others who regard it as pejorative and militant.

greaser, spic, wetback—Derogatory slang terms for Latin Americans. **Greaser** alludes to a greasy look, linked perhaps to oily hair (and hair products) or a fatty Latin diet. **Spic** (possibly derived from *spic*-ghetti, or from *no spica da English*) was an epithet for Italians and later came to refer to any Latinos, especially those from Mexico and Puerto Rica. **Wetback** or *mojado* (meaning *wet* in Spanish) refers to those who cross the Rio Grande by swimming or wading to enter the United States illegally and is used inaccurately by some people to refer to all Mexican Americans.

gringo—Originally derived from the term for *Greek (griego)*, now used in Latin America to refer to any white foreigner, particularly U.S. Americans. *Gringo* can be used neutrally or in a derogatory way.

Hispanic—Considered a term of respect by some **Latinos,** but rejected by others because they feel it recalls the colonization by Spain and ignores the Indian and African roots of many people; it also leaves out Portuguese and Brazilian Americans. Many Hispanics/Latinos prefer to be called by their country of origin (e.g., Cubans or Cuban Americans, Dominicans or Dominican Americans, Puerto Ricans).

La Raza—Literally meaning *the race,* but more accurately meaning *the people*. It is used to refer to Latinos as a group, but more in a cultural than a racial sense.

Latino/a—Terms preferred to **Hispanic** by many Americans who trace their roots to approximately 24 different countries in Central and South America and the Caribbean. The terms refer to cultural background, not to race, as **Latinos** (males) and **Latinas** (females) can be white, black, brown, of Asian complexion, or **mestizo.**

mestizo/a—A person of mixed race or descent, specifically white and Indian. From the Latin *miscere,* to mix, and borrowed from the Spanish *mestizo,* the term has been used in English since the late 1500s. In Latin America, it commonly refers to the offspring of the Spanish and indigenous peoples. In the United States, the word refers primarily to Mexican Americans.

undocumented workers—Mexicans and others who are employed in this country but have not obtained the necessary legal documents from the Immigration and Naturalization Service; generally preferred to the widely used, unfriendly term **illegal aliens.**

History Flashback

Ana García's family is a good example of what author Michael Barone (2001) says about members of the Latino culture in general: "What America's Latinos do more than anything else is work" (161). Ana's father Raúl takes care of the grounds and gardens surrounding luxurious homes. Her mother Carmen and older sister Estela work long hours in the stifling heat of Estela's small factory to create lovely dresses they themselves could never afford. (As Ana indignantly points out, they receive $18 each for dresses that will be sold at Bloomingdale's for $600.)

Ana's family is part of a large and growing Mexican American workforce that has become indispensable to the U.S. economy. Though many men and women of Mexican heritage are employed in white collar or managerial positions, large numbers take "unskilled," low-paying, but nonetheless respectable jobs that few others are willing to do. In cities and towns across the country, they work as maids and janitors, domestic servants and nannies, and drivers and valets. They can be found mowing lawns and cutting shrubs, washing dishes and waiting on tables, and working in unpleasant factories and on construction sites. They also harvest crops, often as seasonal migrants, in the nation's agricultural fields.

Why are Mexican Americans like Ana's family here, and why do they work so hard? First, remember that millions of Mexican Americans were born in the United States, and significant numbers are from families that have been here for generations. As economist Thomas Sowell (1981) clarifies, "Some of the oldest and the newest Americans are from Mexico" (244). Who are these "oldest Americans"?

To understand the early Mexican presence in the United States, let's review a part of history too often missed in schools and universities. Did you know that much of the West and Southwest (California, New Mexico, Arizona, Nevada, Utah, and parts of Colorado, Kansas, Wyoming, and Oklahoma) were part of Mexico until the mid-19th century? If you're surprised, remember that Columbus's expeditions were financed by the Spanish, whose armies, led by conquistadors such as the infamous Hernán Cortés, invaded Central America, Mexico, and the Caribbean in the early 1500s. These conquerors eventually claimed for Spain one of the largest empires in world history, including most of present-day Central and South America—and much of today's American West and Southwest. By the time England established its first permanent colony in Jamestown in 1607, the Spanish had already been a strong colonial power in the hemisphere for almost a century.

The Spanish established a pattern of conquest and settlement vastly different from that of the British on the North Atlantic coast. Because the Spanish came in smaller numbers and mostly without women, a population of mixed offspring of Spanish and Indian blood, called *mestizos,* began to flourish. This explains why today most Mexicans are mestizos, while relatively few North Americans are of dual European and Indian heritage. (African strains are also present in Mexican heritage as a result of the Spanish colonists' importation into their territory of enslaved Africans.)

So how did a huge part of the present-day American West and Southwest become Mexican, and then American? Gradually, Spanish and mestizo missionaries, explorers, and settlers began to move northward, conquering local Indians and expanding the colony of New Spain into areas that now are California, Texas, New Mexico, and beyond (see the map on page 11). Facing considerable resistance from Indian tribes, the Spanish government devised an approach to conquest that was as ingenious as it was brutal—establishing missions to convert the local Indians to Catholicism and erecting *presidios,* or forts, to control them militarily. Spain ruled its vast colony in the New World until 1821, when Mexico won an eleven-year war for independence. At that time, what was formerly the northernmost region of New Spain (in today's American West and Southwest) became Mexican.

But that situation did not last long. The first dispute arose over Texas, which was annexed by the United States in 1845. To learn more about this critical episode in the history of both countries, explore the battle of the Alamo. (See *www.thealamo.org/main.html.*) Tensions between the two countries were further exacerbated by newly elected President James Polk, a firm believer in the concept of Manifest Destiny (see pages 11–12). Having unsuccessfully pressured Mexico to sell some of its land to the United States, Polk called on Congress to declare war on the neighboring country.

The U.S. victory in the hard-fought Mexican American War (1846–48) ultimately established the Rio Grande River as the new boundary between the two countries and determined that California, New Mexico, Arizona, Nevada, Utah, and parts of Colorado, Kansas, Wyoming, and Oklahoma would be incorporated into the United

States. These acquisitions, along with Texas, represented a loss to Mexico of nearly half its territory. In 1853, a remaining strip of land south of the Gila River in present-day Arizona and New Mexico was sold to the United States in the Gadsden Purchase.

As the political boundaries changed, people of Mexican descent, or *mejicanos* (such as *tejanos, californios,* and *nuevomejicanos*), who were living in the West and Southwest suddenly became foreigners in what had been their country. As the saying goes: "We didn't cross the border. The border crossed us." Some of the annexed *mejicanos* left, and many who stayed were gradually dispossessed and deprived of their civil rights. Like the American Indians, they became a conquered people in their own land.

It is not surprising, then, that Mexicans, who possessed a large part of America until it was taken from them by force, might see themselves as entitled to live here. They would not necessarily have the sense that they are invading the United States when they simply continue to cross a border—as individuals, families, and groups—that did not exist prior to 1848 and that, in their minds, was not established by rightful means. Among the newcomers, many like the Garcías still arrive daily, legally or not, primarily to escape poverty and to make a life for themselves and their extended families. In general, their family bonds are strong, and everyone works and sacrifices to provide for each other. Although the film does not give us information about the lives of Ana's parents before they traveled north to Los Angeles, we can write our own flashback based on similar real stories.

We can imagine that the family was very poor and that Raúl García was unable to find work at home. Following the traditional pattern, he traveled north alone, leaving his wife behind. He worked at various part-time jobs and sent most of his money home for several years before being joined by other family members. He chose Los Angeles because friends and acquaintances had already gone there, forming a "chain" of migration whereby those who go first can help newcomers. Having crossed the border illegally, he was constantly on the lookout for immigration officials *(la migra)*. As one of the lucky ones, Raúl was able to obtain his green card (providing permanent residency status, though not citizenship) when he fell under the amnesty granted some 2.7 million undocumented immigrants (not just Mexicans) under the Immigration Reform and Control Act of 1986. Like so many other Mexicans, Ana's father came to the United States hoping to escape poverty and provide a secure, comfortable existence for his family. By the time we meet him in the film, he has come a long way toward achieving this hope.

Now take a moment to think about how Mexican or Mexican American men are commonly depicted in the media, including news articles. What images come to mind? Do you see a rather unkempt fellow with a huge sombrero on his head napping under a tree? Or a group of down-and-out men loitering on a street corner, possibly with beer bottles? Is Raúl García one of these "lazy, good-for-nothing" fellows? Knowing how erroneous and unfair the widespread stereotypes are, we must undo them. In reality, the work ethic of Mexican Americans at all levels of employment is exemplary.

But to recognize this reality would put our government in an uneasy position. For much of the past century, workers from Mexico have been exploited. Imagine for a moment how it might feel to live and work in a foreign country without papers, always fearing that you might be caught and punished or sent home. The harsh truth of U.S. policy and practice concerning Mexican immigration throughout the past century is that whenever Mexicans have been needed as cheap labor, the door quickly opened, and they were allowed to work, regardless of documentation. And whenever they became superfluous, the door slammed shut, and many of those who were already here, even legally, were expelled.

This fluctuating policy first manifested itself on a large scale in the early 1900s, when American employers actively began to recruit Mexican laborers to work on the railroads, in the mines, and in the fields. These Mexicans were generally welcomed, especially since restrictive legislation such as the Chinese Exclusion Act (see page 56) had virtually stopped the influx of workers from Asia. Often housed in the most primitive conditions—in squalid settlements of shacks or tents separated from the rest of society—Mexicans worked long hours for meager pay. Despite harsh conditions, their suffering was tolerable because it enabled them to earn considerably more than they could at home and to send money to their families.

But the warm welcome extended to these workers turned cold during the Great Depression of the 1930s. Suddenly, Mexicans were seen as taking jobs from needy Americans, and by 1940, nearly half a million people of Mexican descent, some of whom were American citizens (this applies particularly to U.S.-born children of immigrants), were deported or pressured into leaving.

The pattern repeated itself when World War II labor shortages brought a renewed demand for agricultural laborers. You might look into the federally organized *bracero* program (*brazo* means *arm* in Spanish, but *bracero* really means *hired hand* in this context) that brought workers in, and the extensive deportation program, called Operation Wetback, that was later put into effect to send these workers home. Compare the p.o.v. presented in the *Handbook of Texas* at *www.tsha.utexas.edu/handbook/online/articles/OO/pqo1.html* (note the capital Os in the URL) with the p.o.v. presented by the United Farmworkers at *www.farmworkers.org/benglish.html*.

Demand for Civil Rights

Resistance to oppression, humiliation, and miserable working conditions became central issues in the Chicano movement *(el movimiento)* of the 1960s. The label *Chicano* signaled a new activism and militancy among Mexican Americans. Inspired by the civil rights movement of that decade, Chicanos developed a broad agenda of goals designed to secure their rightful place in American society, often taking great risks in opposing wealthy and powerful interests.

Of the many prominent Chicano leaders who emerged, the most well known is César Chávez, a modest yet charismatic figure who rose from the poverty of migrant labor to found the nation's first successful union of farm workers, the United Farm Workers of America (UFW). Using nonviolent tactics such as boycotts, strikes, and fasts, Chávez, Dolores Huerta, and other activists captured the attention of the media and involved Americans nationwide in the struggles of the laborers they represented. The 1968 campaign against California's San Joaquin Valley grape growers, who opposed union contracts, proved an enormous success when, for a period of several years, millions of Americans stopped buying grapes in their local grocery stores.

Although much that Chávez fought for was not achievable during his lifetime, the UFW did make improvements in the lot of impoverished agricultural workers who had possessed virtually no rights—no employment benefits (such as health care, disability, or retirement), no seniority system, and no grievance procedures. Huerta and many others carry on the work today. For further information, see *www.lared-latina.com/huerta.html* and *www.ufw.org*.

Mexican Americans Today

As people like Ana and her family learn more about their adopted country, they are becoming more comfortable, integrated, and patriotic. But their adaptation to the new country is different from that of many European immigrants who, for a variety of reasons, have traditionally accepted the melting pot idea, where immigrants leave their languages, customs, and loyalties behind and become Americanized as soon as possible. As Teddy Roosevelt once said, the idea of a "fifty-fifty" allegiance is impossible in this country: "Either a man is an American and nothing else, or he is not an American at all" (Mills 1994, 12). By contrast, Mexican Americans and other Latinos are presenting a bold new challenge to American society by resisting the idea that they need to give up their cultures and ethnicities. The critical question is, why should they? Why not keep traditions, values, and customs that are dear to you—that are an essential part of your identity—while at the same time incorporating a second identity? Why be monocultural if you can be bicultural?

As sensible and desirable as this biculturalism may sound, it is not being viewed positively by many non-Latinos. The use of Spanish in particular can be a polarizing issue. In a country that has long viewed English as the key to acceptance and upward mobility (even though, in legal terms, the United States has no official national language), many English speakers perceive Spanish as a threat. In fact, the number of U.S. residents who speak Spanish as a native language is large and growing; the U.S. Census Bureau reported in its most recent count approximately 28.1 million Spanish speakers, representing a 60 percent growth in ten years. Census figures indicate that a majority of these people speak English very well, but nonetheless some non-Spanish speakers feel offended when Latinos use their native language, interpreting this as ingratitude or a lack of respect for this country. Similarly, some native English speakers resent hearing conversations they do not understand in shops, in the workplace, or on the airwaves. Some may also fear for the unity of a country that does not have an official common language.

Is this rejection of Spanish or Spanish-speaking people an expression of narrow-mindedness and prejudice? In some cases, probably so. But fear can be a controlling factor here. Remember that the myth of the melting pot is still very much alive for many Americans. Non-Latinos may not trust, or know what to expect of, a society that no longer strives for a monoculture but allows instead (or even encourages) the coexistence of a variety of cultures, with their differing ways of life, traditions, and languages. They may also simply reject changes that leave them feeling excluded and uncertain about their own futures.

Without a doubt, unprecedented changes are occurring as Mexican American and other Latino populations are growing in numbers. Demographers predict that if current trends continue, white non-Hispanics will cease to be in the majority around mid-century— for the first time in the history of the nation. What will this mean? The mainstream media have been sounding the alarm for some time, using terms like *Mexamerica* and *Amexica* and referring to the "Latin Americanization" or "browning" of the country. Is this demographic shift a problem? What do you think? Should Euro-Americans and other non-Latinos be concerned? Frightened? Two Anglo students give their views in the shaded box.

Student P.O.V.s

I had no idea that the so-called whitebreads [Anglos] were expected to be a minority in 25–50 years. Also I was surprised to hear that one in eight American families does not speak English at home. . . . This does not bother me, but it made me think about how I am going to have to learn to communicate interculturally in my nursing career. I also began to think that maybe I should find the time to learn another language fluently. Even though I have always wanted to do this at some time in my life, it now seems more urgent, and I feel motivated now to do it for myself and for the people from all different backgrounds that I will be working with in the future.

　—Lorene McClure

One of the most surprising things I learned . . . this week was that by the middle of the 21st century non-white racial and ethnic groups will outnumber whites in the United States. I think I've always realized that the U.S. would not always be a predominantly white society, but I thought it would take much longer for other ethnicities to gain such strength in numbers. I do not think it is necessarily a bad thing that whites are becoming less of a majority in the U.S. . . . when, in fact, whites were not the first inhabitants of this land.

　—Michelle Greenlee

So the question is not *whether* further Latin Americanization of this country will occur but only *how successfully* Americans of all backgrounds will deal with the changes underway. Already, daily life in the United States is being shaped and transformed by rich traditions of Latin music, dance, architecture, literature, fashion, language, food, and arts. And increasingly, Latinos are considered a key factor in the nation's economic growth. Their restaurants, grocery stores, and other businesses—ranging from family-run operations to billion dollar enterprises—have become an essential part of the U.S. economy. Furthermore, as their population continues to expand, Latinos are being viewed—and wooed—as a major source of consumer buying power and as an important constituency of voters.

Along with these momentous changes, the Mexican/Latino image has undergone a transformation in popular culture and the media, as can be seen, for example, by a look at major news magazine cover stories. In the final year of the 20th century, *Newsweek* and *Time* published in the same month favorable cover stories on the excitement being created by talented, popular young Latinos and Latinas in music, sports, and literature. *Newsweek*'s cover pictured three big names—singer Shakira, boxer Oscar de la Hoya, and author Junot Diaz—as examples of how Hispanics are "hip, hot, and making history" (Larmer 1999, 48). The cover headlines stated in large type: "Latin U.S.A.: How Young Hispanics Are Changing America." The cover of *Time* pictured an upbeat Ricky Martin, poised as if to dance. The message was: "We've seen the future. It looks like Ricky Martin. It sings like Marc Anthony. It dances like Jennifer Lopez. ¡Qué Bueno!" (Farley 1999, 75)

But since that intoxicating period, the mainstream press seems to have cooled, and excitement has given way, at least in part, to anxiety. Latinos seem once again to be viewed in many instances as worrisome, even threatening, intruders. Five years into the new millennium, the September 20, 2005 cover of *Time* featured a special investigation on America's border, with a headline announcing that "Even after 9/11, it's outrageously easy to sneak in." Two months later, the November 28, 2005 issue of *U.S. News and World Report* followed with a special story examining the "Border Wars." On the cover, a somewhat frightening nighttime photograph of immigrants being apprehended was accompanied by a heading that read: "The border with Mexico leaks like a sieve. Why the feds can't fix it." Soon after, at a moment that called for celebration, a *Newsweek* cover featured newly elected Los Angeles mayor Antonio Villaraigosa with a vaguely ominous headline about "Latino Power." The feature article dealt with "A Latino Power Surge," telling readers flatly to "get used to it" (Campo-Flores and Fineman 2005, 25).

In light of shifting popular opinion, will the ongoing infusion of ideas, vitality, values, and ways of life from Mexican Americans be appreciated? Welcomed? Resented? Resisted? One can only hope that the points of view of Michelle and Lorene (see Student P.O.V.s on page 82) are not atypical of young adults today. This generation inherits new possibilities but also urgent challenges and problems that should not be ignored or minimized. They include especially

- working with the Mexican government to develop and enforce a sane, humane, workable immigration policy that includes fair and reasonable provisions for guest workers and their employers;

- developing new policies and practices to improve conditions for the nearly eleven million undocumented workers living in the United States today, a majority of whom are Mexican;

- developing fair trade practices and policies that will promote more stable economies in Latin America;

- cooperating with the Mexican government to improve conditions for those living on the border, especially for workers in factories called *maquiladores;*

- finding more humane and workable ways to regulate the border, which continues to be a source of constant conflict (Mexican author Carlos Fuentes says it is a "scar" rather than a border [Fuentes 1992, 342], and Chicana writer Gloria Anzaldúa echoes these sentiments when she calls the area *una herida abierta*—"an open wound" [Anzaldúa 1999, 3]);

- developing new policies and practices to promote multilingualism in the schools and society at large.

The *Newsweek* cover story previously mentioned proclaimed that the new Latin wave "will change how the country looks—and how it looks at itself" (Larmer 48). Certainly the coming decades will be a critical time, as Mexican and other Latino populations continue to grow and establish themselves and as new images confront what seem to be age-old stereotypes.

Cultural Backpacking: Mexican America

Put on your backpack to discover a part of Mexican America that is meaningful to you. Wherever you choose to travel, try to immerse yourself in the experience. You may, for example, visit a museum, memorial, shop, historic site, or neighborhood. You can attend a festival, play, church service, or cultural event or take a Latin dance class. You may go to a restaurant, grocery store, *taquería*, or bakery *(panadería)*. Alternatively, you may choose to do your backpacking in the library or at your computer. Whether your trip is real or virtual, be sure to choose something that gives you new insight into, and appreciation for, Mexican American people and cultures.

When you've completed your backpacking, write a page to describe what you chose and why. What was your experience like, both emotionally and intellectually? What did you come to understand or appreciate about Mexican American culture?

As usual, attach to your essay a picture or photograph. If your backpacking is virtual, include the relevant URL.

Spotlight: Do Real Women Have Curves?

In a gentle, light-hearted way, the makers of *Real Women Have Curves* focus their spotlight on a sensitive topic: women's bodies. What makes a woman beautiful? What makes her sexy and feminine? Specifically, how thin should she be?

The super-thin, Barbie-doll ideal that has been so tenacious in recent decades is actually an aberration in world history. In many countries and cultures, curves in women have been viewed as normal and desirable. An ample, full shape has meant sexual maturity and fertility, indicating good health and prosperity especially in difficult economic times. Thin bodies were likely to be associated with starvation or illness. Cultures in Latin America and Africa in particular have tended to value more generous frames on women, appreciating curves. Whereas women should not necessarily be *too* fat, they should definitely not be *too* thin, either. One Latin American proverb says it succinctly: *Bones are for dogs.*

As a full-bodied young Latina, Ana does not match the standard of beauty prevalent in U.S. mainstream society. Her mother, who does not match it either, is constantly criticizing Ana about her weight. She wants her daughter to be thinner in order to attract a husband, a goal that, in her mind, ought to be of the highest importance for a young woman. Happily, Ana's weight does not seem to bother her young boyfriend, Jimmy; when she turns on the light to allow him to see her naked, he says just the right thing, and in Spanish no less.

An intelligent, strong-willed young woman, Ana is able to resist being defined by others. In the course of the film, she grows into her own beauty, a transformation seen particularly in the underwear scene. In this memorable moment of rebellion, the seamstresses in the stifling factory decide to discard their outer clothing. What results is one of the finest examples in cinema of how ordinary women become more beautiful to themselves and to the audience. Ana's proud and confident stride at the end of the film shows that she accepts and is entirely comfortable with herself as she is.

Unfortunately, the problems that find resolution in the film persist in alarming proportions in the real world. In the United States and many other countries and cultures, media images set standards of female beauty that are not only unhealthy, but also impossible for most women ever to attain. The unfortunate results are eating disorders, liposuctions and other surgeries, and depression. You might look at the National Eating Disorders Association website for additional information *(www.nationaleatingdisorders.org)*.

While there is certainly nothing wrong with trying to look attractive, the film asks us to rethink and expand our definition of what attractive is, not only with regard to our own bodies but in our evaluations and judgments of others. The recently coined term *lookism* refers to prejudice and discrimination based on physical appearance. In an appearance-conscious (or perhaps even appearance-obsessed) culture like that of the United States, physical attributes too often can play a major role—a role that is unearned and unreliable—in one's success, quality of life, and supposed well-being.

As you view or reflect on *Real Women Have Curves,* think of a scene, situation, or relationship in which lookism (or fattism, which is a form of lookism) plays a role. You might ask:

- How is lookism expressed?

- How does lookism affect the person being judged? The person doing the judging? Their relationship?

- Are the characters able to reduce, eliminate, or defy this bias? If so, how?

An example of such a scene: All the lovely dresses being made in the sweatshop are small sizes. Estela defies this bias by making a dress for Ana. Her words are: "Pretty dresses aren't just for skinny girls."

What's Cooking?
Traditional Mexican Recipes

Did you know that foods like corn, tomatoes, squash, chocolate, and avocados entered the European diet from the Aztecs of ancient Mexico? Gastronomic experts and many people believe that Mexican cuisine ranks with the French and Chinese as one of the finest in the world. First, you might watch the delightful film *Tortilla Soup* (2001) for a visual feast (especially the first few minutes). Then find a recipe for a traditional Mexican or Mexican American dish, make it, and share it with your classmates. Write a page about the experience in your film notebook. Two interesting websites are *www.gourmetsleuth.com/mexican_recipes.htm* and *www.texmex.net.*

Lights! Camera! ACTION!

United Students Against Sweatshops (USAS) is an international student movement begun in 1998 to protest sweatshop conditions for workers in the apparel and other industries. Realizing that universities and colleges control several billion dollars of logo apparel, student leaders began to press their administrations to endorse "sweat-free" policies. Students are making a difference! Check the website at *www.studentsagainstsweatshops.org* to learn more and take action.

Your P.O.V.

1. After reading several print or online reviews of *Real Women Have Curves,* write your own review and post it on *www.amazon.com,* on *www.imdb.com,* or on a site of your choosing.

2. Flash forward four years, when Ana has graduated from Columbia University, and imagine a reunion with her mother in New York City. What would they discuss? Write a script of their dialogue. Or write an outline of a plot for the sequel to *Real Women Have Curves.*

3. Find a poem you like that was written in Spanish by a Mexican or Mexican American. Translate it into English, and then write a page or two to explain what you experienced as a translator of a literary text.

4. Design a memorial to honor the immigrants who have come to the United States from the south. Where should it be? You might check the Ellis Island website *(www.ellisisland.org)* to see how European immigrants are being remembered and honored.

5. Locate a newspaper, magazine, and website that present a Mexican American p.o.v., and explain why you chose them. Or do the same with a television show and radio station.

6. If Spanish is your native language, explain to your classmates your personal experiences learning and using both Spanish and English. If you are not a native Spanish speaker but have studied or are studying Spanish now, explain your reasons for doing so. If you are a native speaker of a language other than Spanish or English, what are your views on the debate over whether English should be legalized as the official language of the United States?

7. Imagine that you and your crew have the opportunity to make a film about present-day Mexican American life. Consult the guidelines in Appendix D for further information. Here are some potential topics for consideration:

    a. Spanglish—what is it? How does it work?

    b. Mexican American murals in the United States

    c. the daily life of children of seasonal migrants

    d. a contemporary Latina/o musician

e. sweatshops in the United States (or *maquiladoras* along the border)

f. the *quinceañera* ("Sweet 15") celebration in the United States

g. the nationwide rallies, protests, and strikes culminating in May Day 2006

And Our Mexican American Book Awards Go To . . .

Chicano Popular Culture: Que Hable el Pueblo by Charles M. Tatum (Tucson: University of Arizona Press, 2001). A book that introduces readers to a wide range of exciting popular art forms that Mexican Americans have contributed to American society as a whole. Tatum discusses in separate chapters music; cinema; media (newspapers, radio, and television); popular literature; and popular art, celebrations, and traditions. This is a great overview that leaves the reader eager to know more.

Communicating with the Mexicans (2nd ed.) by John Condon (Yarmouth, ME: Intercultural Press, 1997). Originally published in 1985, a classic that gives the reader plenty of insight into the often profound differences between North American and Mexican cultures. Condon masterfully says a lot in a very few pages; there is no better way to learn in a few hours how to become better neighbors. A recent, more in-depth study that also offers excellent perspectives is *Mexicans and Americans: Cracking the Cultural Code* by Ned Crouch (London: Nicolas Brealy, 2004).

Everything You Need to Know about Latino History by Himilce Novas (New York: Plume, 2003). An engaging book that is good for browsing, reference, or reading in its entirety. A Cuban-born immigrant, Novas shatters myths and misconceptions in question-and-answer format. See also Novas's equally lively and accessible *Everything You Need to Know about Asian American History* (2004).

And Our Mexican American Film Awards Go To . . .

Bread and Roses (2000)—A fight for social-economic justice that has drama and heart. Having crossed the border illegally to join her sister in Los Angeles, the lovely Maya is pleased to have a job as a janitor. She soon becomes politicized, joining a young, charming labor union organizer and other exploited compatriots to fight for workers' rights. Though a bit didactic, this is a powerful and interesting film. Directed by Ken Loach.

El Norte (1983)—Heartbreaking story of a brother and sister from Guatemala who travel north to Los Angeles in hopes of realizing their dreams. This is an unforgettable film that shows the harsh realities of border crossings and immigrant life. The scenes with Lupe Ontiveros as the maid are cross-cultural gems. The video can be hard to find, but it's well worth the search. Scenes of violence in Guatemala and of the border crossing are disturbing. Directed by Mexican American Gregory Nava.

Lone Star (1996)—Complex and absorbing tale of interracial and interpersonal tensions in a present-day border town. This fascinating story of deeply buried family secrets, including a long-unsolved murder, serves as a backdrop to a keen examination of how diverse groups of people coexist in regions where Mexico and the United States come together. Directed by John Sayles.

Spanglish (2004)—A refreshingly different look at family and parenting through bicultural lenses. Flor, a stunningly attractive Mexican mother who speaks no English, migrates to Los Angeles with her daughter, eventually becoming a housekeeper for a wealthy Anglo family. When the two families are forced to live together under one roof for the summer, cultural and personal values collide. Directed by James L. Brooks.

5

Irish American Culture:

Far and Away

Setting the Scene:
Freewriting and Discussion

Courtesy of Library of Congress

Study the picture. Then freewrite your observations and reactions in your film notebook. Who do you think these people are, and where are they? When do you think the photograph was taken? How do you imagine the people feel? What awaits them? How might you feel if you were one of these immigrants moving to a foreign land with little money and few possessions? Share your thoughts with a partner or with the class as a whole.

Sneak Preview

About the Film

Far and Away (1992) tells the story of two young Irish immigrants, Joseph Donelly (played by Tom Cruise) and Shannon Christie (played by Nicole Kidman), who leave home in the early 1890s to search for new opportunities in America. After landing in Boston and experiencing the hard life of penniless newcomers, they eventually make their way separately west to Oklahoma Territory, where they take part in the historic land rush of 1893.

Overall, the film gives a good sense of the experiences of late 19th- and early 20th-century European immigrants to the United States. It can help us understand the motivation and feel the emotions of the millions of Irish and other immigrants who, to the present day, dream of a better life in America, uproot themselves from their homelands, face disillusionment and enormous hardships upon arrival, and eventually prevail.

The broad outlines of the plot are taken directly from Irish immigrant history. As in the chapter on *The Long Walk Home,* we will look at *Far and Away* in terms of its historical accuracy. The film has three sections: life in Ireland, the journey aboard ship, and life in America.

In the first section, we meet Joseph Donelly and his family, typical members of an entire class of poverty-stricken, Catholic tenant farmers in Ireland who can never hope to own their own land and who are at the mercy of the wealthy Protestant landowning class, as exemplified by the Christie family. The middle section shows Shannon and Joseph on their way to America. This part is decidedly atypical, as the journey of our two main characters is depicted as much more luxurious than the transit of most Irish immigrants (especially from earlier times), who traveled for four to six weeks on so-called coffin ships in wretched, unsafe, unhealthy conditions. In the final section, the two young people make their way in the new country, receiving a full initiation into the underside, and the opportunities, of American life.

As we've seen to be the case with so many other ethnic groups, the depiction of Irish Americans in film has relied heavily on negative stereotypes. Irish men have routinely been portrayed as quick-tempered drunkards—like the men in the saloon in *Far and Away*— and they play the parts of tough urban criminals or hoodlums in films like *The Public Enemy* (1931), *Mystic River* (2003), and *Gangs of New York*

(2002). But they are also brave, big-hearted heroes, such as the brothers in the movie *The Sullivans* (1944), the Catholic priest in *Boys Town* (1938), and the boxer in *Cinderella Man* (2005).

Stereotypical depictions of women show long-suffering mothers who try to keep peace in their own raucous, violent, poverty-stricken homes—similar to Angela in *Angela's Ashes*. But there are also many strong, independent Irish American women in film who give a sense of the determination and pluck of the historical immigrants—women like Shannon in *Far and Away*, Sarah in *In America* (2003), Maggie Fitzgerald in *Million Dollar Baby* (2004), and Mae Braddock in *Cinderella Man*.

Whatever their on-camera roles, the Irish have shown themselves for decades to be gifted, charismatic actors, and they have also long been creative forces behind the scenes. Having brought to America their rich theatrical and literary tradition, many Irish found a place in film production and performance. Among the dozens of major film stars you may know are Spencer Tracy, Mickey Rooney, Bing Crosby, James Cagney, Art Carney, Ronald Reagan, Helen Hayes, Grace Kelly, and Maureen O'Hara. Check the database on the website *www.irishfilm.net* for excellent information on films about the Irish and Irish Americans.

In recent years there has been an upswing in Irish American pride and a renewed interest in things Irish. For example, you may be familiar with the popular dance group Riverdance *(www.riverdance.com)* or with traditional Irish musicians like those featured on websites such as *www.shamrockirishmusic.org* and *www.npr.org/programs/thistle*. Novels such as Frank McCourt's *Angela's Ashes* (1999) and works of nonfiction like Thomas Cahill's *How the Irish Saved Civilization* (1995) have been huge bestsellers.

About the Filmmakers and Actors of *Far and Away*

With *Far and Away*, director and former child actor Ron Howard—known for directing *Cocoon* (1985), *Apollo 13* (1995), *A Beautiful Mind* (2001), and many other films—pursued a longtime personal passion. As one of approximately 45 million Americans of Irish descent living in the United States today (one in every six Americans can claim full or partial Irish heritage), Oklahoma-born Howard longed to turn the events of his own family history into an epic film. He says his "romance with Ireland" began when, at a very young age, he stopped there briefly with his parents on a flight to Vienna (Dolman and Howard 1992, viii). As a young boy, he also heard stories from his Irish great-grandmother about her husband, who took part in the 1893 Oklahoma land rush and who, in her memory, rode out in front. Interestingly, four other Howard ancestors also competed in this race for land, but only one of the five successfully staked a claim.

Of his fascination for this period in history and excitement about capturing it on film, Howard says:

> As a kid I always had the dream of being able to take a time capsule back and see what it was like on the prairie, see what it was like as a pioneer. And here it was. That was what all those ancestors of mine had been through. This is what it looked like. This is what they did. (120)

At the same time, Howard had no illusions about the fact that to "get financing in Hollywood for a film about Irish immigrants would be next to impossible" (ix). The topic was very ambitious, and the prospect of attracting a large audience was uncertain. Despite many frustrations and setbacks, Howard and screenwriter Bob Dolman persisted for eight years to see the complicated and often dangerous film through to its conclusion.

Far and Away is unique in that it makes use of expensive, seldom-used 65-millimeter film, which, because of its extra width, is suited to panoramic scenes like the land rush. Cinematographer Mikael Salomon's spectacular re-creation of this one event took months to plan and required 800 extras, 400 horses, and 200 wagons.

The two stars, Australian Nicole Kidman and American Tom Cruise, had to be taught to speak with Irish accents. (One might ask why Irish actors were not chosen. Given the financial risks being taken, Howard may have felt that he needed these internationally known stars for publicity. Even so, *Far and Away* was not a huge hit at the time, nor is it especially well-known today.) Dialect coach Tim Monich explains that "Tom uses the earthy, plain lyricism of the rural western part of the country," whereas the "precise, clipped speech that Nicole uses . . . still distinguishes upper-class Irish Protestants and gives them the name of 'West Brits.'" (51). Check with cultural insiders to get their p.o.v. on the accuracy of the film characters' accents.

Who's Who in the Film

Joseph Donelly (Tom Cruise)—Catholic son of poor peasant farmer

Shannon Christie (Nicole Kidman)—Protestant daughter of wealthy landowner

Daniel Christie (Robert Prosky)—Shannon's father and landowner

Nora Christie (Barbara Babcock)—Shannon's mother

Stephen (Thomas Gibson)—Shannon's fiancé and bailiff for Daniel Christie

Mike Kelly (Colm Meaney)—Boston political boss

Director—Ron Howard

Screenwriter—Bob Dolman

Terms to Know

Anglo, Anglo American, Anglo Saxon, Euro American, European American—Common terms, often used interchangeably, to refer to white, English-speaking Americans of European (if not always of Anglo-Saxon) origin. The Angles and Saxons were Germanic tribes that ruled England beginning in the 5th century. Thus, in a strict historical sense, the terms **Anglo** and **Anglo Saxon** apply only to those of British heritage, but they are often used more broadly. Irish generally do not wish to be called **Anglos**.

Caucasian—Anthropological term for **white** people that is now discredited but is still seen on questionnaires and heard in everyday speech. The concept comes from anthropologist Johann Friedrich Blumenbach (1752–1840), who thought the first humans (whom he believed to be white) lived in the region of the Caucasus Mountains, located between the Black and Caspian Seas.

mick, paddy—Derogatory nicknames for Irishmen or Irish Americans. **Mick** derives from the Irish name Michael and also perhaps from the prefix *Mc*, commonly found in many Irish surnames. **Paddy**, an old nickname for Patrick, came to be used as a slur for the Irish, particularly males, beginning in the mid-18th century.

Scotch Irish (Scots Irish) Americans—Protestant Americans whose ancestors migrated first from Scotland to Ulster (Northern Ireland), primarily in the 1600s, and then again to North America, mostly in the 1700s. Scotch Irish have tended to emphasize their origins as being distinct from, and superior to, other (Catholic) Irish, even to the extent of claiming to be a separate race.

WASP—Acronym for **White Anglo Saxon Protestant.** Technically applies to those of English descent, perhaps Scottish or Welsh, but not Irish. When used by critics, the term suggests a certain smug, self-satisfied, patrician attitude, but it can also be used without apology by self-identified WASPs.

white—Most widely accepted term for those of largely European descent whose skin color approximates, though is not truly, white.

History Flashback

In entertaining and vivid fashion, *Far and Away* re-creates the experiences of late 19th-century Irish immigrants. Though European and white, the Irish never shared the advantages of settlers from England or other northern European countries. A look into Irish history will reveal a subjugated, impoverished people ruled for centuries by English conquerors. Not until 1921 did any part of Ireland gain its independence, when the Irish Free State was created in the south. See the map at *www.ireland-map.co.uk/index.htm*. But the six largely Protestant counties of northern Ireland remained under British jurisdiction, and strife and violence continue to this day over the question of whether these counties will be reunited with the rest of the island.

Irish immigration to the United States is marked by a single catastrophic event: the Potato Famine of the mid-1800s. The harvest of this staple food had been unreliable before, and a devastating blight ruined much of it in 1845 and successive years, resulting in unparalleled hardship and famine for the largely rural population.

Accordingly, we can separate Irish immigration into three distinct periods: before the great famine of 1845–51; during the two famine decades of the 1850s and 1860s; and post-famine, which is the time period of *Far and Away*. In the pre-famine period, both Catholic and Protestant Irish (also called Scotch Irish) came to America in small numbers from the 1600s onward. (For information on the Scotch Irish, see *www.ulsternation.org.uk/ulster's%20contribution%20to%20america.htm*.) Then the great famine resulted in a massive migration, primarily of Irish Catholics. The statistics are staggering. Of an estimated eight mil-

lion people living in the country in 1840, more than one million perished of hunger and hunger-related diseases. Faced with starvation or
departure, huge numbers left during the famine decades, and a
smaller but significant exodus continued into the next century, total-
ing an estimated four million people who went mostly to the United
States, but also to Canada and Australia. By 1900 the population of
Ireland had fallen to four million, half of the pre-famine figure, and
today it is approximately 5.2 million. Among the 19th-century Irish
immigrants were many families, but also large numbers of single
women, an unusual occurrence in U.S. immigration history.

As destitute, unskilled workers and as Catholics, the Irish who
arrived in America during the famine era were made universally
unwelcome. The extreme antipathy between Protestant English and
Catholic Irish in the old world carried across the ocean to the eastern
shores of America, where Catholics were a despised minority. Boston
was not yet an Irish town, nor were there other settlements of compatriots the new arrivals could join. An estimated one-third of the
arrivals spoke little or no English—their native language was Irish, also
called Gaelic—and many could not read or write any language. Among
the population at large, negative stereotypes of drunken brutes pre-
vailed, and discrimination was rampant. Want ads and signs proclaiming "No Irish Need Apply" were a common sight; an advertisement
from the *Daily Sun* newspaper of May 11, 1853, reads: "Woman
wanted—to do general housework. . . . English, Scotch, Welsh, or
German, or any country or color except Irish" (Graves 2003, 65).

The story of this group of mid-century newcomers is one of inde-
scribable hardship and sacrifice. Although totally unequipped for
urban life, they were afraid to move inland and trust their fate again
to farming, as so many Germans did. (In this sense, Joseph's hunger
for land is not typical.) Nor could they scrape together the money to
leave the city of their debarkation. As author William V. Shannon
says, "The Irish were a rural people in Ireland and became a city people in the United States" (Barone 2001, 30).

In *Ethnic America: A History* (1981), Thomas Sowell describes the
situation in vivid language:

> They crowded into the poorest quality housing—far worse than
> slum housing today—and lived under conditions that readily
> communicated disease, fire, and such social problems as vio-
> lence, alcoholism, and crime. . . . The jobs the Irish did find

were those considered too hard, too menial, too dirty, or too dangerous for others. The hardships of their lives may be summed up in the 19th century observation that 'You seldom see a gray-haired Irishman' (17).

Even in their undesirable jobs, the Irish had to compete with the Chinese and blacks, resulting in ugly animosities and rivalries. In an unfortunate chapter of Irish American history, many workers used their whiteness against those in their same economic class rather than joining together in a common cause.

For Irish immigrants like Joseph and Shannon, who arrived in the post-famine period at the end of the 19th century, the situation was somewhat different, both at home in Ireland and in the United States. The worst years of starvation had passed, but Irish Catholics still lived in extreme deprivation. Though families like those we see in Joseph's village were legally free, they lived as a conquered people in their own country, with few rights in the areas of politics, religion, and education. As we learn at the beginning of the film, they were unable to own their own land but had to pay rent to Protestant landlords. In the final decades of the century, anger toward these landowners was growing dramatically, and violence was escalating, as evidenced in the section of the film where a wealthy landlord tries to ride through the village in a fancy carriage.

The funeral scene in which Stephen Chase, the bailiff for Daniel Christie, appears is a turning point for Joseph. As Christie's employee, Stephen has the disagreeable job of collecting rent from the peasants, who in bad times could not afford to pay. In a dramatic and cruel gesture, Stephen slaps his notice of eviction on the lid of the coffin bearing Joseph's father. Historically, poor peasants were often evicted from the land, and their homes were sometimes destroyed, as occurs in the film. In return, despised landlords like Christie experienced so-called "outrages" at the hands of angry individuals or groups. Their mansions were burned, their animals killed, and occasionally they were shot. So it would not have been unusual for a man like Joseph to set out to take revenge on Christie. In doing so he becomes part of a group of underground resisters who burn down the Christie mansion later in the film. Historically, such clandestine groups actively opposed their oppressors and committed vigilante acts of violence.

As is memorably evident from the moment Joseph catches a glimpse of the Christie mansion, he and his landlord belong to two deeply divided classes. Joseph's story is typical of the majority, whereas families like the wealthy Christies were rare at the turn of the century. Originally from England, the Christies may well have been living in Ireland for more than 100 years, adopting Irish ways and becoming "almost more Irish than the Irish" (Dolman and Howard 20). But their religion, wealth, and sense of superiority kept them apart from the people whose lives they controlled. Surprisingly, Daniel Christie turned out not to be the ogre Joseph imagined him to be, and Shannon, though definitely rich and spoiled, had feminist ideas not entirely in keeping with her life of privilege. America tempts her as a way of escaping the boredom and stuffiness of her upper-class life.

The voyage that wealthy Shannon and her reluctant "servant" Joseph take on the first-class deck of the ship was certainly more pleasant than the transatlantic travel most Irish experienced. Actually, however, by the time of our story even the lower classes no longer faced perilous voyages, partly because steam ships had cut the travel time to America to two weeks. And the arrival in the new country, however frightening and harsh it might have been at the end of the century, was much easier than in earlier times. By now, Boston was an Irish city, with plenty of people available for advice and various kinds of help.

Of course, as we see in the film when Shannon's spoons are stolen, help was not always what it seemed, and newcomers were easily exploited. Discrimination was still a harsh reality as well, but the immigrants had organized themselves politically and socially for mutual gain and protection. Having resisted oppression in the old country for so long, they brought with them grass-roots organizational skills, including methods of circumventing what they regarded as oppressive authority, and a gritty courage that helped them assert themselves in American politics. They gravitated toward so-called political machines, becoming powerful forces in Boston and other cities. Used in this sense, a machine is an unofficial, well-organized political group that functions, not always in legal or ethical ways, to gain and exercise power. In the film, Mike Kelly, a ward (or neighborhood) "boss" who is part of a political machine, secures votes for his party's candidates in exchange for providing jobs and other favors. Though corrupt, the machines undoubtedly provided useful services to many who would otherwise have been excluded from the system.

How do the lives of Shannon and Joseph in Boston compare with the historical experiences of Irish newcomers? Again, the filmmakers strive to stay true to historical events and achieve authenticity in sets, costumes, and small details—like the charming appearance of the lamplighter on the Boston street. The two travelers' arrival into the confusing, bustling port seems quite realistic. Their employment in the chicken factory is typical of the harsh working conditions of the time (although, unlike Shannon, most Irish women entered domestic service in jobs shunned by other immigrant groups). The room shared by the "brother and sister" in Molly's brothel is typically cramped and unpleasant, though it was much better than what many others before them had endured. And Joseph's new-found, lucrative occupation as a bare-knuckle boxer is true to part of the Irish experience.

The film's vivid boxing scenes are noteworthy as examples of how the sport began in America. It probably grew from spontaneous brawls in pubs and social clubs, like the one Joseph frequents. Boxers stood toe-to-toe with upheld hands and exchanged punches until one went down, marking the end of a round. One immigrant group would often compete against another, as in the scene where Joseph challenges the Italian champion. Real-life, celebrated Irish champions include names such as John L. Sullivan and "Gentleman" Jim Corbett.

After leaving Boston, Joseph finds work as a manual laborer in those occupations where the Irish made enormous contributions to the building of America. In Pennsylvania, he digs coal and helps construct a bridge, and he travels south to the Ozarks to work on the railroad. At that time, railroad work, especially the laying of dynamite needed to cut through mountains, was so dangerous that a common expression suggested that there was an Irishman "buried under every tie."

The culmination of the film, when Joseph and Shannon, the Christies, and Stephen all meet again and risk everything in their gamble for a new life, is a cinematic tour de force. The production crew studied epic scenes in *Ben-Hur* (1959) and *Cimarron* (1960) to learn more about staging such a large-scale operation, and their successful recreation is reminiscent of Kevin Costner's breathtaking buffalo chase seen by viewers just two years earlier in *Dances with Wolves* (1990).

What was this rather strange phenomenon of the land rush all about? As railroad companies extended lines into increasingly remote areas, they and other business interests pressured the federal government to open more territories to settlement. Between 1889 and 1893, the government sponsored several free runs for land in the Oklahoma Territory. The one we see, the final and largest of the Oklahoma runs, took place on September 16, 1893. A million acres were to be given away, and of the 100,000 people who were expected to compete, only one in eight could hope to succeed. To attract settlers to the vast new territories and encourage them to vie for land, millions of advertisements, brochures, and pamphlets, like the one Shannon shows Joseph early in the film, were typically printed in a variety of languages and circulated throughout America and northern Europe.

When the filming of the long-awaited scene was finally to begin, Howard was overcome with emotion:

> Right before we were about to roll, I actually thought to myself, try to take a picture, try to remember this moment. Because you are one lucky son of a bitch to get to do this. It was the closest I've ever come to being too emotional to say 'roll the cameras.' (120)

Cruise says that he, too, was totally carried away by the excitement: "What a thrill! I was completely caught up in the moment, all I could think about was getting to that piece of land and staking my claim" (129).

Although the portrayal of events encourages us to celebrate the way the elderly Christies are able to outwit the racers and begin a new life as homesteaders, the historical reality sheds a negative light on their deception. Many such cheaters, called "Sooners," actually sneaked on to the unassigned lands and hid on their "claim" before the start of the race. Some were successful, but others were detected and evicted, or worse. One body, for example, was found next to a stake on which an attached piece of paper read "Death to All Sooners."

Another unfortunate perspective often overlooked in accounts of these races for glory is that the riders were competing for stolen land. Ron Howard was well aware of the tragedy of the situation:

> While researching the film we had discovered some disheartening facts about the Oklahoma Land Runs. They were a fiasco in many ways—a publicity stunt, backed by government and railroad companies, to lure settlers west onto land that was taken from Native Americans. (xi)

How does Howard include this p.o.v. in the film? Do you think it was necessary for him to include it? If so, do you think what he showed was sufficient?

The movie suggests that Joseph and Shannon will live happily ever after, but for most Irish the American Dream took longer to achieve. Through decades of struggle, Irish Americans gradually improved their lots, becoming respected as municipal employees (the Irish cop and Irish fireman were fixtures in major cities), playing an important role in the American Catholic Church, and achieving particular success in politics. The Irish Catholic political tradition reached its pinnacle in 1960 when John F. Kennedy, whose paternal great-grandfather came to the United States in 1848, became the first Irish Catholic to be elected president of the United States.

As the Irish rose along the economic and social ladder, other new immigrant groups—Poles, Italians, Jews, and Greeks—quickly took their place at the bottom, beginning the experience of their own arduous climb upward. Typically, the more recent waves of newcomers often settled in the same neighborhoods the previous groups had vacated. In this and other ways, patterns of immigration have repeated themselves again and again in American history.

Diversity Detective: Explore Your Family History

Some of you may have spent a lot of time looking into your family background, and others may have spent only a little. Whatever your ethnicity or nationality—and however much you may already know about your heritage—use this detective exercise to deepen your knowledge. Your assignment is simply to research part of your family history that interests you and produce an album (or the beginnings of one) with photos, documents, and text. Realize that whatever you are able to record and document can become a gift to your family and something to preserve for future generations.

Ideally, you might visit parents or other family members in person to speak with them and perhaps collect relevant items. If you are an international student or are attending a college or university far from your home, you might write, call, or e-mail a relative. If you are of mixed heritage, you might choose to focus on one part of your family background.

First, take about an hour to draw your family tree according to whatever knowledge you currently have. If you already possess a chart or drawing, locate it if you can and refresh your knowledge.

Then think about how to increase your knowledge of your family background. Is there someone (e.g., a parent, grandparent, or elderly aunt) you might visit or contact to inquire about your family? For example, you might think about interviewing the oldest living person in your family. Are there family records or photographs you might take a closer look at? You can begin to gather photographs, not only of people, but of schools, homes, farms, places of birth and burial sites, places of worship, and places of employment. This collection, even if small, could be made into an album, electronic file, or video to share with family and others.

You can also begin to collect letters, diaries, and e-mails. In our electronic age, it's always a good idea to preserve at least one sample of a family member's handwriting. Also, you might be interested in recording family members' voices as part of oral histories. Depending on where your detective work leads you, you might collect maps, newspaper articles, and original documents (or copies of documents) like military records and marriage certificates. Favorite family recipes are also great to include.

If your parents or earlier generations were immigrants to this or another country, you can attempt to find out about their lives before and after immigrating. You might also look at how subsequent generations have preserved the cultures of their ancestors' places of origin. If you are Native American or an indigenous person from another country, or if your ancestors have lived in the same place for many generations, see how much you can learn about who they were and what their lives were like.

Whatever your background, the following questions may give you further ideas for your detective work:*

- Describe the places where previous generations lived; borrow and copy photos of their places of residence, streets, villages, or neighborhoods.
- Describe the modes of transportation used by your ancestors.
- Describe equipment, tools, or machines used by your ancestors and tell the role they played in their lives.
- Describe your ancestors' religious practices.
- Describe your ancestors' possessions, including clothing and jewelry, artifacts, and furnishings. If some articles have been

....
*Adapted from Valerie Holladay, "Easy Steps to Writing Your Family History," *Ancestry* 21, no. 4 (July/August 2003): 17.

handed down and are available, take pictures and tell as much of the story associated with the possessions as you can.

- Record family stories, lore, and jokes, even if they may not be true.

- Find out about creative abilities or skills that your ancestors possessed, and tell about their accomplishments.

- Describe the work done by your ancestors, professionally and in the home.

A word of caution: Every family has its troubles, secrets, lies, and painful memories. Some things you learn may be difficult or shocking for you, and some topics may be sensitive, or even too painful, for family members to speak about. Please show care and respect as you go about your investigations. Painful memories of separation or divorce, illness and death, or conflicts and feuds are to be treated with sensitivity.

If you are adopted, you might find family research to be useful and valuable, or you might decide not to pursue it at this time. You can, of course, choose to investigate the lives and background of your adoptive parent or parents, since biology is not our sole, or sometimes even our preferred, definition of family.

When you complete your detective work, you may be asked to report to the class what you learned about yourself and your family, and what method you used to delve into your family history.

If for any reason you prefer not to research your family background, or if you are unable to do so, you may work individually or with classmates on an assignment from the **Your P.O.V.** list at the end of the chapter.

Spotlight: When Did the Irish Become White?

What does it mean to say someone is white? Since the country was founded, the definition has undergone frequent change, and it remains unclear and in flux. How dark can a person be and still qualify as white? Are Italians and Greeks white? Are Jews and Arab Americans? These and other groups that are unthinkingly classified as white today were originally seen differently.

In fact, founding father Benjamin Franklin thought of white as referring only to those of Anglo-Saxon descent, all others being "swarthy" or "tawny" inferiors. In a 1751 essay, he wrote: "Spaniards, Italians, French, Russians, and Swedes are generally of what we call a swarthy complexion; as are the Germans also, the Saxons only excepted, who with the English, make the principal body of white people on the face of the Earth." Furthermore, Franklin asked why this new country should "darken its people," when there was "so fair an opportunity, by excluding all Blacks and Tawnys, of increasing the lovely White" (Labaree 1961, 234).

How do you react to the fact that Franklin did not consider Swedes, French, or Germans to be white? Notions similar to Franklin's "lovely Whites" have persisted down through American history, and only gradually has the category of white expanded to include non–Anglo-Saxon Protestants, amidst considerable controversy and confusion. One of myriad examples of how "white" has meant different, often contradictory, things socially and legally is that in 1910 an immigrant from India was light enough to convince one court that he was white, but ten years later the United States Supreme Court ruled that another Indian immigrant was not. At stake were rights and benefits such as entering the country, holding jobs, and becoming citizens.

Just like the legal action brought by Indians, immigrants of Arab (see page 121), Japanese, Afghan, and Armenian descent sued in U.S. courts from the mid-1900s to the mid-20th century to prove themselves white. Irish were long considered as belonging to a race other than white. That they were seen, at least by one employer, as being of a different "color" from English, Scotch, Welsh, or German is evidenced, for example, in the wording of the advertisement quoted on page 97. The story of how Irish Catholics gradually gained entry into the white race—both nobly and ignobly—is told by Noel Ignatiev in his important work *How the Irish Became White* (1995). A related study is *Are Italians White? How Race Is Made in America* (2003), compiled by editors Jennifer Guglielmo and Salvatore Salerno.

The category white is still undergoing change today. Statistics and studies reveal that new immigrants often self-identify as white because they see it as synonymous with being American and having better opportunities. Wanting to belong, to be accepted, and to fit in, newcomers are further expanding the definition and making white an extremely diverse category. A fairly recent phenomenon is the growth of so-called White Studies at colleges and universities. For further information, see *www.euroamerican.org* or *www. uwm.edu/~gjay/Whiteness/index.html*.

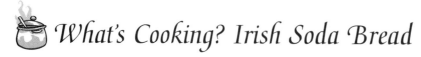

What's Cooking? Irish Soda Bread

St. Patrick's Day is a time when many Irish Americans look to their roots and prepare foods from the old country. One of our students reported that in her family Irish Soda Bread is a St. Patrick's Day tradition. Look up a traditional Irish recipe, prepare the dish (and share it with your class), and write a page describing the experience. See *www.irelandseye.com/aarticles/culture/recipes/index.shtm*.

Lights! Camera! ACTION!

Check the website of Global Exchange, a non-profit organization that promotes peace, human rights, and ecological sustainability. Of special interest are their many study tours, called reality tours. One of their regular Ireland tours, held in Dublin, focuses on "A Lasting Peace—with Justice." You might consider becoming a member of Global Exchange, bringing a speaker to your campus, becoming an intern or volunteer, or supporting the organization in other ways. See *www.globalexchange.org*.

Your P.O.V.

1. Imagine you have the opportunity to spend two weeks in Ireland. Where would you go, and why?
2. Imagine you have been hired to organize a weekend or week-long festival celebrating Irish American culture and tradition. What events would you include? Design a program for the festival.

3. Find a person who self-identifies as Irish or Irish American, and ask if you might spend some time talking with the person. Consult the guidelines for intercultural chats and interviews in Appendix C.

4. If you are not Catholic, visit a Catholic church, school, or university, and write a page to describe your experience. Find someone who will accompany you to a Mass. See *www. americancatholic.org/default.asp* and consult the guidelines in Appendix B.

5. Imagine that you and your crew are making a film on Irish American life and culture today. Consult the guidelines in Appendix D for further information. Here are some potential topics for consideration:

   a. The Irish Heritage Trail in Boston. Be sure to follow the live links at the *www.irishheritagetrail.com*.

   b. St. Patrick's Day customs and parades in cities across the United States. How do they differ? For example, in San Antonio, Texas, the river is dyed green.

   c. Irish music (an excellent resource for live music links is *www.liveireland.com*).

   d. The Irish language (two sites that offer enjoyable language lessons with useful phrases, games, and pronunciation tips are *www.daltai.com* and *www.standingstones.com/gaelpron.html*).

   e. The story of Irish maids in the United States.

   f. Irish American life and news. A comprehensive list of news services can be found at *www.world-newspapers.com/ ireland.html*.

And Our Irish American Book Awards Go To . . .

Irish America: Coming into Clover by Maureen Dezell (New York: Anchor Books, 2000). A fresh, intelligent look beyond the clichés and myths to discover who the Irish American Catholics really are. "This is a book about an Irish America that isn't on parade on St. Patrick's Day," says author Dezell (1).

The Irish in America, edited by Michael Coffey (New York: Hyperion, 1997). A splendid compilation of more than 100 photographs and two dozen essays about all things Irish American. Included are contributions by well-known Irish American writers, actors, musicians, and others. This book is both a good read and a valuable source of information on Irish American history, community, politics, arts, and culture.

Out of Ireland: The Story of Irish Emigration to America by Kirby Miller and Paul Wagner (Niwot, CO: Roberts Rinehart, 1997). Another wonderful book with incredible, rare photographs. This tale of immigration is personalized, using actual letters written home.

And Our Irish American Film Awards Go To . . .

In America (2002)—A poignant and heartwarming story of modern-day immigration. Brokenhearted by the loss of their five-year-old son, an Irish family immigrates in the 1980s to the slums of New York. Trying to escape the pain of their past, they eventually find healing in the form of a friendship with an unusual neighbor. Directed by Jim Sheridan.

On the Waterfront (1954)—A story of Irish longshoremen victimized by their corrupt union, and considered one of the great films of all times. Marlon Brando delivers an unforgettable performance as an ex-prizefighter and exploited dockworker. Directed by Elia Kazan.

This Is My Father (1998)—The portrait of a lonely and disillusioned Chicago high school teacher who realizes he can only answer questions about his past by going back to his mother's village in Ireland. An intriguing film about the search for the truth. Directed by Paul Quinn.

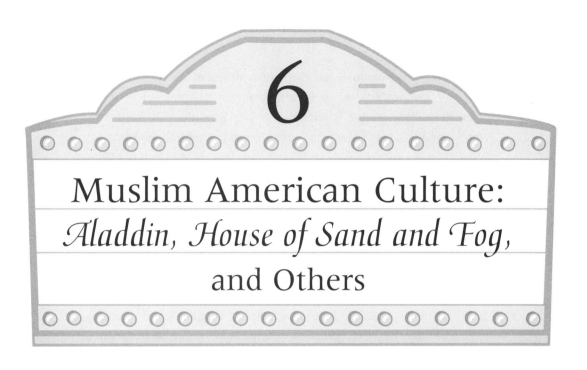

6

Muslim American Culture:
Aladdin, House of Sand and Fog,
and Others

Setting the Scene:
Freewriting and Discussion

Study these two photographs. Freewrite your reactions, and then share them with a classmate. You might consider the following questions: Does it surprise you that these images were taken in the United States? Did you expect them to be from another country? If so, where? Does the woman in *hijab* seem different to you from the image of Muslim women generally depicted in the media? If so, please explain and give a possible reason. How do you think this woman and this place of worship are viewed in their neighborhoods? Would you want to meet the woman? Visit this place of prayer? Why or why not?

Sneak Preview

Aladdin and Others

Take a moment to recall a film you have seen that deals with Muslims or Arabs in America. Can you think of any? As we began on our search, we expected to find at least a few films that would allow for an exploration of Arab and Muslim cultures in the United States as well as for a discussion of contemporary realities subsequent to September 11, 2001.

To our amazement, we could not find a suitable film. We scoured all the sources we know; consulted with knowledgeable colleagues; and viewed many films that we quickly rejected because of their lack of insight, care, and authenticity in depicting the cultures in question. Though films that stereotype, bash, or misrepresent cultures—and there are many of those where Muslims and Arabs are concerned—can be used as illuminating negative examples, we had hoped to avoid them.

In his classic book entitled *Reel Bad Arabs: How Hollywood Vilifies a People* (2001), Lebanese American scholar Jack Shaheen gives a fascinating and comprehensive analysis of the film industry's ongoing defamation of Arabs. He relates that for twenty years he and his wife "searched for, collected, and studied motion pictures related to Arab portraits and themes" (12). They discovered that "Hollywood has projected Arabs as villains in more than 900 feature films" (13). Among the worst offenders are widely known films such as *The Black Stallion* (1979), *True Lies* (1994), and *Rules of Engagement* (2000).

Shaheen advises us to "pay special attention to those Arabs you *do not see* on movie screens" (13). He points out that "images of ordinary Arab men, women, and children, living ordinary lives" are missing—movies that show friends, social occasions, and family events (13). He summarizes: "All I ask of filmmakers is to be even-handed, to project Arabs as they do other people—no better, no worse" (35).

Does Shaheen not seem to be calling for the very type of film we are studying in other chapters of this book—like *Smoke Signals* (1998), *The Joy Luck Club* (1993), and *The Wedding Banquet* (1993)? Where is the Arab or Muslim American equivalent? Where are the Muslim and Arab American directors, screenwriters, and actors? Where is an Arab or Muslim p.o.v.?

There are at least a few Arab Americans who have had significant acting or directing careers in Hollywood. Four actors come to mind (though their Arab identities have often been irrelevant to their roles): Danny Thomas (the star, from black-and-white TV days, of the long-running sitcom *Make Room for Daddy*), Jamie Farr (the cross-dressing corporal on *MASH*); F. Murray Abraham (the hardworking and versatile actor who was so memorable in *Chariots of Fire* [1981]), and Tony Shalhoub (the brilliant but sorrowful obsessive-compulsive detective on the TV series *Monk*).

Behind the camera, there is Syrian-born Moustapha Akkad, who is known for directing and producing two historical epics that portray Muslim heroism: *The Message* (1976), which deals with the Prophet Muhammad and the birth of Islam, and *Lion of the Desert* (1981), which tells of the Libyan resistance leader, Omar Mukhtar. (Since these two films are set outside of the United States, they were not selected as suitable for our purposes.) Financial considerations caused Akkad to turn to a different genre—the horror film—and he spent many of his years in the movie industry as executive producer of the movies in the *Halloween* series.

Given the lack of "even-handed" films available at the present time, we suggest a different type of assignment in this chapter. First, complete the *Aladdin* (1992) section with your entire class. Then follow the instructions given at the end of **Sneak Preview**.

We assume that many of you have seen this Disney film in which Robin Williams is the entertaining, manic voice of the genie of the lamp. For this exercise, you'll view only the first two or three minutes of the movie. Before doing so, do you know where the story comes from? *Aladdin and the Enchanted Lamp* is one of the most popular of the many folktales of Indian, Persian, and Arabic origin that form the collection known as *The Arabian Nights* or *The Thousand and One Nights*. This collection and the stories within it have gone through various shapes and retellings in different languages for centuries, with the first Arabic version appearing about 850 CE. What is common to all the collections is the unforgettable frame story of the thousand and one nights that holds the tales together.

In the frame story, known throughout the world, we meet the beautiful heroine Scheherazade (Shahrizad), who lived long ago in a kingdom ruled by King Shahriyar. Having been betrayed by his Queen, whom he immediately put to death, the King "made it his custom to take a virgin in marriage to his bed each night, and kill her the next morning" (Dawood 1973, 13). This continued for three years, causing people to flee the kingdom with their daughters. Over her father's protestations, the exceptionally talented and courageous Scheherazade saw it as her fate to go to the king voluntarily, either to die, or to live and be the means of "deliverance" for the people (13). "Versed in the wisdom of the poets," Scheherazade told the King such spellbinding stories each night that he longed for more, keeping her alive for 1,001 nights and eventually making her his Queen (13).

With this enchanting backdrop in mind, view the first few minutes of the film, paying special attention to the lyrics of "Arabian Nights" sung by the storyteller. What exactly does he say? In *Reel Bad Arabs*, Shaheen explains that the original lyrics, heard by audiences when the film appeared in movie theaters in 1992, were somewhat different from the lines we hear now. In the original song, the storyteller says he comes from a "faraway" land where "caravan camels roam." This is a place, he informs us in the next two lines, where they "cut off your ear" if they "don't like your face," a practice he admits is *barbaric*.

In response to criticism and pressure from Arab American groups, Disney executives agreed to change the two offensive lines prior to the release of the video the following year. So the part about cutting off ears was deleted in the video version, but not the "barbaric" line. Why do you think Disney would insist on introducing children to an entire culture and civilization with the term *barbaric?*

An analysis of other Disney films such as *Dumbo* (1941), *The Lion King* (1994), and *Pocahontas* (1995) reveals that this disrespectful language is not an aberration, and in fact Disney has been faulted repeatedly for promoting ethnic and gender stereotypes. In the case of *Aladdin*, an ostensibly entertaining film intended for children serves as an unsuspected—and consequently insidious—vehicle for the denigration of Arab culture. For more details on the film as a whole see *Reel Bad Arabs.* Two interesting articles on Disney's stereotypes are found at *www.stanford.edu/~jdiop/index_files/Page656.html* and *www.gseis.ucla.edu/courses/ed253a/Giroux/Giroux2.html.*

You might also turn to Carlos E. Cortés's *The Children Are Watching: How the Media Teach about Diversity* (2000) for an illuminating, highly readable analysis of the unfortunate cultural lessons children and adults alike are learning every day from movies, television, and other mass media.

Clearly, *Aladdin* is not a film about Muslim Americans, but we chose it to present in this chapter because it has the potential to influence Americans' perceptions of Arab and Muslim cultures for generations (as profoundly as the 1962 epic *Lawrence of Arabia*).

Of the six other films we've suggested for you to select from, no single one matched our criteria sufficiently to stand alone in this chapter. (Two are documentaries, one takes place in France, and three deal with Muslims who are not Arabs.) Together, however, they offer a splendid picture of Muslim issues and life as portrayed in cinema. We value these films as excellent examples of enlightened, fair-minded portrayals of Arab and Muslim people.

Working with a partner or small group, choose one of the six that interests you most. Be sure to read the **History Flashback** before making your choice. Your task is to watch your movie, find out as much information about it as you can, and prepare a short presentation to the class in which you show a clip (preferably of no more than five minutes) that gives a Muslim or Arab p.o.v. In your presentation, explain why you chose the clip; talk about the p.o.v.; and evaluate your film or clip in terms of the insight, care, and authenticity with which it presents the themes and characters (or people in the case of a documentary), giving it one to five stars. Be aware that you may need to provide a little background and plot information before showing your clip so that others will understand it. If you are Muslim and know of a different film clip you would like to present, please speak with your instructor about using it.

Movie Options

1. *Control Room* (2004)—If you're interested in politics and the media, you'll be fascinated by this documentary about the United States' war with Iraq as reported by Al-Jazeera, a highly popular satellite news channel in the Arab world. *Control Room* is all about p.o.v., revealing how the same news events are perceived and reported from different cultural perspectives. An eye-opener. Directed by Jehane Noujaim.

2. *House of Sand and Fog* (2003)—Based on a novel of the same title by Andre Dubus III, this is an intricate and powerful film

about the conflict that arises when an Anglo housecleaner, through a bureaucratic error, loses her San Francisco house to a family from Iran. These characters are not villains, but rather people trying desperately to hold their lives together. Should you select this film for your presentation or simply decide to watch it on your own, you should know that it is intense and may be quite disturbing. Directed by Vadim Perelman.

3. *Inside Mecca* (2003)—This one-hour documentary takes us inside Islam's holy city of Mecca, which few non-Muslims have ever seen. An all-Muslim film crew was allowed access to the city during the events of the five-day *hajj*—the annual pilgrimage that is required, if possible, of every Muslim once in a lifetime. We experience the *hajj* through the eyes of the film crew and of three extraordinary pilgrims, one from South Africa, one from Malaysia, and one from the United States. The photography is extraordinary.

4. *Malcolm X* (1992)—In this film, African American director Spike Lee delivers a powerful version of the life of Malcolm X (played by Denzel Washington), from his early days as a street hustler, to his emergence as brilliant orator and revolutionary leader, to his assassination. Pay particular attention to the latter part of the film in which Malcolm X travels to Mecca.

5. *Monsieur Ibrahim* (2003)—Set in Paris in the 1960s, this is the story of a remarkable bond that develops between a Jewish boy (played by Pierre Boulanger) and an elderly Muslim (played by Omar Sharif) who owns the neighborhood grocery shop. A beautiful, tender film, Monsieur Ibrahim is the best example we have found of the type of movie that needs to be made in the United States. The scene depicting the whirling dervishes is unique in all of cinema. Directed by François Dupeyron and filmed in French with English subtitles.

6. *The War Within* (2005)—A film about terrorism unlike others produced to date, this is a brilliant look at the human side of Muslim attacks on America. We get to know the point of view of Hassan, a Pakistani engineering student in Paris, who becomes convinced that he must join with other radicals in their training to become suicide bombers. We also see the p.o.v. of an Americanized Pakistani family with whom Hassan stays in New Jersey as he prepares to carry out his deadly mission. Directed by Joseph Castelo.

Terms to Know

Allah—The Arabic word for *God.* Allah is viewed by Muslims as the creator of everything in the universe.

ayatollah—An honorific title for a high-ranking Shiite clergyman who is widely acknowledged for his wisdom, scholarship, preaching, and teaching. There is no prescribed path to the ranking, nor is there an official ceremony for the bestowing of this title.

hajj—The pilgrimage to Mecca, in Saudi Arabia, that all Muslims are required to take at least once in their lifetime, provided they have sufficient health and financial means.

hijab—Used in a broad sense to refer to the Islamic practice of dressing modestly. Hijab is interpreted differently in different locations and varies widely. It can be a simple **headscarf** or other type of head covering worn by Muslim women. The **chador,** used primarily in Iran, covers the woman entirely except for her hands and part, or all, of her face. A chador that covers the face as well, except for a net-like opening for the eyes, is called a (full or Afghan) **burqa.** In Saudi Arabia, women are expected to wear an **abaya,** or black cloak and veil, while out in public. Hijab for men in Saudi Arabia usually consists of the **thobe** (an ankle-length white shirt) and a cotton skullcap. Many Muslim men wear full beards as part of their commitment to hijab. Muslims wearing hijab-style dress often cite the pride they feel presenting themselves to the public as honorable, faithful followers of Islam. Hijab is seen by these adherents as a way to honor Allah's will. To see some samples of modern, beautiful hijab, go to *www.alhannah.com/jilbab.html.*

imam—Leader of worship, or leader of the Muslim community.

Islam—Meaning *submission* (to the will of Allah), a monotheistic faith (one of the three Abrahamic religions along with Christianity and Judaism) that accounts for about one-fifth of the world's faithful.

jihad—A widely misunderstood word, the literal meaning of which is "struggle." Though in a contemporary context it is usually equated with military struggle and translated as *holy war,* its pure meaning refers more to inner struggle, such as the effort to behave morally and gain spiritual enlightenment. The most important jihad is thought to be the struggle within oneself.

Ka'aba—Considered to be the holiest site in Islam. Located in the central courtyard of the Grand Mosque in Mecca, it is a large, cube-shaped structure.

Koran—See **Qur'an** below.

masjid—Literally *place for prostration,* the Arabic word for **mosque.**

Mecca (Makkah)—The capital city of Saudi Arabia's Makkah province. Mecca is the destination for many Muslims worldwide during the annual **hajj.**

Mohammedan—An antiquated term viewed as being derogatory today.

mu'azzin (muezzin)—Literally *chanter,* the person who calls Muslims to prayer five times daily.

Muslim (can also be spelled **Moslem,** but Muslim is closer to the pronunciation of the Arabic word)—Literally *one who submits,* a person who believes in **Islam.**

Qur'an (Koran)—The holy book of Islam believed to be the Word of Allah as revealed to the Prophet Muhammad; it contains 114 **surahs,** or chapters.

raghead, towelhead, camel jockey—Highly derogatory terms for Arabs. **Raghead** and **towelhead** allude to the headdress worn by Gulf Arab men; the terms are sometimes used to refer to Indian Sikh men as well, who wear turbans.

Salam alaikum—Standard Islamic greeting meaning *peace be with you,* the response being **alaikum salam** *(peace be with you also).*

Sharia—The entire body of Islamic law, pertaining to both religious rituals and to many aspects of everyday life.

sheikh—The head or leader of an Arab family, tribe, or village. Can be used pejoratively to refer, for example, to any Arab in headdress.

Shi'a (Shi'ite)—Meaning *partisans of Ali,* the branch of Islam that advocates that Ali, the Prophet's son-in-law, was his rightful successor, and that only his descendants can qualify as imams. Shi'as, comprising about 15 percent of all Muslims, are found primarily in Lebanon, Iraq, the Arabian Gulf, and Iran.

Sunni (Sunnite)—Meaning *orthodox,* the branch of Islam, comprising about 85 percent of all Muslims, which advocates that Muhammad's successors should be elected rather than qualifying on the basis of blood ties to the Prophet's son-in-law Ali.

Sufism—Tradition within Islam that espouses mystical approaches to the understanding of God.

ummah—The Muslim community.

History Flashback

"The twenty-first century will be the century of Islam." So begins the introduction to an illuminating collection of essays entitled *Inside Islam: The Faith, the People, and the Conflicts of the World's Fastest-Growing Religion* (Miller and Kenedi 2002, 1). The author of the introduction, Akbar S. Ahmed, says that understanding Islam is "imperative to anyone wanting to make sense of living in the twenty-first century" (1). He tells us to consider the facts: a "population of 1.3 billion and growing; 55 states [countries in which Muslims are the majority]—and one of them nuclear; about 25 million living permanently in the West . . . ; and a religion that comes with commitment and passion" (1). Let us add to these facts that one in five people on earth is Muslim and that demographers predict this will become one in four by mid-century.

Surely, Ahmed is right that we all need to know more about Islam. But how will this happen? In her landmark book, *A New Religious America: How a "Christian Country" Has Become the World's Most Religiously Diverse Nation* (2001), Diana L. Eck explains that there are obstacles: "Islam is the religious tradition about which many Americans have the most negative stereotypes—extremist terrorism, saber-rattling jihad, and the oppression of women" (232). Undoing such stereotypes and learning anew about this world religion and its adherents will take an effort, especially since we receive much misinformation and see primarily negative images in the media, "creating a view of Islam as dangerous, subversive, highly political, and anti-American" (223). Stories of everyday people like ourselves going about their business in peaceful ways do not make the headlines. Present-day relations between Muslim American communities and the population at large can be characterized by a mutual lack of trust as well as a huge communication gap.

As you will see in this chapter, many Muslim organizations and individuals are undertaking in the most sincere, serious way to explain who they are and educate the general public. For example, some of the websites you will explore contain a wealth of thoughtfully assembled information and resources. (Our favorite is the Arab American Institute site, in particular "About Arab Americans" at *www.aaiusa.org/about_arab_americans.htm*.) But Muslims cannot succeed in creating bonds and allies by themselves, especially since they have to deal with their own pain and anger, with feelings of being "misunderstood, maligned by the media, and subject to continuous low-level harassment" (Eck 232). If Muslims are indeed taking a first step to reach out, we each have decisions to make as to our response.

First, some basic information: Islam, which means *surrender* or *submission*—understood in this context to mean submission to God—is a monotheistic, or one-God, religion that arose under the leadership of the Prophet Muhammad ibn Abdallah (570–632). A wealthy, respected Arab merchant, Muhammad brought to the polytheistic tribes of Arabia a faith built upon the teachings of the Jews and Christians. As Iranian-born Vartan Gregorian (2003) clearly explains, "Contrary to what many believe, Allah was not a new god, but simply the Arabic word for God—the God of Abraham, Moses, Jesus, and Muhammad" (5). Muslims honor the earlier prophets but believe that Muhammad was the greatest, and the last, prophet.

The Qur'an, Islam's holy book, is believed to be the literal word of Allah that was revealed to Muhammad in Arabic by the Archangel Gabriel and later compiled in written form. Muslims believe the Qur'an complete and makes perfect the revelations given to the prophets of the Old and New Testaments. It is considered to be indescribably beautiful when recited in Arabic.

The Five Pillars of Faith—the fundamental principles that are to be observed by all Muslims—include

1. professing belief in Allah as the one true God *(shahadah);*
2. reciting prayers five times daily in the direction of Mecca *(salah);*
3. giving alms and caring for the less fortunate *(zakah);*
4. fasting from dusk until dawn during the month of Ramadan, a practice intended to remind the faithful of the sufferings of the poor and hungry *(sawm);*
5. making a pilgrimage to the holy city of Mecca at least once, finances and health permitting *(hajj).*

For more information, see *http://islam101.com.* Another interesting site is *www.islamonline.net/english/aboutus.shtml.*

What is the difference between Arabs and Muslims? An easy way to remember is to associate Arabs with a language (Arabic) and Muslims with a religion (Islam). Arabs—generally defined as native Arabic speakers and their descendants—live primarily in twenty countries stretching from the Middle East to North Africa. Study the map on page 119, and then locate these countries on a larger map that includes

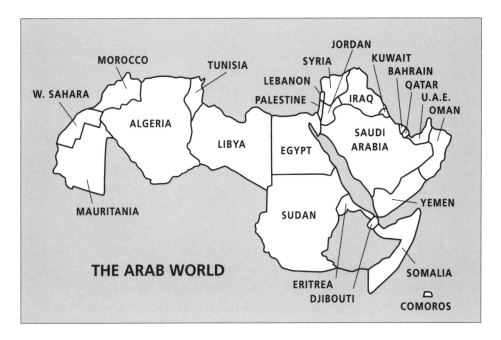

THE ARAB WORLD

adjoining countries and bodies of water. Work with a partner to make sure you can place the Arab world in a context that includes neighbors like Spain, Turkey, Ethiopia, and Iran. Can you make a guess where the largest concentration of Arab people is found outside this region? Answer: in the greater Detroit area of Michigan, where there are currently an estimated 300,000 Arab Americans.

Are most Arabs Muslims? Yes, the religion practiced by an estimated 95 percent of Arabs is Islam, but there are also Arab Christians and some Arab Jews. Given that not even 5 percent of Arabs worldwide are Christian, it is noteworthy that Christians make up more than 50 percent of the Arab American population.

If most Arabs are Muslims, is the reverse true? No. Less than 20 percent of Muslims speak Arabic as their native language. And most Muslims live outside the Arab world. The Muslim population in the United States, for example, is significant and growing.

There are an estimated seven million Muslims in America today, but statistics are unreliable, perhaps in part because many Muslims are hesitant to participate in surveys. It is generally believed they are the second largest religious group after Christians, with the Jewish population now third. Across the country there are more than 1,200 mosques, and the number of Islamic schools, businesses, and publications is growing steadily.

In the following short historical overview, we will look at four different groups of Muslim Americans: (1) Arab immigrants and their descendants, (2) non-Arab immigrants and their descendants, (3) African Americans, and (4) Anglo and other converts.

1. Arab Americans

Before reading further, take the short quiz on Arab Americans at *www.aaiusa.org/quiz.htm*. How well did you do on the quiz? More important than your score on the first try is the goal that by the end of this chapter you should be able to answer most of the questions with confidence.

The Arab American Institute estimates that there are 3.5 million people of Arab descent living in the United States today, most of whom arrived during the 20th century. The first of two waves of Arab immigrants came from Greater Syria, now known as Syria and Lebanon, in the decades from 1890–1940. (Please note that some historians describe three or four waves, and the exact meaning of *wave* is rather imprecise.) As was the case with so many other immigrant groups, the first to leave were mostly young, unmarried males with little education, taking the risk of departing their homelands for the unknown with the intent to return after a few years. Motivated primarily by the promise of economic opportunity, many of them worked at first as peddlers and later as merchants and shopkeepers in urban areas. They sent money home to their extended families and were able to pay for some relatives to join them.

Why was peddler the chosen occupation of so many? Remember that this is a time before convenience stores (and superstores) were located within easy distance of most rural Americans. As explained by Michael W. Suleiman (1999), being a peddler

> did not require much training, capital, or knowledge of English. With a few words of English learned on the run, a suitcase *(Kashshi)* full of notions (e.g., needles, thread, lace) provided by a better-established fellow Lebanese or other Arab supplier . . . many new arrivals often were on the road hawking their wares only a day or so after they landed in America. Success in peddling required thrift, hard work, very long hours, the stamina to endure harsh travel conditions (mostly walking the countryside on unpaved roads), and not infrequently the taunting and insults from children or disgruntled customers. (4)

Settlements, sometimes known as Little Syrias, began to grow in cities like Toledo, Ohio, and Detroit-Dearborn, Michigan. Though the first wave of Arabs was predominately Christian, some Muslims who came in this early period did establish several mosques in the 1920s.

Suleiman says that the opportunities for early Arab immigrants were accompanied by hardship and an unwelcome mat. Often facing prejudice and hostility, they suffered an especially severe blow when U.S. authorities began in 1909 to deny them the right to naturalization and citizenship because they were not considered to be white. This classification and rejection "traumatized" (7) the Arab communities and has remained a source of anxiety and confusion to the present day. Legal rulings have gone back and forth, resulting in the feeling among many Arab Americans that they are "honorary whites" or "white but not quite." Some Arab Americans express the preference to be seen as "people of color" (15).

From the post–World War II period to today, a second group of more educated, affluent Arabs has come to the United States for largely political reasons. To cite a few examples, America was seen as a refuge for Palestinians displaced by the creation of Israel in 1948, for Egyptians and Iraqis leaving political and social turmoil at home, for Lebanese and Yemenis fleeing civil war, for Yugoslavian and Albanian Muslims fleeing communism, and for those escaping the extended regional war between Iran and Iraq.

Possessing an Arab or pan-Arab identity to a greater extent than those in the first wave (who generally called themselves Syrians), immigrants from the second wave have generally been more eager to preserve their languages, ethnic traditions, and personal ties to their countries of origin. A testament to this developing identity is the establishment of the first-ever Arab American National Museum, inaugurated in Dearborn, Michigan, in 2005 *(www.theaanm.org).* Still, however, it is important to know that many Arabs and Arab Americans identify themselves with their country of origin rather than seeing themselves as Arab. They might say, for example, "I am Egyptian, and I speak Arabic."

Overall, Americans of Arab descent have been a success story, achieving high levels of education and meaningful employment and making substantial contributions to their communities and the society at large. Yet they remain quite unknown. How aware are you of the role Arab Americans play in public life? Team up with a classmate, or sit quietly by yourself for a few minutes, and try to think of three

Arab Americans you know of from contemporary U.S. life. Then refer to the excellent brochure at *www.aaiusa.org/PDF/Cas.Broch.(AAIF-V).pdf* put together by Casey Kasem, veteran disc jockey and host of *The American Top 40 Countdown* radio show. (Sorry, but he can't be counted as one of the three.)

2. Muslim Americans from Non-Arab Countries

Earlier in this chapter you learned that most Muslims live outside the Arab world. Are you able to name at least three of the ten non-Arab countries in the world in which the largest numbers of Muslims live? Jot down your answers and see the list at the end of this chapter.

Can you think of any movies that include Muslims from these countries who have immigrated to the United States? We did find a few feature films that deal with Muslims from Iran, and we have chosen one entitled *House of Sand and Fog* for this chapter. But with a single exception—the remarkable film *The War Within* that focuses on Pakistani Muslims—we searched in vain for suitable films about Muslim Americans from other non-Arab countries. Are we to believe that there are no other stories to tell about Muslims originally from South Asia (e.g., India, Bangladesh, Pakistan, and Afghanistan), Southeast Asia (Malaysia, Indonesia, and the Philippines), sub-Saharan Africa (Nigeria, Senegal, and the Ivory Coast), Eastern Europe (Bosnia/Herzegovina and Albania), or Turkey? Non-Arab Muslims remain virtually unrepresented in feature films. What does this mean? How might it feel for the many Muslim Americans who never see their lives reflected on the big screen? It is as if they are invisible.

If you choose to watch *House of Sand and Fog,* take careful note of the fact that, contrary to general opinion, Iranians are not Arabs; they are Persians whose native language is Farsi. Iranians are a fairly recent presence in the United States, immigrating primarily for reasons of economics, politics, and educational opportunity. The largest group, including the family you will see in the film *House of Sand and Fog,* came after the 1978–79 revolution in Iran, which toppled Shah Reza Pahlavi *(www.rezapahlavi.org)* and replaced his government with that of the Muslim fundamentalist Ayatollah Khomeni. In the film, Colonel Massoud Amir Behrani had served in a high-level position in the Shah's air force as a purchaser of fighter planes before fleeing with his family to California. Struggling to find a new existence, he is working at two jobs—one as a garbage collector on a highway crew and one as a cashier in a convenience store—when we first meet him in the film. Be aware that *House of Sand and Fog* is a disturbing film.

The same is true for *The War Within*, which contains torture scenes at the beginning and in flashbacks. If you choose this film, it's important to realize that the people who abduct, imprison, and torture Hassan are Western intelligence operators who suspect him of committing, or having knowledge of, Islamist terrorist activities. On a first viewing, this may not be clear. Also, be sure to watch the DVD special feature with audio commentary by writer/director Joseph Castelo and writer/actor Ayad Akhtar, who plays Hassan.

3. African American Muslims

Two widely known films about African American Muslims are *Malcolm X* (1992) and *Ali* (2001). You are undoubtedly familiar with the two real-life figures—Malcolm X (born Malcolm Little) and Muhammad Ali (born Cassius Clay)—on which the films are based. And you may have heard of other prominent Americans who converted to Islam, such as basketball star Kareem Abdul-Jabbar (born Lew Alcindor). Have you wondered why these African American men changed their religion?

Few people know that Islam is far from a new religion among America's black population. Fascinating research is now revealing considerable information about the enslaved persons who were taken from West Africa in the 19th, and even the 18th, centuries and who brought their religion of Islam with them. As Allen Austin points out in *African Muslims in Antebellum America* (1997), African Muslims are a "proud people" who "until very recently had been almost completely neglected by modern America's eagle-eyed historians" (4). If you have seen Steven Spielberg's film *Amistad* (1997), you may recall the scene where Muslims pray on the deck of the slave ship.

Today, African Americans constitute from 25–40 percent of all Muslims in this country. There are perhaps twenty different groups. The Nation of Islam (NOI), led by the controversial Louis Farrakhan, receives the most attention in the press. Founded in 1930 in Detroit by a mysterious figure named "Master" W. Fard (who dropped from sight without explanation in 1934), it grew quickly from a black nationalist cult to a mass movement under the new leadership of Elijah Muhammad. This strong and charismatic figure led his group of Black Muslims, as they called themselves, for 40 years until his death in 1975.

Following Master Fard's intention that the NOI actually form a separate nation, Elijah Muhammad advocated complete racial, religious, and economic separation from whites, based on the conviction that Caucasians had proved themselves throughout American history to be the enemy or, in his words, the "white devil." Accordingly, black people were to learn to make themselves independent. They should "discover themselves, elevate their distinguished men and women . . . give outlets to their talented youth, and assume the contours of a nation." An important strategy was to "buy black," meaning that members were urged to own, operate, and patronize their own businesses and other organizations such as schools and hospitals (quotations from *www.noi.org*).

The Black Muslim message of self-reliance, along with an emphasis on self-discipline and hard work, held great appeal for many African Americans, including those whose lives seemed without hope. The NOI has wisely sought converts on the streets and in the prisons. In terms of the religious doctrine itself, followers believe in Allah and the Koran, but they take a separate path in proclaiming that Master Fard was "Allah in person" and that Elijah Muhammad was his Messenger. For traditional, orthodox Muslims worldwide, this view can be seen as heresy; the principles most central to the faith are that there is only one God and that Muhammad was the last prophet, or messenger. (To learn more about the NOI, see *www.noi.org*.)

Among those who became increasingly disenchanted with the NOI was W.D. Muhammad, Elijah's son. When his father died in 1975, W.D. initially assumed the highest leadership role, but after a few years of strife he left with thousands of followers to practice orthodox Sunni Islam under the umbrella known today as the Muslim American Society. (Meanwhile, Louis Farrakhan took leadership of the old NOI in 1978, continuing in the tradition and spirit of Elijah.)

The loosely organized Muslim American Society has a larger following than the NOI and more places of worship. After a lifetime of service, W.D. Muhammad stepped down in 2003. To learn more about the Muslim American Society, check *www.masnet.org*.

What was the role of Malcolm X in the Black Muslim movement? After a long period of passionate involvement and brilliant leadership, Malcolm X, like W.D. Muhammad, broke with the NOI. Those of you who choose to watch the biographical film can report on his path.

4. Anglo Converts and Others

There is a small but growing group of Anglo and other converts to Islam, estimated to comprise 1–2 percent of the total population of American Muslims. As an example, if you choose to watch the National Geographic film *Inside Mecca* (2003), you will have the opportunity to hear from a white woman from Texas who has found her life's meaning in Islam.

What is it, we might ask, that draws people from all parts of the world to Islam? Why is this religion growing so rapidly? Experts in the field cite its simplicity; its appeal to the mind and to the heart; and its willingness to embrace as equals people of all backgrounds, ethnicities, nationalities, and economic classes. Along with its own great prophet Muhammad, it honors the prophets of the Judeo-Christian tradition, from Abraham and Moses to Jesus, who is respected as a prophet but is not seen as divine. Though adherents of Islam speak more than 60 languages, they are united in prayer by the classical Arabic of the Qur'an, which they learn to read and chant (though most do not speak it). Finally, the religion of Allah appeals to disenchanted urban youth—and many other disempowered people—in the United States and other countries who seek the discipline, meaning, and hope this religion offers.

Cultural Backpacking: Visiting a Mosque

If you are non-Muslim, this is an opportunity for you to visit a mosque *(masjid)*, the Muslim place of worship. Visiting a place of worship different from your own can be a powerful and memorable experience, often awakening one's curiosity as well as replacing ignorance and fear with a more realistic and open attitude.

Ideally, a Muslim classmate or acquaintance can accompany you on your visit. Perhaps you can consult with your college or university chaplain for assistance and information.

What to know: Please read the guidelines for visits to places of worship in Appendix B. Also, consult if possible with someone knowledgeable of etiquette. Be sure to call the mosque ahead of time to inquire about whether you may visit and about the best date and time. The Friday mid-day service is often recommended. Some mosques may be able to provide a tour or include you in a scheduled open house.

Etiquette requires modest dress for men and women. Women should wear loose clothing covering the whole body and a scarf covering the head and neck. Footwear must be removed upon entering a mosque and can usually be placed on a shoe rack at the entrance. For further information, see "So, You Want to Go to the Mosque" at *www.modernmuslima.com/tomasjid.htm.*

By the end of your backpacking trip, whether real or virtual, you should have gained factual knowledge. For example, you should have a basic familiarity with the typical parts of a mosque and their functions, the architectural elements, and the significance of certain rituals. What would you like to learn more about?

Equally important are your emotional reactions. Be observant, but also allow your feelings to play a role as you breathe in the atmosphere of the mosque and its surroundings. Afterward, reflect on how you felt. Were you comfortable? What caught your attention, and why? What did you find interesting? Did anything bother you? What sensory impressions did you receive? Did you interact with anyone and, if so, what happened? Did you feel welcome? Would you return to this or another mosque? Please write a page or two in your film notebook to present to the class or a small group.

If you are unable to make a visit in person, choose one mosque you would like to visit some day, either in the United States or in another country, and explore it online. Obtain a few photographs, and make a brief presentation to your class (or to a small group), explaining why you chose this particular mosque and what you learned about it. If you would have been able to visit, what in particular would you have wanted to see and experience?

If you are Muslim, you might wish to fulfill the assignment by assisting others in the class. Or you might like to visit a non-Muslim place of worship, perhaps with a classmate.

If your own religious or spiritual beliefs make it too difficult or uncomfortable for you to complete this assignment, please speak with your instructor about choosing additional p.o.v. work instead from the suggestions on pages 131–32.

Poet's P.O.V.

In her letter *To Any Would-Be Terrorists* (2006), Palestinian American poet Naomi Shihab Nye refers to a great Arab scholar, Dr. Salma Jayyusi, who said, "If we read one another, we won't kill one another." Nye explains that "poetry humanizes us in a way that news, or even religion, has a harder time doing." She offers potential terrorists some advice: "Read American poetry" *(www.arches.uga.edu/~godlas/shihabnye.html).*

One of Nye's own poems begins with these four lines:

This plane has landed thanks to God and his mercy.
That's what they say in Jordan when the plane sets down.

What do they say in our country? Don't stand up till we tell you.
Stay in your seats. Things may have shifted. (Nye 13)

What do these lines say to you about different ways of viewing the world? A popular and engaging speaker, Nye is perhaps the best-known among a group of Arab American authors who are gaining increased acclaim. You might want to look at her writings, such as *Words under the Words* (1995), along with those of a fellow Palestinian American, the exciting female hip-hop poet Suheir Hammad. Also of interest are the novels of two Jordanian Americans: Diana Abu-Jaber's *Arabian Jazz* (1993) and *Crescent* (2003), and Laila Halaby's *West of the Jordan* (2003).

Spotlight: Profiling

Profiling, or racial profiling, is "any action undertaken for reasons of safety, security, or public protection that relies on stereotypes about race, color, ethnicity, ancestry, religion, or place of origin, or a combination of these, rather than on reasonable suspicion, to single out an individual for greater scrutiny or different treatment" (quotation from *www.stopracialprofiling.ca*).

If you have seen artists' (or computer) sketches of suspected criminals based on descriptions provided by victims or witnesses, this is not the type of profiling we are discussing. Nor are we speaking of criminal profiling, such as done from collected evidence by behavioral profilers at crime scenes. Rather, we are talking about the tendency to view an entire group of people with heightened suspicion and also to treat individuals thought to belong to that group with unwarranted mistrust and scrutiny.

Racial profiling has long been a serious problem for African Americans and Latinos in this country, who can be thought by law enforcement officials to look "suspicious" even when they are simply shopping, walking, or driving. There are numerous stories of innocent people being falsely accused, mishandled, humiliated, or arrested—and in tragic cases beaten, shot, or killed—simply because they were (or were thought to be) of the same racial or ethnic background as a suspected criminal or they "looked like" they might be troublemakers.

Since September 11, 2001, racial and ethnic profiling has taken on new meaning in the search for suspected terrorists. Airline passengers, in particular, have been subject to increased scrutiny, especially those who "look" Muslim or Arab. A survey conducted by the Arab American Institute Foundation in 2002 revealed that 78 percent of Arab Americans felt that racial profiling had increased since September 11 (see *www.aaiusa.org/PDF/poll%20report.pdf*). Amnesty International reports that current practices targeting people of Middle Eastern descent and other racial minorities as part of the war on terror appear to "violate protections against discrimination under U.S. and international law" (quotation from *www.amnestyusa.org/racial_profiling/index.do*).

The legal issues are in fact paramount. Much debate has centered on the Patriot Act of 2001, which grants federal law enforcement officers new powers in an effort to "deter and punish terrorist acts in the United States and around the world." The Patriot Act is viewed by advocates as a necessary, justifiable response to a situation of national urgency and by opponents as an alarming erosion and violation of civil liberties. Highly controversial provisions include the federal government's expanded ability to monitor Internet use and to use wiretaps. The Patriot Act is a complicated document that few people have actually read. Even if we were to read and study it carefully, we would have no way of knowing whether government and law enforcement officials are using these extended powers responsibly.

A poignant perspective on profiling is presented by Lebanese

American Elmaz Abinader in her essay "Profile of an Arab Daughter" (2005). Being subjected after September 11 to airport searches for the first time in her life, she recalls a time when her Girl Scout leader came up with the idea of making silhouettes of the girls' profiles to be pasted onto white construction paper. "The other girls had gentle lines of faces, silky hair, slender noses," she recalls (38). As she waited at the end of the line, Elmaz found herself trembling and wanting to run away. Imagining what her profile would look like, she thought: "the only one with a sharp hook nose, a sharp chin. . . . Somewhere in the construction paper portrait, my dark eyes would be revealed and my life would be uncovered" (38–39).

In her essay, Abinader says that "history is a poor teacher" (40). Have we forgotten, she wonders, how Jews were sent to concentration camps in Europe and Japanese Americans to internment camps in the United States? In fact, having experienced the disastrous effects of profiling when they were imprisoned in camps during World War II, Japanese individuals and groups have spoken out boldly against targeting Muslims and have opposed the Patriot Act. See, for example, the resolution passed unanimously by the national board of the Japanese American Citizens League (JACL) in November 2003 *(www.jacl.org/news_and_current_events/Patriot_II_Act_resolution.pdf)*.

Some Jewish organizations are also speaking out. The Jewish Social Policy Action Network (JSPAN), for example, is taking a stand as "members of a minority that has been the victim of terrorist attacks and government oppression over many years in many places." JSPAN has recommended that an independent monitor be appointed to watch over the administration's use of the Patriot Act. (See *www.jspan.org/?cat=11#policy.*)

Have you ever been profiled? If so, write a page or two in your film notebook describing the incident, and talk about your feelings then and now. If you have not been profiled or simply prefer another assignment, describe the p.o.v. of someone who has been profiled or who fears it. You may describe a real-life situation (there are many on the Internet and elsewhere) or one that you imagine.

Insiders' P.O.V.s on Hijab

Many things attracted me to Islam—and that's a long story—but one feature that I especially appreciated was the religion's respect for women. In Islam, women were not sex objects to be ogled; their bodies were not to be put on display for male approval or rejection. The hijab was a concrete statement that told people: women's bodies are sacred. . . . Islam offered me a freedom that secular America did not. It allowed me to stop feeling inferior, to stop competing with other women, and to focus on intellectual and spiritual matters.

> —Maureen (Dickerson 31)

My name is Fairuz. I was born in and now live in Egypt. I am a respected professional with a good paying job. I went to the United States for college, but returned right after graduation. . . . It was at that time I decided to wear the hijab. My friends from the United States do not understand my decision. . . . [T]hey see traditional Muslim dress as a symbol of women's oppression, as a sign of backwardness and silence. I expect that many of you feel the same way. . . . What you don't understand is that I have made this choice willingly, intelligently, consciously, and freely. I have lived in the United States. I have seen what the West has to offer. . . . And I have chosen modest dress and the hijab instead of tight skirts, plunging necklines, and . . . high-heeled shoes. . . . I am upset that "the veil" is misunderstood in so many ways. . . . My hijab symbolizes devotion, discipline, reflection, and freedom. But nobody asks me. You just assume that I am oppressed, and with that assumption you oppress me much more than my veil does!

> —Fairuz (37–38)

Lights! Camera! ACTION!

Arabic has generally not been widely taught in U.S. schools and universities. In the most recent nationwide survey (2002), Arabic ranked thirteenth out of fifteen languages in numbers of students enrolled with 10,584—or less than 1 percent of the total—and with fewer students than Latin, Ancient Greek, and Biblical Hebrew (Association of Departments of Foreign Languages).

Even if you can only spare a little time, take a course, or some lessons, in Arabic. You might begin by looking at the websites at *http://i-cias.com/babel/arabic/index.htm* and *www.rosettastone.com*.

 # What's Cooking? Baklava

Diana Abu-Jaber's *The Language of Baklava: A Memoir* (2005) is a humorous look at what it was like to grow up with a Jordanian father who loved to cook. For wonderful insights into the link between food and culture—and for amazing recipes like Subsistence Tabbouleh ("for when everything is falling apart and there's no time to cook" [143]) and Poetic Baklava (for "when you need to serenade someone" [192])—read this book! Also be sure to check out *Arabic Slice* at *www.arabicslice.com/main.html*.

Your P.O.V.

1. Write a review of your film for publication in a newspaper, or post it on the Internet.
2. Request a chat or interview with a Muslim student or acquaintance. Please follow the guidelines in Appendix C.
3. Spend some time exploring the U.S. State Department website on Muslim life at *http://usinfo.state.gov/products/pubs/muslimlife*. Write a page or two in your film notebook giving your impressions of this site.

4. Design a poster, button, T-shirt, or bumper sticker expressing your views on the Patriot Act.

5. Assume that you are responsible for planning an Islamic Awareness Weekend or Week for your campus. What activities and events would you include?

6. You and your team of filmmakers have become interested in present-day Muslim life in America. Consult the guidelines in Appendix D. Here are some potential topics for consideration:

   a. the comedienne Shazia Mirza, a Pakistani from Birmingham, England, who is becoming the world's best-known Muslim comic, and/or the group called "Allah Made Me Funny" *(www.allahmademefunny.com)*

   b. forms of Arab music and dance *(http://youth.ibn.net/music.asp)*

   c. Muslim student associations *(www.msa-natl.org)*

   d. Muslim women's p.o.v.s on wearing the hijab

And Our Muslim American Book Awards Go To . . .

Funny in Farsi: A Memoir of Growing Up Iranian in America by Firoozeh Dumas (New York: Random House, 2004). A touching and frequently humorous biography from an Iranian American woman. In a series of short vignettes, Dumas takes us on a journey from Iran to California, from her first painfully awkward moments of intercultural misunderstandings to her marriage to a Frenchman. The author's disarming use of humor allows her to address a number of sensitive topics in an appropriate and accessible way.

A New Religious America: How a "Christian Country" Has Become the World's Most Religiously Diverse Nation by Diana Eck (San Francisco: Harper, 2001). A courageous and beautifully written book that explores the faiths of the "other America," including Muslims, Jews, Hindus, and Buddhists. Eck is a gifted storyteller who weaves in colorful personal experiences from her travels across the country to learn firsthand about religious diversity. In a post-September 11 era, this call for openness and understanding is essential reading.

***The Trouble with Islam Today: A Muslim's Call for Reform in Her
Faith*** by Irshad Manji (New York: St. Martin's Griffin, 2003). A thor-
ough and timely examination into the role of Islam in the world
today. Respected journalist, feminist, and human rights activist Manji,
herself a Muslim, argues that Muslims worldwide need to reexamine
their faith and belief systems with a critical eye and overcome the
insularity that has shut them off from the world at large. Though this
may seem like heresy to the faithful, the author's message is ultimately a positive one: Islam, and its image in the world, can be
returned to the peaceful and positive force for unification and tolerance once envisioned by its founders.

Why I Am a Muslim: An American Odyssey by Asma Gull Hasan
(London: Element Books, 2004). A delightful and informative short
book about a woman's choice to be a Muslim. Hasan goes beyond the
default explanation of being born a Muslim to share her personal reasons for choosing the Islamic faith: her desire to have a direct relationship with God, her reverence for the rich mystical tradition of Sufism,
and her belief that being a Muslim makes her a better American (and
vice-versa), to name but a few. This is an inspiring and eye-opening
look at the religion from a young woman's point of view. Hasan's
American Muslims: The New Generation (2001) is also excellent.

And Our Muslim American Film Awards Go To . . .

As you have seen in this chapter, feature films of high quality about
Muslim Americans are virtually nonexistent. This situation is reminiscent of the days when there were few feature films by and about the
other groups you have studied in this book. The Hollywood image of
Asian Americans, African Americans, Latinos, gays and lesbians, and
other minority groups has changed slowly, but you have seen that
progress is being made. Depictions of Muslim and Arab Americans are
clearly stuck in the old, negative patterns. In fact, one critic speaks of
how Hollywood is now playing "Cowboys and Arabs" (Goodstein
1998, AR17). When and how will this change?

To learn about some viable alternatives to the films being produced
in the U.S. movie industry, check the following websites. There are

many outstanding American and Canadian documentaries as well as wonderful foreign feature films about Arabs and Muslims. You might explore some feature films from Arab countries as well as from Iran, Turkey, and other countries of the Muslim world. Of special interest are films like *Monsieur Ibrahim* that deal with Muslims in France. With its history of colonialism in Algeria and large immigrant population of Muslims from north Africa, France has been in the forefront of portraying new realities—in films like *Salut Cousin!* (1996) and *Bye-Bye* (1995). We also recommend *Ali: Fear Eats the Soul* (1974) and the award-winning *Head-On* (2004) from Germany as well as *East Is East* (1999) from England.

Websites:

www.al-bab.com/media/cinema/cinema.htm (Arab Cinema)
www.arabfilm.com (Arab Film Distributors)
www.aff.org (Annual Arab Film Festival)

Non-Arab Countries with the Largest Muslim Populations*:
Indonesia—213 million
Pakistan—157.6 million
India—129.6 milion
Bangladesh—119.8 million
Turkey—69.52 million
Iran—66.7 million
Nigeria—64.4 million
Ethiopia—36.5 million
Afghanistan—29.6 million
China—26 million
Uzbekistan—23.6 million

....
*Compiled and estimated from the *CIA World Factbook 2005 (www.cia.gov/cia/publications/ factbook)*.

Gay
Culture:
The Wedding Banquet

Setting the Scene: Freewriting and Discussion

Perhaps you are familiar with the Safe Zone triangle represented here. Especially in colleges and universities, it can be found attached to the doors of offices and dorm rooms. It signals that the person inside is sensitive to issues faced by people who are gay, lesbian, bisexual, or transgendered (GLBT) and considers himself or herself an ally.

Whatever your own sexual orientation, take a few minutes to sit quietly and freewrite in your film notebook about how you might feel seeing a Safe Zone triangle displayed on a door you are about to enter. How would you feel about the person displaying it? Would you be willing to post such a symbol on your door? Why or why not? Can you imagine why the presence of the triangle might be needed, useful, or appreciated by GLBT people?

Sneak Preview

About the Film

Historically, gays have either been ignored in cinema or portrayed in disparaging, superficial ways. Often they have been depicted as evil, predatory, or perverted; sometimes they have been included simply for laughs. But *The Wedding Banquet* (1993) distinguishes itself as one of the first of a rapidly growing number of films to present gay characters in non-stereotypical fashion. It was awarded a Golden Bear, the top prize at the Berlin Film Festival, and it won five prizes, including Best Film and Best Director, at the Golden Horse Awards in Hong Kong. Filmed in English and Chinese (with English subtitles), it is dedicated to a real-life gay couple whose story inspired the film.

Restricted to an incredibly low budget of $750,000, the filmmakers were surprised and delighted by the financial and popular success worldwide of *The Wedding Banquet*. In terms of the cost-to-earnings ratio, it was said to be the most successful movie of 1993 in the United States, outperforming even *Jurassic Park* (1993). It was also the biggest box-office hit ever in director Ang Lee's native Taiwan, making history there as the first film in which two men kissed. The resounding success in the same year of *The Wedding Banquet* and *The Joy Luck Club* (1993) demonstrated that Asian American films could appeal to huge mainstream audiences and be enormously profitable as well.

As you watch the film, your main focus will be on gay issues. However, this is not the only cultural controversy Lee presents; he also takes on interracial romance in the relationship between the lead characters, and he addresses sensitive matters of international politics, intermingling the three topics in a sophisticated way. The international theme has to do with the fact that the two Chinese characters, Wai-Tung and Wei-Wei, are from different Chinas. Wei-Wei is from the communist mainland, the giant of a nation which, at the time of the appearance of the film in 1993, was suffering from monumental economic and political problems and felt inferior to its neighbor—the modern, wealthy, industrialized, democratic island nation of Taiwan. Although to many American and other viewers, the Chinese in the film are seen simply as Chinese, more knowledgeable viewers can catch many references to how the two cultures—mainland China and Taiwan—differ.

Insiders would probably understand, for example, the political humor in the scene when Wai-Tung announces himself on the loft apartment intercom as the "nasty landlord," to which his tenant Wei-Wei quickly replies, "This floor has been liberated." (In other words, now that the communists are in power, she doesn't have to be afraid of his threats.) Insiders would also relate to the fact that the Taiwanese-born Wai-Tung is the one who is a U.S. citizen, whereas Wei-Wei, from the lesser advantaged mainland, is in need of a fake marriage to obtain the all-important green card and avoid deportation. And they would likely recognize Lee's audacity in creating Wai-Tung's character as a homosexual, thereby bringing into question the age-old Confucian requirement that Chinese males produce an heir. The director leaves no doubt that he intended for the character Wai-Tung to present, in his words, "the ultimate challenge to the patriarchal tradition" (Berry 1993a, 41).

Lee knew that American and other international audiences would not necessarily relate to all the tensions played out between the characters from the two Chinas. But he also knew that Taiwanese audiences, for example, might not understand some of the nuances of American life and culture that make the film special for audiences here, like the marriage ceremony at city hall and Wai-Tung's joke that he might not even be able to afford a "vacation in the Poconos" if a business deal doesn't go through. The film is so rich in its cultural portrayal that, in fact, it's not possible or even important for everyone to understand everything. If, however, you're interested in knowing more about the distinctly Chinese aspects of the film, you might speak with a cultural insider, read more about Lee himself, or check websites such as *www.eslisland.com/intro/history.html* and *www.gio.gov.tw/taiwan-website/5-gp/rocprc*.

Though not gay himself, Lee possesses a remarkable sensitivity to the process of coming out. In a sense the entire film is about the emotional and practical difficulties created by staying "in the closet." The scene in which Simon and Wai-Tung's apartment needs to be redecorated overnight shows with gentle humor how hard it can be to handle the lies, complications, and awkward problems of a closeted life. Lee also knows about the conflicts that arise between partners when, like Simon and Wai-Tung, they're at different stages in their ability, or desire, to come out. Perhaps most impressive is Lee's ability to portray the agony of the moment when a person comes out to an unaccepting loved one. The hospital scene between Wai-Tung and his mother is simply masterful and will leave no viewer unmoved.

Given the director's clever and subtle approach to his themes, the ending may come as a bit of a surprise. Is it just another happy ending? See whether you agree with Lee's p.o.v. regarding the ending. Normally a man of mild demeanor, he says it annoys, even infuriates, him when people say that the film has a happy Hollywood ending. "To me," he explains, "the film has more pain than humor" (Berry 1993b, 52). The happy ending, he says, is a myth. According to Lee, "it's very sad and sentimental, because everybody has to give up so much to get the happy ending" (Berry 1993a, 41).

About the Filmmakers and Actors of *The Wedding Banquet*

Ang Lee's rise as a leading contemporary filmmaker was not without enormous personal and financial struggles. Born in Taiwan in 1954, he was the oldest son in the family, meaning that, according to Chinese tradition, the responsibility to conform lay on his shoulders. His father was a high school principal who hoped that his son would follow in his footsteps and become a teacher. However, Lee's artistic talents and creative nature did not fit in with the family's plans for him. After failing the highly competitive university entrance exams, he decided to set out on his own, enrolling as a drama student at the Taipei Academy of Arts in Taiwan. He continued his studies in the United States, receiving a bachelor's degree in theater from the University of Illinois and a master's degree in film from New York University. Lee then "spent the next six years writing scripts, cooking dinner for his wife, a microbiologist, and his two sons and waiting for his big break" (Schamus 1994, iv).

The big break came in 1990, when producers Ted Hope and John Schamus were seeking a new director and teamed up with Lee for *Pushing Hands* (1992), the first in a trilogy of films dealing with Chinese themes that also included *The Wedding Banquet* (1993) and *Eat Drink Man Woman* (1994).

Schamus admires Lee's combination of gentleness and determination and speaks of the respect the director gets from his actors and crew on the set. His approach elicits excellent performances from a cast that includes noted Taiwanese actors Sihung Lung (Mr. Gao) and Ah-Lei Gua (Mrs. Gao) as well as the hugely popular Taiwanese singer/television star May Chin (Wei-Wei), who was elected to her country's parliament. Lee took a risk with first-time actors Winston Chao (Wai-Tung), a former airline steward and model who read about the production in the newspaper, and Mitchell Lichtenstein (Simon), an openly gay man who is the son of artist Roy Lichtenstein. The role of Wai-Tung was especially difficult to cast, Lee says, since it's "hard to find a good actor who is charming, speaks English and Mandarin Chinese, and doesn't mind portraying a gay character" (Shapiro 1993, 19). Lee himself appears in a cameo role at the banquet, commenting that the raucous goings-on reflect "five thousand years of sexual oppression" in China.

Since making his three Chinese American films, Lee has demonstrated enormous talent in so-called crossover films. *Sense and Sensibility* (1995), his first Hollywood mainstream movie, was widely praised, receiving a Best Picture Oscar nomination. Collaborating once again with Schamus, Lee directed the critically well-received films *The Ice Storm* (1997) and *Ride with the Devil* (1999). But it was *Crouching Tiger, Hidden Dragon* (2000), a stunningly original martial arts romance, that made film history for him, winning dozens of prestigious international awards and becoming the highest grossing foreign language film ever released in America.

With his landmark movie *Brokeback Mountain* (2005), Lee has again shown the ability to capture the attention and respect of critics and audiences worldwide. This film places him firmly in the group of elite contemporary directors, as evidenced by his 2006 Oscar for Best Director.

Who's Who in the Film

Wai-Tung Gao (Winston Chao)—gay Taiwanese American real estate entrepreneur

Simon (Mitchell Lichtenstein)—Wai-Tung's lover

Mr. Gao (Sihung Lung)—Wai-Tung's father

Mrs. Gao (Ah-Lei Gua)—Wai-Tung's mother

Wei-Wei (May Chin)—mainland Chinese artist who marries Wai-Tung

Little Sister Mao (Vanessa Yang)—opera singer chosen by computer to marry Wai-Tung

Bob Law (Yung-Teh Hsu)—friend of Wai-Tung

Old Chen (Tien Pien)—owner of China Palace who knew Mr. Gao in China

Director—Ang Lee

Screenplay writers—Ang Lee, Neil Peng, and James Schamus

Terms to Know

bisexual or **bi**—Person whose romantic and sexual feelings are for members of both sexes.

come out or **come out of the closet**—Terms referring to the process of disclosing one's homosexuality to others and of accepting it oneself. Coming out is not a single act, but a lifelong, often painful, process.

don't ask, don't tell—Originally, the nickname of a law enacted in 1993 that replaced a previous ban on gays serving in the military. Basically, the law says gays and bisexuals are allowed to serve as long as they stay in the closet, and the military, for its part, agrees not to inquire about sexual orientation. There is widespread opposition to "don't ask, don't tell" among gays and heterosexuals.

faggot, fag, homo, pansy, fairy, fruit, flamer—Epithets for gay men; insulting words for lesbians include **dyke, butch, lesbo,** and **lezzy.**

gender—One's psychological and emotional identity as a male or female, in contrast with one's biological sex. One is born with a sex but raised with a gender.

GLBT—Acronym for people who are not straight (gays, lesbians, bisexuals, and transgendered people).

heterosexism—Prejudice against gays resulting from the often unquestioned assumption that everyone is heterosexual; analogous to other -isms such as racism, sexism, and ageism; also called **heterosexual bias.**

heterosexual or **straight**—Person whose romantic and sexual feelings are for members of the opposite sex.

heterosexual privilege—Benefits that heterosexuals enjoy in society simply because of their sexual orientation.

homophobia, homophobic (adj.)—Deep-seated fear and accompanying hatred of homosexuality and homosexuals.

homosexual or **gay**—Used to refer both to men and women whose romantic and sexual feelings are for members of the same sex.

in the closet (being in the closet)—Hiding one's homosexuality from others and possibly from oneself.

lesbian—Woman who is homosexual. The word derives from the Greek island of Lesbos, home of the poet Sappho, whose lyrics celebrated love between women.

lover, **significant other**, **other (better) half**, **(domestic) partner**, **(longtime) companion**—Terms used to refer to individuals in a same-sex relationship. None of these terms is completely adequate, since **lover** has sexual connotations some gays dislike; **significant other** and **other (better) half** are also used by heterosexuals; **domestic partner** refers more to the legalities of those living together than to the emotional realm; **partner** seems like a business or professional relationship; and **longtime companion** seems too much like merely a friend.

metrosexual—Young, straight, urban male who might be perceived as gay by virtue of being affluent, appearance conscious, and sensitive to emotions.

outing—Refers to the act or process of coming out of the closet. Gays can out themselves, but the term is more commonly associated with the practice of deliberately revealing a closeted person's homosexuality against his or her will. The motives for doing so include personal malice, monetary profit, or the wish to embarrass and expose a person in public life. When gays are outed by other gays, it is often done to expose hypocrisy (especially if the closeted person has taken anti-gay stands in public) or to gain acceptance by showing that gays hold more prominent and prestigious positions than is commonly known.

queer—A disparaging term, but now preferred by some gays and lesbians to *gay* or *homosexual*. They feel that by reclaiming the term, they can transform it from a hateful word into a proud self-description.

sexual orientation—One's sexual inclinations; usually preferred by homosexuals to *sexual preference*, since the latter indicates there is choice, whereas many gays and lesbians believe they were born homosexual.

special rights—Term often used by critics of gays to suggest that in working toward equal rights (in the workplace, the military, etc.), gays are really asking for extra benefits, in other words, *special rights*.

straight but not narrow—Slogan often seen on buttons and T-shirts to indicate that the wearer is heterosexual but an ally of GLBT people.

transgendered or **trans**—Broad term for people who consider themselves to be of the opposite gender from their biological sex.

Trans people may feel born into or trapped in the wrong bodies. They may be **cross-dressers,** and they may or may not seek surgery and other medical procedures to bring their bodies into conformity with their psychological and emotional selves. The term **transsexual** is often applied to those who have undergone medical treatment.

transvestite—Person who dresses in clothing of the opposite gender; also referred to as **cross-dressing**. Male transvestites are sometimes referred to as **drag queens.** Males who cross-dress to perform in public are known as **female impersonators.** Transvestites may be heterosexual, homosexual, or bisexual.

History Flashback

While a personal rather than a political film, *The Wedding Banquet* (1993) can be understood as a Taiwanese American director's eloquent statement in favor of full acceptance of gays, whether in more tradition-bound societies like his country of birth or in more future-oriented societies such as his adopted home.

A look at the history of homosexuality reveals that the lives of the two men as depicted in the film, while complicated and difficult, nonetheless represent enormous progress in society's acceptance of gays. This history is not easily written, for as one scholar succinctly states, "Sex has no history" (Halperin 1993, 416). Obstacles to constructing such a history include the absence of documentation and records; the reluctance of some universities to legitimize research on homosexuality and of some publishers to issue works; and the unwillingness on the part of many people to divulge information related to their personal, private behavior. Because gays have been persecuted and oppressed in so many societies, they have kept much of what might be critical to an understanding of gay history hidden from view, leading some scholars to speak of the "hidden history" of homosexuals.

Despite these difficulties, over the past several decades historians and biographers have produced a substantial body of material to reclaim and illuminate the homosexual past. Though gay history may be faced with particularly stubborn obstacles, remember that in the United States all minority histories—those of African Americans,

Asian Americans, women, and others—have been long neglected in favor of the dominant story, which is white, Christian, heterosexual, and male. As is stated in an African proverb, *Until the lion writes his own story, the tale of the hunt will always glorify the hunter.* But in our own time, much excitement is being generated by so-called revisionist history— the new sets of stories and truths as well as the new interpretations of our collective past that are steadily emerging (see page 42).

Scholars generally agree that homosexuality—in a wide variety of forms—has been known across virtually all cultures and time periods. We must be careful, however, not to apply the word *homosexuality* in its modern sense to non-Western, traditional, or early societies, where same-sex love or same-sex unions were understood very differently from today's notions. The ancient Greeks, for example, did not have a word for homosexuality (nor did the Hebrews or Romans). What was practiced and legitimized was a certain form of love between an older, usually well-to-do man and a youth, resembling a tutelage or initiation into manhood.

As a further example, in many Native American societies, the *berdache* (a gender-mixed person who was usually a man but could be a woman) wore clothing of the opposite gender, had sexual and marital relations with the same gender, and assumed ceremonial roles in sacred rituals. Berdaches confound modern notions of heterosexuality and homosexuality, since they were seen as neither sex, or both, or in-between, being described by many Indians as "half men, half women." While some tribes looked down on berdaches, others, such as the Navajo, revered them.

Ancient Greece and Native America offer only two of numerous examples of societies able to accept and even appreciate forms of same-sex love. Overwhelmingly, however, homosexual love in Western societies has been feared, banned, and punished, leading some to speak of gay history simply as a "history of persecution." The church, the law, and medical science have all shared in condemning homosexuality, defining it in religious terms as a sin, in legal terms as a crime, and in medical terms as a disease.

Our modern understanding of homosexuality began to emerge in the late 19th century. The term *homosexual* itself was first used in a pamphlet written in 1869 by a Hungarian physician, Károly Kertbeny. The first human rights organization for homosexuals, the Scientific Humanitarian Committee, was founded in Germany in 1896. In the United States, the first gay men's organization, called the Mattachine

Society, was founded much later, in 1955, followed by the first lesbian organization, the Daughters of Bilitis.

The gay and lesbian rights movement can be said to have begun in earnest in 1969, when the Stonewall riot took place in Greenwich Village, New York. (See *www.planetout.com/news/history/archive/06211999.html.*) The police raid on the Stonewall gay bar on June 27–28 was not noteworthy in itself, since raids in which police harassed or arrested homosexual patrons were a common occurrence. Nor was resistance by gays to discriminatory acts unusual—many examples can be cited. But somehow the week of protest and riots that followed the Stonewall raid became the symbol for the new movement. A consciousness of gay liberation, gay power, and gay civil rights emerged, clearly inspired by gains in civil rights achieved by other groups in the 1960s.

The decade following Stonewall was a period of unprecedented activism and change. Gay rights groups and organizations were formed in communities and on campuses across the United States, including major national organizations such as the National Gay and Lesbian Task Force *(www.thetaskforce.org)* and the Lambda Legal Defense and Education Fund *(www.lambdalegal.org).* The so-called gay liberation press was founded and began to flourish, with publications like *The Advocate* (which is among the stack of Wai-Tung's unread magazines) gaining readers nationwide. (See *www.advocate.com.*) Pressure brought to bear on the American Psychiatric Association resulted in the removal of homosexuality from its list of mental disorders in 1973. Lesbian/Gay Pride Day festivals and other parades and demonstrations made gays more visible and brought gay issues before the general public. The election to public office of two openly gay candidates, Elaine Noble in New York in 1974 and Harvey Milk in San Francisco in 1977, were considered major victories in the realm of politics. (See *www.time.com/time/time100/heroes/profile/milk01.html.*)

After having made considerable progress, the gay community suffered a tremendous setback in the 1980s with the outbreak of the AIDS (acquired immune deficiency syndrome) epidemic. A disease of the immune system, AIDS damages the body's ability to fight other diseases. Because the virus can be transmitted through blood or semen, gay men are especially susceptible to it. AIDS is not a disease restricted to homosexuals, however, and can be spread by intravenous drug use, by blood transfusions, and in other ways. Outside the

United States AIDS is primarily a heterosexual disease, reaching alarming proportions. According to the United Nations, in 2005 there were 40.3 million people worldwide living with AIDS or the HIV virus that causes it.

Although the epidemic resulted in a new wave of fear and intolerance—gays were fired, denied housing, and refused health insurance—there were some positive effects as well. The deaths of tens of thousands of gay men, though an unequaled tragedy for the gay community, also galvanized many gays and lesbians to come out of the closet and become socially and politically active. Gays moved into the forefront of efforts to combat the disease, promoting educational efforts, advocating the use of condoms and other safe-sex practices, and raising funds and lobbying for medical research. Their often publicized struggles to care for dying friends and partners revealed them to the public as caring and compassionate people.

A unique symbol of this compassion is the Names Project AIDS Memorial Quilt *(www.aidsquilt.org)*. Begun in 1985, this work of art now contains about 46,000 three-by-six-foot individual panels, each one commemorating the lives of people who died of AIDS-related complications. There are more than 82,800 names. Sewn together by lovers, friends, and family members—and including panels from all the states and many countries—the quilt has been displayed at numerous National Marches on Washington for Gay, Lesbian, and Bisexual Rights. It also tours the world in smaller segments.

As the gay community struggled with the AIDS crisis, it also faced a determined backlash from right-wing individuals and groups determined to halt the progress of previous years. One of the first to gain nationwide attention for her opposition to gay rights was Anita Bryant, well known as a pop singer, publicist for Florida orange juice, and born-again Christian. Save Our Children, the organization she founded in 1977, paved the way for many subsequent groups that opposed homosexuality under the guise of family values. The explosive growth of the so-called religious right (this term encompasses a variety of organizations such as the Christian Coalition and the Traditional Values Coalition), combined with the lack of political support for gays during the Reagan years, made the 1980s a time of formidable opposition.

Having made enormous strides since Stonewall, the gay community still has a long way to go. Arduous struggles continue for what many gays and lesbians view as basic rights, including legally accepted marriages, antidiscrimination laws in the workplace, domestic partner benefits (such as health insurance), and full acceptance in the military. Gays and lesbians are still the frequent target of verbal abuse, street violence, and other hate crimes. They have also had to mobilize against well-organized groups that have brought antigay ballot measures to voters in Maine, Colorado, Oregon, and elsewhere. For information on numerous groups that are actively opposing equal rights for gays, see *www.turnleft.com/out/knowthy_orgs.html*. To learn about four groups that support gays, see *www.rainbowbaptists.org* (Baptists), *www.ecwr.org* (Evangelical Christians), *www.keshetrabbis.org* (Conservative Rabbis), and *www.gsanetwork.org* (Gay-Straight Alliance Network for Youth Activists).

Diversity Detective: Same-Sex Marriage

The most dramatic recent development in acceptance of gays in U.S. society has been the move toward same-sex marriage. Your detective firm has been given the task of putting together an overview of the legal status of same-sex marriage in the United States and abroad. Read the following background information and then follow the instructions.

Worldwide, the first country to legalize same-sex marriage was the Netherlands. Having taken this step in 2001, Dutch people on the whole no longer see the issue as controversial. As Anne-Marie Thus, the Dutch spouse of Helene Faasen, says, "It's really become less of something that you need to explain. We're totally ordinary. We take our children to preschool every day. People know they don't have to be afraid of us." A middle-class couple, Thus works in a home for the elderly, and her partner is employed as a notary. Their two young children, Thus's biological offspring, have been legally adopted by Faasen. "With marriage," explains Faasen, "you have a whole range of legal issues settled right in one go. Child care, life insurance, health insurance, pension, inheritance. Otherwise you're left taking care of those things bit by bit, where it's possible" (*www.cbsnews.com* 2004).

Working individually or with a partner or small group, choose a place in the world to investigate. It can be your home state or country or another place. Coordinate with others in your class to make sure you haven't chosen the same location, and then research the legal situation for homosexuals. Are they allowed to marry? Adopt children? Enter into so-called civil unions? Is homosexuality legal? If not, what are the penalties? How do you think GLBT people are viewed by the general population in the place you have chosen? Further information on the history and status of same-sex marriage in different states of the United States can be found at *www.gay-civil-unions.com/HTML/Contents.htm*. International information is available at this site and also at *www.freedomtomarry.org*.

In addition to the organizations mentioned on page 146, other useful groups and sites to consult include

- Gay and Lesbian Alliance against Defamation (GLAAD) *(www.glaad.org)*;
- Parents and Friends of Lesbians and Gays (PFLAG) *(www.pflag.org)*;
- Gay and Lesbian Advocates and Defenders *(www.glad.org)*. (Note this is not the same as the Gay and Lesbian Alliance against Defamation at *www.glaad.org*.)

When you have finished your investigation, write a page in your film notebook to present to the class and then assemble all the results in a report.

Student's P.O.V.

I have many different issues about homosexuality and have many friends who are gay. I am a Christian and do read the Bible, and yes it does state "one man and one woman," but I believe that we are to judge no one but ourselves, and the Bible also states that. I just try to accept people for who they are and not judge. For me, this is a way to have a happier life. It does seem to me that homosexuality must be something you are born with and not a choice, because why would someone want to be different, and choose to be discriminated against and ridiculed? People have the God-given right to be who they want to be, and it isn't for anyone to judge except for the Creator Himself.

—Name withheld

Spotlight: Why Do We Speak of Gay Culture?

As we discuss *The Wedding Banquet,* you might be surprised by our frequent references to gay culture. Traditionally, culture has been defined as "a learned set of shared interpretations about beliefs, values, and norms, which affect the behaviors of a relatively large group of people" (Lustig and Koester 2003, 27). Those who belong to a specific culture generally hold in common their language, history, and customs, which they pass from generation to generation, and they often live in geographically defined areas.

Of course, this description does not apply neatly to GLBT people or the gay community. Nonetheless, many gays and lesbians—as well as researchers—believe the concept of gay culture is appropriate, and in recent years it has become more widely accepted.

Homosexuals do, for example, have a sense of shared history. They also have a sense of geographical place, having carved out gay neighborhoods in many major cities, such as Greenwich Village in Manhattan (where Simon and Wai-Tung live), the Castro area of San Francisco, and South Beach in Miami. Gay neighborhoods have sprung up to serve many purposes: here GLBT people can meet and socialize, feel comfortable and safe, and come together to achieve political goals.

Gays and lesbians have distinct patterns of communication by which they meet and recognize each other. This is expressed humorously in the notion that there is "gaydar," a built-in way that gays detect other gays as if by radar. The patterns consist primarily of nonverbal cues such as posture, voice, eye contact, dress, and touch. In exaggerated form, they constitute the basis for stereotypes of gay behavior, particularly of men.

Gay culture abounds with symbols, such as the rainbow, the stud earring in the right ear for men (although now stud earrings are worn by many heterosexual men as well), and the color lavender. The pink inverted triangle, which gays were forced to wear in the concentration camps of Nazi Germany, has become a political symbol, and the red ribbon is a sign of support for AIDS victims and AIDS research. The website at *http://jasewells.com/gayicons* provides additional information on these symbols.

A further rationale for using the term *culture* is that homosexuals, like many ethnic, religious, and other minority cultures, experience oppression and discrimination by virtue of being different from the mainstream. Living outside the locus of power, gays and members of many other subcultures derive a sense of unity and solidarity from joining together for moral support as well as for political and social action.

To learn more about gay culture, you might take a look at some of the leading gay publications such as *The Advocate, Poz, Out, Girlfriends, Curve, Genre,* and the *Gay and Lesbian Review.* A growing trend is the publication of free weekly, monthly, and quarterly papers that cater to GLBT populations. You might obtain copies of such publications to find out about important issues in your local gay community.

As you think about gay culture in this chapter, remember that culture is not easy to define. There is no accepted checklist of characteristics that must be present. Anthropologists offer us many different definitions and hundreds of books on the topic. Does a culture have to have its own foods, language, customs, and dress? Are its common values and ideals what are most significant? In her book *The Gay and Lesbian Liberation Movement* (1992), Margaret Cruikshank says that the phrase *gay culture* designates "attitudes, values, tastes, artistic and literary works, groups and organizations, common experiences, festivals, special events, rituals, and their sense of a shared history" (119).

A final important aspect of a culture is that people identify with it. You might wear red shoes frequently, for example, without seeing yourself as part of a red-shoe subculture. But your Birkenstocks® might well link you with a certain subculture. If you see your personal identity as being tied to dancing ballet, practicing Catholicism, or living on a farm—and if you feel a sense of shared identity with others like you—one can argue that you are then part of a particular culture or subculture. This same idea applies to Deaf culture, discussed in the next chapter.

Again, if your particular culture or subculture is one that has been oppressed or marginalized, you are probably aware of types of discrimination that others may not see. In the case of sexual orientation, heterosexuals enjoy many benefits that are often denied to homosexuals. They range from big things, such as being welcomed into a wide variety of apartment buildings or neighborhoods, to smaller ones, such as being able to greet a friend openly in the street or to find appropriate greeting cards for a partner or spouse.

Can you and your classmates think of other heterosexual benefits beyond those mentioned in this chapter? If you're having difficulty, try to obtain an insider's p.o.v. If your campus has a gay and bisexual student organization, you might invite members to speak to your class. Or there may be students in your class who are gay or bisexual (and perhaps already "out" on campus) who can be of assistance. If there is no gay student group on your campus, you can invite to class a representative from PFLAG or a similar organization.

Student's P.O.V.

I still cry when I think about the senseless death of Matthew Shepard.

It's been nearly seven years since Shepard's death on October 12, 1998—five days after this kind and compassionate 21-year-old college student was attacked and left for dead in rural Wyoming. He was lured from a bar near the University of Wyoming by two men claiming to be gay, who beat him severely enough to cause permanent, inoperable brain damage, and then tied him to a post in near-freezing winter temperatures.

I'd like to think Matthew is the only one, that such ignorance and violence is an anomaly. But I know better. I'm not the most "out" person on the planet, and I am far from what anyone would call "loud and proud" about my sexual orientation. But in my short 32 years of life, I have been heckled and threatened with bodily harm, received hate mail, been spat upon, suffered vandalism, and generally been hated for no better reason than being gay.

I understand that there are people who disagree with the "gay lifestyle" and see it as an unforgivable sin. That's okay with me—people are entitled to their own opinions. What's not okay, however, is when opinions lead to violence. It is an absolute tragedy that people like Matthew Shepard had to die because somebody's hate led to uncontrollable violence. But what would be even more tragic is if we learn nothing from his death.

—Name withheld

Lights! Camera! ACTION!

As you have learned in this chapter, hate crimes are still being perpetrated, causing many people who are "different" to live in fear. One of the most active and successful groups opposing hate crimes is the Southern Poverty Law Center, located in Montgomery, Alabama. Read about their Intelligence Project *(www.splcenter.org/intel/intpro.jsp)* and think about how you could lend support. You might attend a meeting of a gay-straight alliance or check out the action suggestions in the Fahy book listed in **Our Film Awards.**

Your P.O.V.

1. Design a poster, button, or other artwork to advocate for gay rights or AIDS awareness.

2. Imagine you lived in a totally non-homophobic society. Describe what life might be like and how it would be different from your own society.

3. Note that in his first appearance Simon wears a Keith Haring T-shirt. (See *www.haring.com*.) Imagine you were to wear for a day a T-shirt expressing gay pride. How might you feel? What reactions might you get from others?

4. Imagine that Wai-Tung and his mother send e-mails back and forth to each other after the parents' visit. Write the messages.

5. Imagine a sequel to *The Wedding Banquet* in which the baby is featured as a teenager living with Wai-Tung, Wei-Wei, and Simon. Describe the major plot elements.

6. You are a heterosexual who is unsure about your feelings toward gays. Imagine that you receive a letter in which a sibling or close friend comes out to you. Write your reply. Or imagine that you are a parent and your daughter or son comes out to you in a letter. Write your response.

7. Take a look at some of the books that explain homosexuality to

children, such as *Daddy's Roommate* (1990) by Michael Willhoite, *Heather Has Two Mommies* (1989) by Leslea Newman, and *The Daddy Machine* (2004) by Johnny Valentine. Write a page or two giving your reaction to at least two books of your choosing.

8. You and your crew have become interested in shooting a film on gay culture. Consult the guidelines in Appendix D for further information. Here are some potential topics for consideration:

a. children of gays and lesbians

b. the everyday situation of gays in the military

c. the debate about homosexuals that is occurring within the Christian church or in another religious faith

d. gay-friendly or gay-hostile corporations and other places of employment

e. the ongoing story of the AIDS quilt (Watch the documentary *Common Threads: Stories from the Quilt* [1989] as part of your research.)

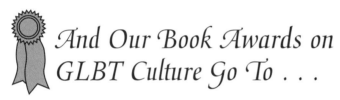

And Our Book Awards on GLBT Culture Go To . . .

How to Make the World a Better Place for Gays and Lesbians by Una Fahy (New York: Warner Books, 1995.) A useful and practical handbook for anybody—gay or straight—committed to bettering the world by confronting and overcoming homophobia. Fahy has compiled in 50 short, accessible chapters 50 concrete ways to bring about change.

Is It a Choice? Answers to 300 of the Most Frequently Asked Questions about Gays and Lesbians (2nd ed.) by Eric Marcus (San Francisco: HarperSanFrancisco, 1999). Full of good information—as the title suggests. Are you born gay? What should you do if you think your child is gay or lesbian? Why do gay and lesbian people feel they need laws to protect them against discrimination? Marcus answers many questions and addresses in a straightforward way topics such as coming out, activism, AIDS, sex, and family life. A must-read for anyone who has been curious but hesitant to ask.

*What the Bible **Really** Says about Homosexuality* by Daniel A. Helminiak (San Francisco: Almo Square Press, 1995). A strong case, based on contemporary Biblical scholarship, that "the Bible supplies no real basis for the condemnation of homosexuality" (14). The author argues for an historical-critical approach that puts the literal words of the Bible back into their original context in order to understand what was really being said. Thoroughly researched and well documented, this examination of Biblical passages related to homosexuality is informative for all readers, Christian and non-Christian alike.

And Our Film Awards on GLBT Culture Go To . . .

Brokeback Mountain (2006)—A tender and unusual love story based on a short story by E. Annie Proulx. Popularly known as the "gay cowboy movie," *Brokeback Mountain* explores the 20-year passionate relationship between a ranch hand and a rodeo cowboy. An often breathtaking Wyoming landscape provides the setting against which their love develops and then struggles from the complications created by their wives, children, and lives of pretense. Directed by Ang Lee.

The Incredibly True Adventure of Two Girls in Love (1995)—An engaging lesbian romantic comedy about two teenage girls from different racial and socioeconomic backgrounds who fall in love. Directed by Maria Maggenti.

The Laramie Project (2002)—A vivid and stunning dramatization of the murder of University of Wyoming student Matthew Shepard. A young gay man, Shepard became an icon for both the gay community and anti-hate-crime advocates when he was brutalized and left for dead near Laramie in 1998. His death shocked the nation. This film examines, through fictional reenactments (based on more than 200 interviews) mixed with real news reports, the attitudes and reactions of residents of Laramie, asking how such violence could come to be in such a "normal" town. Directed by Moisés Kaufman.

Philadelphia (1993)—The story of a successful corporate attorney (Tom Hanks) who is battling AIDS. When he is fired from his firm, he decides to sue for discrimination. This is an important mainstream film about biases against people with AIDS. Directed by Jonathan Demme.

8

Deaf Culture:
Children of a Lesser God

Setting the Scene:
Freewriting and Discussion

Take a look at the photographs of Erin Fleming, a hearing college student who is studying American Sign Language (ASL). Then freewrite your ideas as to how learning ASL might expand one's world.

Expand

Your

Life

Sneak Preview

About the Film

Set at a fictitious school for the deaf in Maine but filmed in New Brunswick, Canada, *Children of a Lesser God* (1986) focuses on the changes in the lives of the two main characters, one deaf and one hearing. The hearing character, James Leeds (played by William Hurt), is a newly appointed, ambitious speech teacher. Using innovative techniques, he sets out to teach his deaf students to speak with their voices—instead of communicating through sign language—and he also tries to force his ideas on Sarah Norman (played by deaf actress Marlee Matlin), a deaf graduate who is now the school's janitor. Despite considerable pressure, Sarah refuses to cooperate, insisting on her right to sign rather than to lip-read and speak.

Director Randa Haines sees the film as being about "two people from two different cultures":

> I saw the deafness as a metaphor for the things in each person which separate us from other people, the barriers that we have built up around us, the way in which none of us can ever really experience the way another person hears or sees the world. All of us are, in a sense, deaf to what's inside other people's heads. (Attanasio 1986, F1)

Highly selective about her work, Haines chooses only those projects about which she is passionate. The theme that interests her most, she says, is "the struggle to communicate" (Spotnitz 1992, 18). As she explains, "I'm always attracted to stories that reflect how very much alone we are in life and the never-ending need to connect" (quotation from *www.filmbug.com/db/35906*).

Based on an award-winning play of the same name by hearing playwright Mark Medoff, the film was a landmark in Deaf history and in the cinema: for the first time, large audiences experienced deaf and hearing-impaired actors in major film roles. (By contrast, in the famous film *The Miracle* Worker [1962], the hearing and sighted actress Patty Duke was cast as Helen Keller.) Furthermore, Marlee Matlin's unforgettable performance as a beautiful, proud woman in possession of an amazing language helped give the deaf a new image. Matlin's rapid, spirited signing fascinated viewers, and her strong personality as Sarah allowed no room for pity. Reviewer Jack Knoll (1986) from *Newsweek* described Matlin's performance as "so good— sensitive, sharp, funny—that she's likely to be the first deaf actress to get an Oscar nomination," and she did, in fact, win Best Actress in 1987 for her role in *Children of a Lesser God* (77).

For Haines, bridging the communication gap between signing actors and hearing audiences was undoubtedly her most difficult challenge. She decided to have James, who understands sign language, translate Sarah's words and voice them through most of the movie. Haines introduces this strategy early in the film with James's line, "I'm a speech teacher—I like to hear my own voice." Though Haines received praise from reviewers for the film as a whole, not everyone was happy with this approach. Critic Dave Kehr (1986) faults her for "using Hurt as an audience identification figure and keeping Matlin at arm's length. . . . Because we are unable to understand her language, she remains an exotic, remote, strange figure" (7A). Roger Ebert agrees: "By telling the whole story from Hurt's point of view, the movie makes the woman into the stubborn object, the challenge, the problem, which is the very process it wants to object to" (*http:rogerebert.suntimes.com*). What do you think? Does it matter that Sarah's language is filtered through James? Is Ebert right that the "whole story" is told from Hurt's point of view? If you had been the director of *Children of a Lesser God*, would you have made the same decision as Haines, or are there other options?

About the Director and Actors of *Children of a Lesser God*

Randa Haines always imagined herself as an actor, and she made her first onstage appearance at age ten. But after studying acting for a brief period with Lee Strasberg, she realized that she preferred working with scripts and directing. Beginning in 1981, she directed episodes of the hit television series *Hill Street Blues,* and she received wide acclaim for her sensitive, skillful treatment of incest as director of the television feature *Something about Amelia* (1984). Haines was finally able to realize her creative vision in *Children of a Lesser God.*

Extremely successful, it was the first film directed by a woman ever to receive a Best Picture Oscar nomination.

Haines and her crew knew from the outset that the success of the film depended on finding the right person for the female lead, and a six-month international search led them to the yet undiscovered nineteen-year-old Marlee Matlin, who was playing the supporting role of Lydia in a Chicago stage production of *Children*. Born hearing in 1965 to a Jewish family of Russian and Polish heritage, Matlin had become almost completely deaf at eighteen months old when she contracted the roseola virus. Determined that their daughter would not be denied opportunities for a good education and a successful future, her parents placed her in the public school system that was not always a supportive place for deaf children. But for Matlin it was the right choice, since, as she says, "I dealt with the outside world from the age of three. I was not shut out" (Walker 1989, 43).

Outside of school, Matlin starred in stage productions of the *Wizard of Oz, Mary Poppins,* and *Peter Pan* as part of a children's theater group at a local center for deafness that her mother had helped to found. Not initially planning to be an actress, Matlin studied criminal justice briefly at a junior college but quit when she learned her deafness would be an obstacle to becoming a police officer. Her big break came with *Children,* which brought her overnight success.

Despite stardom and widespread recognition for her talent, sensitivity, and charisma, Matlin faced an uncertain future as a deaf actress. There were very few roles available, and some observers predicted that her career was over. But Matlin has proven them wrong, resolutely carving out a new place for herself. Since *Children,* she has performed in a substantial number of movies and television productions, most notably in roles where her deafness is incidental. In the television series *The West Wing,* for example, she played a savvy political analyst who happened to be deaf.

Matlin is very much a public figure, working steadfastly on behalf of the deaf and also for other charities and humanitarian causes. She played a key role in bringing about federal legislation enacted in 1993 requiring that all televisions manufactured in the United States be equipped with closed-caption technology, and she has actively promoted the subtitling and closed-captioning of old movies. She is especially committed to children's causes, working actively to assist children with AIDS and other serious illnesses. Her children's books include *Deaf Child Crossing* (2002) and *Nobody's Perfect* (2006), and she teaches sign language to children in a video series called *Baby Einstein*.

In addition to hiring Matlin, the filmmakers were committed to casting other hearing-impaired actors in the relevant supporting roles. In total, ten hearing-impaired actors receive billing. To handle communication on the set, Haines hired an interpreter for Matlin, a second interpreter for the other actors, and a hearing-impaired technical adviser. Haines learned some basic sign language, and William Hurt learned to be a fairly proficient signer.

The choice of Hurt for the lead role of James Leeds was never in doubt for Haines and her producer, Patrick Palmer. Having studied drama at Julliard, Hurt had won the Best Actor award for *Kiss of the Spider Woman* in 1985 and was recognized as an enormous talent.

Who's Who in the Film

Sarah Norman (Marlee Matlin)—deaf custodian and former pupil at the school

James Leeds (William Hurt)—new speech teacher

Curtis Franklin (Philip Bosco)—school superintendent

Mrs. Norman (Piper Laurie)—Sarah's mother

Marian Loesser (Linda Bove)—deaf woman at party

Lydia (Allison Gompf)—deaf student who sings the lead in the group No-Tones

Johnny (John F. Cleary)—deaf student who refuses to speak

William (John Limnidis)—deaf student and football player

Orin (Bob Hiltermann)—deaf teacher

Director—Randa Haines

Screenwriters—Hesper Anderson and Mark Medoff

Terms to Know

closed-captions—Captions that appear only if a decoder box or chip is used. The decoder can be attached to, or built into, television sets.

CODA—Acronym for Children of deaf adults, that is, hearing children of deaf parents. Many CODAs grow up bicultural and bilingual.

deaf—(lower-case spelling)—Audiological condition of deafness.

Deaf (capitalized)—Deaf culture and those individuals who identify themselves with it.

deaf and dumb—Term that is no longer acceptable but was widely used historically to refer to deaf people who did not possess spoken language and therefore were considered stupid.

deaf mute—A person who is incapable of speech. The term has fallen out of favor.

Deaf of hearing parents—Term used to refer to a deaf child of hearing parents.

late deafened—A person who becomes deaf later in life due to genetics, gradual hearing loss, or an accident.

mother father deaf—Sign used in the Deaf community to mean a hearing child of Deaf parents.

open captions—Captions that are part of the picture (similar to subtitles), and thus decoders are not needed.

oralism—A pedagogical approach that focuses on lip reading and vocalization. In the 1800s, oralism referred to the movement that mandated speech rather than sign for deaf individuals.

person with a disability—Term preferred to **handicapped person** or **disabled person** because it places emphasis on the person rather than the disability. Many deaf people do not consider themselves as having a disability.

PSE (Pidgin Sign English)—A combination of ASL and other signing systems that follow English grammatical word order.

SEE (Signing Exact English or **Signed English)**—Uses signs that represent English words in English grammatical order.

TTY—The device (teletypewriter) that enables deaf people to make phone calls. Resembling a typewriter with a small screen, it allows each person with a TTY to type and receive messages. It is commonly referred to by hearing people as **TDD** (telecommunication device for the deaf), whereas the deaf prefer TTY.

History Flashback

The history of deafness in the United States is marked not only by ignorance and misconceptions on the part of the hearing world but also by persistent attempts to control the deaf and force them to accept spoken language. For much of early U.S. history, deaf people experienced abuse, neglect, poverty, and discrimination. Because speech is so closely tied to notions of intellect, deaf persons were generally considered inferior and stupid (as evidenced by the long-used phrase *deaf and dumb*, which meant *deaf and mute*) and were badly mistreated.

In the 1820s conditions for the deaf began to improve because of the efforts of one man. The story, a beloved part of deaf history, begins when Thomas Hopkins Gallaudet, a minister in Hartford, Connecticut, was observing some children playing in his garden and noticed that one little girl, Alice, was left out. Upon learning that the girl was deaf, he talked with her father, the surgeon Mason Cogswell, about setting up what would become the first permanent American school for the deaf.

Sponsored by Cogswell, Gallaudet sailed in 1816 for Europe to learn about teaching methods known to be more progressive than in America. He first went to England, but the turning point came when he visited the Institute of Deaf Mutes in Paris, founded in 1755 by the Abbé de L'Epée. This visionary man had observed and learned the sign language of orphaned deaf children, given them shelter, and helped them develop a system of French Sign Language that could be used within the wider society. At the institute, Gallaudet met the brilliant young deaf teacher Laurent Clerc, who was to play a critical role in deaf history in the United States. Though Clerc had never traveled outside France or even ventured much beyond the institute, he accompanied Gallaudet back to Connecticut.

By the following year the two men had raised sufficient funds to found, with Cogswell, the American Asylum for the Deaf and Dumb in Hartford. Clerc's French Sign Language was blended with indigenous sign languages already used by deaf Americans to create a unique language, known as American Sign Language (ASL). The success of the Hartford asylum led to the opening of other such schools around the country. In 1864 the U.S. Congress created the first college for the deaf in the world, known today as Gallaudet University, in Washington, DC. (See *www.gallaudet.edu*.)

But this "golden age" enjoyed by the American deaf was short-lived. A new movement called oralism, which required the deaf to read lips and vocalize (a physical near-impossibility for many), was gaining support. Well-known inventor and speech expert Alexander Graham Bell lent his considerable prestige to the effort to force the deaf to speak. At the International Congress of Educators for the Deaf held in 1880 in Milan, Italy, the delegates—only one of whom was deaf—prescribed oralism as the universal teaching method for the deaf, and an edict was passed to ban the use of sign language.

As a result of the Milan Congress, ASL was banned from U.S. schools, effectively stripping deaf students of their native language. Disobedient students had their hands strapped or tied down to keep them from signing. The number of deaf teachers decreased rapidly, giving control of deaf education to the hearing. Rather than bringing about improved standards, the new restrictions caused education for the deaf to suffer and literacy to decline.

Not until 80 years later, in 1960, did ASL receive further consideration as the language of the deaf. In that year linguist William Stokoe of Gallaudet University published brilliant new research, demonstrating in undeniable fashion that ASL is a genuine language in its own right, with a sophisticated vocabulary and grammar, rather than (as was believed at the time) a primitive and random assortment of gestures. So revolutionary were Stokoe's findings that at first it was hard even for many deaf people to understand and believe his claim that ASL was equal to spoken language.

Stokoe's work helped promote a growing consciousness of deaf pride in the wake of the civil rights movement of the 1960s. Yet the landmark event for deaf rights did not occur until 1988, when Gallaudet University experienced for the first time in its 124-year history the possibility of naming a deaf president. As the day of the decision approached, thousands of students, faculty, staff, and alumni, wearing buttons that read "DEAF PRESIDENT NOW," gathered for a rally. One of the speakers, Professor Allen Sussman, realized that history was being made. By calling the event "the first deaf civil rights activity," he clarified for many people the link between civil rights and the treatment of the deaf (Shapiro 1993, 77).

A few days later, when the board of directors chose the lone hearing person from among the three candidates, the campus erupted in protest. Students boycotted classes and began working to gain support from deaf organizations across the country. They organized marches on the White House and the Capitol, receiving wide coverage in the national media. After a highly emotional week of resistance, the newly hired hearing president was forced to resign in favor of one of the two deaf finalists, the popular dean I. King Jordan.

The Gallaudet Revolution was pivotal not only in instilling a new sense of pride in the deaf community, but also in giving powerful impetus to the disability rights movement across the country. In 1990, just two years after the successful protest, the landmark Americans with Disabilities Act (ADA) was passed. The ADA both protected "qualified individuals" with disabilities from discrimination in the workplace and empowered physically disabled individuals by facilitating their access to public buildings and transportation systems. Specifically, deaf people's lives were greatly enhanced by newly mandated technology such as closed-captioning and the relay telephone system (see Insider's P.O.V. on pages 171–72). Two subsequent key pieces of legislation that also affected deaf people were the Individuals with Disabilities Education Act in 1997 (IDEA) and the Newborn Infant Hearing Screening and Intervention Act (1999).

Deaf Culture

In the decades since Stokoe, the Gallaudet protest, and the ADA, deaf history can be characterized by the development of a new sense of identity among the deaf. For the first time, deaf people are defining for themselves who they are. The idea of a Deaf culture (spelled with a capital D to indicate the cultural rather than the audiological condition) has gained widespread acceptance.

This idea may seem unusual at first because we so often link the idea of culture with ethnic or national identity and with shared geographical space. Yet the Deaf most definitely see themselves as belonging to a culture (or subculture) with its own language, nonverbal behavior, values, socializing patterns, etiquette, humor, history, traditions, arts and entertainment, and social and political organizations. Moreover, part of Deaf culture and consciousness is, like that of many other subcultures, a sense of what authors Harlan Lane, Robert Hoffmeister, and Ben Bahan (1966) call "shared oppression" (159).

Viewing Deafness as a culture produces a profound shift in thinking away from old models that define it as a handicap, disability, or illness to be cured. As Edward Dolnick (1993) explains in his article "Deafness as Culture," many deaf people now see themselves simply as a "linguistic minority (speaking American Sign Language)" (37). They are "no more in need of a cure for their condition than are Haitians or Hispanics" (37). Actor John Limnidis (who appears in *Children*) proclaims, "Deafness is not a handicap. It's a culture, a language, and I'm proud to be deaf. If there was a medication that could be given to deaf people to make them hear, I wouldn't take it. Never" (Shapiro 85).

Certainly the key to Deaf culture is sign language, which you will learn more about later in the chapter. Through signing, with its specific hand and body movements and facial expressions, Deaf people create common bonds and form a community. They share and pass on their history, values, and traditions, and they express themselves artistically. Because sign language is spatial rather than written, Deaf arts are often very different from hearing arts. Mime, visual poetry, theater, and storytelling are highly valued among the Deaf. Other flourishing Deaf art forms that do not depend on the written word are dance, sculpture, and crafts.

Also essential to Deaf culture and identity are residential schools for the deaf, such as the one depicted in the film. Unlike most children in the world, deaf children born to hearing parents cannot learn language and culture from them. At deaf schools they develop bonds with others like themselves, and they learn unique social patterns, including specific styles of greetings, farewells, and touching. For example, Deaf people cannot use their voices or make sounds to get each other's attention, so they wave their arms in the other person's visual field or touch the other person in a prescribed, appropriate way. Residential schools are so important that Deaf people usually mention the name of their school when introducing themselves.

Another part of Deaf culture is Deaf humor, which tends to be visually based, making use of mime and gesture. Many comical stories and jokes focus on deafness itself, on the Deaf outwitting the hearing, and on the daily hazards Deaf people have to overcome. The small book *Deaf Culture Our Way* (1994) by Roy Holcomb contains lots of anecdotes and amusing incidents.

In his article, "Deaf Is Beautiful," Andrew Solomon (1994) describes his perception of the Deaf community as "close, closed, and affectionate." Attending a reception for hundreds of Deaf people, he observes "inviolable bonds of love that are rare in hearing culture." His astonishing statement that "it is impossible, when you are among them, not to wish that you were Deaf," illustrates the transformation taking place in how the Deaf are viewed by the hearing and in how they view themselves (44–45).

Cultural Backpacking: Deaf Culture

This time, you will venture into the culture of the Deaf. Before you set out, you'll need to know a little about Deaf/hearing cultural etiquette. First, and most important, try to relax. Hearing people are usually quite nervous in their first encounters with people who are Deaf. Even if you know just a little ASL, by all means use it. Deaf people will be delighted that you have made an effort to learn *their* language. When conversing with a Deaf person, be aware of your appearance and body language. For example, simple things such as wearing sunglasses, wearing a baseball cap low over your eyes, chewing gum, covering your mouth, or not making eye contact can impede conversation. Don't assume that a deaf person lip-reads, but you may certainly inquire. If you're talking with a person who reads lips, speak normally, neither raising your voice nor exaggerating your words.

If lip-reading is not a possibility, please do not end the conversation there. Be resourceful, and use all means possible to communicate. Have a pen and paper handy or, failing that, use the palm of your hand as a writing pad! Finally, one very important rule—be totally honest if you do not understand a deaf person. It is considered extremely rude for hearing people to smile and nod as if they understand the conversation when they don't. Usually deaf people are patient and will sign more slowly or modify their communication for you. If you want to learn more about Deaf culture and etiquette, consult videos such as *Deaf Culture Lecture #81: Cultural Differences* (1994) by Sign Enhancers and *An Introduction to the Deaf Community* by Sign Media (1993).

Equipped with these basic guidelines, you might check to see if there is a Deaf residential school in your area that you might visit. Look as well for Deaf coffee houses and other meeting places, which often grow up in areas where there are residential schools. Alternatively, take a virtual tour of the Kendall Demonstration Elementary School and the Model Secondary School for the Deaf at the Laurent Clerc National Deaf Education Center *(http://clerccenter.gallaudet.edu)*.

Visiting a Deaf theater production will provide you with yet another wonderful glimpse into Deaf culture. Keep an eye open in your own community for Deaf theater performances, most of which are interpreted for the hearing audience. Alternatively, take a virtual tour of The National Theater of the Deaf to learn about its history, mission, and forthcoming productions at *www.ntd.org/about.htm.*

Spotlight: Protecting Your Hearing

The startling headline on a cover of *Newsweek* (2005) reads, "How to Keep Your Hearing: Why Young People Are at Risk." Apparently, too many people are now "living loudly"; in fact, almost everyone is "caught in the constant roar of the 21st century" (Noonan 2005, 44).

The human ear is a finely tuned instrument, originally serving to warn our ancestors of impending danger from the slightest sound—"the snap of twigs in the forest, the rustle of grass on the savannah" (46). But the excessive noise of modern life, whether urban (traffic, construction, sirens) or rural (farm machinery, power tools, snowmobiles), is causing steady damage to our ears.

One of the main offenders is loud music. Rockers who play or listen to music at high volumes are especially at risk, as is the Walkman® (or the more recent iPod®) generation. "The ubiquitous music players, which send sound directly down the ear canal, are a potential problem for millions of Americans, young and old" (47).

The statistics are sobering: More than 28 million Americans experience some degree of hearing loss. The problem is only expected to get worse, with predictions that there may be 78 million Americans who will live with mild to severe loss of hearing by 2030.

Of course, hearing loss does occur as a natural part of aging, but there is no need to accelerate that process. What can be done? The National Institutes of Health (NIH) runs a campaign called "Wise Ears" that dispenses advice about care and protection. (See *www.nidcd.nih.gov/health/hearing/wiseears.asp.*) For example, earplugs should be worn to avoid prolonged exposure to excessive noise, and the volume on personal listening devices should be kept fairly low. Dr. Peter Rabinowitz at the Yale School of Medicine suggests that taking care of one's ears is just part of a larger approach to general health. "If you are watching your diet, if you are exercising," he says, "then protecting your hearing should be part of your lifestyle" (49).

Student's P.O.V

For as long as I can remember I have been enchanted by sign language. As a child, my mother and father would scold me for staring at people in restaurants and stores who used their hands to communicate.

I enrolled in a semester-long sign language course my sophomore year of high school. After the first day of class, I knew that I had a passion for sign language. For my required senior project, I decided to combine my three favorite things—gymnastics, children, and sign language. I called my project the Twist and Tumble Gymnastics Camp for Deaf Children. The project was a success and ultimately changed my life. From that point on, I knew I wanted to spend my life working with Deaf children.

Many hearing people assume that the Deaf find their inability to hear to be a burden and a source of shame. However, nothing could be further from the truth. Within the Deaf culture there is a profound sense of pride and appreciation for being Deaf. In fact, I have never met a Deaf individual who, if given the opportunity, would become hearing.

Although I primarily live within the hearing world, I feel a strong connection to my Deaf friends and a desire to continue to strengthen that bond.

Being able to take Sign Language at college has opened doors for me on and off campus and allowed me to continue to pursue my goals. Whether I end up as an interpreter for Deaf Children, a teacher for the Deaf, or an adoptive parent of a Deaf child, I know that the experiences within the Deaf community have had a profound effect on who I am and the joy with which I choose to look at life.

—Erin Fleming, ASL student

Poet's P.O.V.

The Deaf Experience

Robert Panara

Looking at the speaker
thru uncomprehending
eyes
trying to decipher
the word
unheard
the sleight of tongue
and talking mouth
which opens
and shuts
instamatically
enigmatically
traumatically . . .

Reaction
in action
a flutter of fingers
a show of hands
the mimic movement
of silent symphony
suddenly
shattered
with cymbalic force
endorsed
of course
by smug recourse
to verbal intercourse.

Robert Panara, one of the best-known Deaf writers in the United States, has received numerous awards for his teaching and poetry. You can find several of his poems along with many other fine writings in *No Walls of Stone: An Anthology of Literature by Deaf and Hard of Hearing Writers* (Jepson 1992).

Lights! Camera! ACTION! Learning Sign Language

Read the following section in preparation for a lesson in ASL.

Hearing people generally misunderstand sign language. Undoubtedly, part of the confusion comes from the fact that it is extremely difficult for a hearing person to imagine how language can be created manually, other than by stringing word pictures together. Sign language, however, is not a sequence of word pictures. While some signs look like the objects they represent (e.g., a house is made with two hands formed into the shape of a roof and then moved down to shape walls), most do not. If they did, after all, a hearing person would be able to understand signing (such as Sarah's signing in the film) quite easily. Much to the contrary, the task of learning sign is long, complicated, and arduous.

What makes ASL so difficult for the hearing to learn and understand is that it is spatial rather than linear. Whereas in spoken language, meaning is created by combining specific sounds into words arranged in a certain order, in ASL meaning is created in three dimensions. That is, the shape and orientation of the hands, their movement, and their location in relation to the body all work together in a three-dimensional mode to create meaning. Additionally, eye and eyebrow movements, facial expressions, and the tilt of the head play a role. The grammar and syntax (arrangement of words or signs into sentences) of ASL are radically different from English as well. As Matthew Moore and Linda Levitan, authors of *For Hearing People Only* (1993), explain, "With ASL you have to abandon 'English thinking' and think visually. It's not easy" (53).

Thus ASL is not a way to communicate in English through signs. In fact, one of the most startling realizations for hearing people is that children who grow up in a signing environment from birth have no knowledge of English. They are not thinking in English (or any other spoken language) or translating from English—rather, they are thinking in sign. If they wish to understand English, they must learn it, as hearing people might learn a foreign language. And in order to read,

Sign Language Alphabet

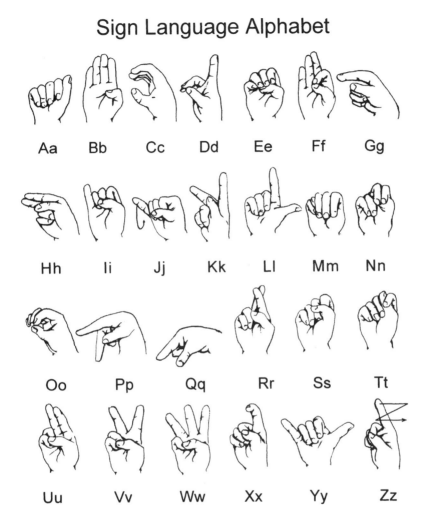

they must first learn English or another written language, since sign languages cannot be written.

Another surprising realization for hearing people is that there is not a universal sign language. Just as there is no universal spoken language, deaf people in different parts of the world sign differently. They use French Sign, British Sign, Israeli Sign, and so on. In fact, there is even such a thing as a regional accent in sign.

As Lou Ann Walker explains in *A Loss for Words* (1987), the creativity of ASL can be remarkable, resembling sculpture. She explains:

To sign *flower growing*, you delicately place the fingertips at each side of the nose as if sniffing the flower, then you push the fingertips of one hand up through the thumb and first finger of the other. The flower can bloom fast or fade, or, with several quick bursts, it can be a whole field of daffodils. (47–48)

You should know that ASL is not the only language of the deaf in the United States; rather, various new signing methods and philosophies have been developed in the past several decades. The approach called Total Communication, for example, encourages the use of all means available to communicate, including ASL, English, and finger spelling.

If you are a hearing student, we invite you to explore the world of sign language. If you are Deaf, we ask you to help your hearing peers enter your world. Arrange with your instructor to spend a class period learning sign language, either from a knowledgeable person in your class or from an invited guest, preferably an ASL teacher or sign language interpreter in your community. In the absence of a knowledgeable person, or if you are taking this class online, you can use a DVD, such as *Signing Made Easy!: How to Talk to a Person Who Can't Hear* (2005) or a website such as *http://lifeprint.com* or *www.lessontutor.com/eesASL1.html.*

- Begin by working in pairs or small groups, and learn to sign your first names using the manual alphabet that appears on page 169. This alphabet is used primarily for proper names and words that have no easy translation from English.

- Now learn a few simple phrases (greetings, apologies, thanks) in ASL with the appropriate facial expressions.

After the sign language lesson, write a page in your film notebook. How did it feel to be using signs rather than words? What insights into Deaf culture did you obtain from this brief introduction? Would you like to learn more sign language? Explain your reasons.

If you are motivated to take further action, inquire into whether public events at your campus, place of worship, or community that are not currently signed might be signed in the future.

Insider's P.O.V. (via Video Relay System)— A Sign of the Times

While Sandra was working on this chapter, she e-mailed her Deaf colleague, Fred Farrior, who teaches ASL, to ask if he would consider writing an Insider's P.O.V. "Sure," replied Fred, "but why don't I call you tonight so that you can experience the video teleconferencing relay firsthand!" So that evening Sandra received a call from Fred via the video relay service. Over high-speed Internet, a relay interpreter signed Sandra's questions to Fred and voiced Fred's answers for her. Here is a transcription of part of the conversation:

Sandra: Fred, what are some of the biggest technological changes that have enhanced your life?

Fred: Well, going back to the '80s, some Deaf communities got TTY (teletypewriter telecommunications) so they could communicate with one another. These were just local services and the Deaf community had to pay for them—you can just imagine, the phone bills were very expensive! But then sixteen years ago, as a result of the Americans with Disabilities Act in 1990, we got the TTY relay service paid for by the federal government. It was wonderful! We could make our own phone calls to anyone we wanted. You can imagine the freedom—I could just pick up the phone, dial the relay service, and type in my message. The relay interpreter would speak my words to the hearing person on the other end of the phone and then type the response for me. It was great. I could call businesses, organizations, schools, friends. If there was an emergency, I could dial 911 and get help through the relay interpreter, whereas before I would have to run to a neighbor or go out in the street to get help. Sometimes hearing people did not want to get involved.

Sandra: And how are we talking now?

Fred: In 2000, we got video phones through high-speed Internet. Truly amazing! That's what you and I are using right now. There is a little camera over my screen. I dial up the relay person, who is a qualified ASL interpreter. She can see me signing on the screen, and I can see her on my video screen. She then interprets for you on the other end of the phone—just like we are doing right now. Of course, if I am calling a deaf person, I just contact them directly over this high-speed Internet system-DSL, and I sign with that person directly via the screen—just like we are having a face-to-face conversation.

Sandra: As you know Fred, Ellen, my coauthor, and I are into movies. How do you go about watching first-run movies?

Fred: No problem! I subscribe to a publication entitled *Deaf Events*. I read it online to find out about the latest movies with open captioning—then I just choose to go to the theater on the particular nights that the movie is being shown "open-captioned." Deaf people these days are flocking to open-captioned movies.

Sandra: What would you most like hearing people to know about the Deaf?

Fred: I realize that hearing people often see deaf people as handicapped. Hearing people say, "You can't do this, you can't do that." I just wish hearing people would understand that we deaf people can do everything that hearing people can do except, of course, hear.

Sandra: Do you see progress being made in how deaf people are growing up now compared to when you were young?

Fred: The young generation today can't believe the atrocities that we had to live with. Young deaf people have grown up in a different environment and feel they CAN do everything. Ten years from now there will be at least one person in stores, hospitals, courtrooms, and businesses who will be able to communicate with deaf people—due to the acceptance of ASL as a second language and the introduction of Deaf Studies programs.

As you can tell, the services that Fred mentioned have already made a huge difference in the independence of deaf people. However, not all forms of technology have met with approval from the Deaf community. One of the most heated controversies affecting deaf people today surrounds what is called a cochlear implant, an electronic aid that provides profoundly deaf people with a sense of hearing. (See *www.cochlearwar.com*.) The implant is not a simple solution, however. Sounds heard by people with an implant seem to be different from those heard by a hearing person, so, for example, Deaf children need intensive speech therapy to learn to understand what they hear and to be able to produce recognizable speech. Requiring an expensive surgical procedure, the implant is regarded by many Deaf people as invasive and ethically questionable. They are angered by the hearing world's eagerness to "fix" their deafness, when in fact they view it as part of their identity rather than as a problem. Many others, both deaf and hearing, disagree, asking why a profoundly deaf child or adult should not be given the chance to hear if that possibility exists.

✺ Your P.O.V.

1. Try to experience silence as James does at the end of the movie. Place yourself in as quiet of a place as possible, and imagine how it would be always to be surrounded by this silence. Try to view the silence not as a void but simply as a different world. Write a film notebook entry in prose or poetry about the experience.

2. You are Johnny. What are you thinking as you watch your classmates interact with Mr. Leeds? Alternatively, imagine you are Sarah watching from the back of the room as the students perform for their parents, teachers, and peers. What is going through your mind? Freewrite your thoughts.

3. At the end of the film James asks Sarah, "Do you think that we could find a place where we can meet, not in silence and not in sound?" In your opinion, is such a meeting place possible? If not, why not? If so, imagine what it might be like in a poem or short narrative.

4. Write a poem or draw an illustration to show Sarah's thoughts and feelings as she swims in the pool.

5. If you are hearing, spend at least five minutes listening without the sound to a television anchor person delivering a news broadcast. Reflect on the experience in your film notebook.

6. Imagine that you and your film crew have an assignment to make a film on Deaf life and culture today. Consult the

guidelines in Appendix D for further information. Here are some potential topics for consideration:

a. student life at Gallaudet University

b. theater for the Deaf

c. Deaf humor

d. the heated controversy over cochlear implants

e. CODAs

And Our Deaf Culture Book Awards Go To . . .

For Hearing People Only: Answers to Some of the Most Commonly Asked Questions about the Deaf Community, Its Culture, and the "Deaf Reality" (3rd ed.) by Matthew S. Moore and Linda Levitan (Rochester, NY: Deaf Life Press, 2003). Everything you wanted to know and ask about deafness and Deaf culture. The authors provide answers to questions such as "What bothers a deaf person most about hearing people?" and "Why don't all universities accept ASL as a foreign language?" This classic book dispels myths and promotes excellent discussion.

Mother Father Deaf: Living between Sound and Silence by Paul Preston (Cambridge, MA: Harvard University Press, 1995). Profoundly moving stories of children who occupy two worlds—hearing and deaf. Author and anthropologist Preston shares tender recollections of his own childhood experiences and those of 150 other CODAs whom he interviewed. This is one of several excellent books written by hearing children of deaf parents. See also *A Loss for Words* (1986) by Lou Ann Walker and *Train Go Sorry* (1994) by Leah Hager Cohen.

Seeing Voices: A Journey into the World of the Deaf by Oliver Sacks (Berkeley: University of California Press, 1989). A fascinating read for anyone interested in the capacities of the human mind, pre-lingual deafness, and the development of sign language. A renowned neurologist and acclaimed author, Sacks traces the history of Deaf culture and details the suffering of Deaf people due to lack of tolerance and understanding on the part of the hearing.

And Our Deaf Culture Film Awards Go To . . .

Beyond Silence (1996)—Story of a young gifted musician whose struggle for independence is difficult for her deaf parents to grasp (German with English subtitles). Directed by Caroline Link.

The Heart Is a Lonely Hunter (1968)—Heartwarming drama of the relationship between a troubled adolescent girl and a lonely deaf man. Directed by Robert Ellis Miller.

Mr. Holland's Opus (1995)—The story of a teacher whose whole life revolves around music and how he comes to terms with the way that his deaf son can experience the one thing he lives for. Directed by Stephen Herek.

9

Creating Community:
What's Cooking?

Setting the Scene: Freewriting and Discussion

Work with a partner to exchange ideas on the How to Build Global Community poster on page 177. Talk about which suggestions you like best and why. Then come up with two suggestions you would like to add to the list. You might create a class poster made up of your own suggestions.

Sneak Preview

About the Film

As if to announce that America had something bold and special cooking (but not melting) at the beginning of the new millennium, *What's Cooking?* was released in the year 2000. Set in West Los Angeles, where many ethnic groups live and interact, the film revolves around four different families—African American, Jewish, Mexican American, and Vietnamese American—all preparing to celebrate Thanksgiving in their own way. The film is a celebration of food, family, tradition, and difference.

Like *The Joy Luck Club* (1993), there are four story lines in *What's Cooking?* that are intertwined and at times hard to follow, and there are a lot of characters—41 speaking parts to be exact. The first few minutes at the beginning set the tone for the film. With "The Star Spangled Banner" playing in the background, we are treated to a visual delight of colorful street life in different ethnic neighborhoods, viewed in part from the inside of a bus (where the director is seated in a blue dress). This is everyday life in one of America's most diverse cities, brimming with energy and contradictions—and totally alive. At one point the camera focuses on a poster mounted on the side of the bus showing an all-American, Anglo nuclear family posed around a turkey. When the bus stops, the same poster appears on a bench, this time showing a proud all-American Latino family posed in front of their turkey.

As Thanksgiving dinner approaches, all four families are experiencing tension and near-crisis. Some of the conflicts are humorous, some serious. The Latina mother Lizzy, recently separated from her philandering husband, has found a new boyfriend whom she wants her family to meet for the first time at dinner. But, without her knowledge, her son has invited her estranged husband to dinner, too.

In the African American family, the mother Audrey contends with a controlling

HOW TO BUILD GLOBAL COMMUNITY

Think of no one as "them"
Don't confuse your comfort with your safety
Talk to strangers
Imagine other cultures through their art, poetry and novels
Listen to music you don't understand · Dance to it
Act locally
Notice the workings of power & privilege in your culture
Question consumption
Know how your lettuce and coffee are grown: wake up and smell the exploitation
Look for fair trade and union labels
Help build economies from the bottom up
Acquire few needs
Learn a second (or third) language
Visit people, places, and cultures - not tourist attractions
Learn people's history · Re-define progress
Know physical and political geography
Play games from other cultures · Watch films with subtitles
Know your heritage
Honor everyone's holidays
Look at the moon and imagine someone else, someone else, looking at it too
Read the UN's Universal Declaration of Human Rights
Understand the global economy in terms of people, land and water
Know where your bank banks
Never believe you have a right to anyone else's resources
Refuse to wear corporate logos: defy corporate domination
Question military/corporate connections
Don't confuse money with wealth, or time with money
Have a pen/email pal · Honor indigenous cultures
Judge governance by how well it meets all people's needs
Be skeptical about what you read
Eat adventurously · Enjoy vegetables, beans and grains in your diet
Choose curiosity over certainty
Know where your water comes from and where your wastes go
Pledge allegiance to the earth: question nationalism
Think South, Central and North – there are many Americans
Assume that many others share your dreams
Know that no one is silent though many are not heard
Work to change this

Source: Melinda Levine/SCWCommunity © 2002. *www.syrculturalworkers.com**

....

*Syracuse Cultural Workers "Tools for Change" catalog is 32 color pages of feminist, progressive, multicultural resources to help change the world and sustain activism. The Peace Calendar, Women Artists Datebook, over 100 posters on social, cultural and political themes, holiday cards for Solstice, Christmas, Chanukah, Kwanzaa, plus buttons, stickers, T-shirts, notecards, postcards, and books. Great fundraising products. Box 6367, Syracuse, NY 13217 (315) 474-1132; Free Fax (877) 265-5399. 24-hour ordering—Visa/MC. email: *scw@syrculturalworkers.org*

mother-in-law, marital problems, and a painful clash between her husband and son.

The Jewish parents struggle to accept the relationship between
their daughter Rachel and her lesbian partner, Carla, both of whom
arrive from San Francisco for Thanksgiving dinner with feelings of
anxiety and discomfort.

In the Vietnamese family, the three Americanized children seem to
be losing their parents' cherished Asian traditions. Younger son Joey
is hanging with the wrong crowd, has been suspended from school,
and has hidden a gun under his bed. Punkish daughter Jenny has a
white boyfriend and is discovered to have a condom in her coat
pocket. And older son Jimmy claims to be too busy studying for
midterms to come home from college for Thanksgiving, which he
prefers to spend with his Latina girlfriend Sofia—who happens to be
the daughter of Lizzy.

This crossover from one household to another is just one of the
many complications that make *What's Cooking?* an intriguing film.
With its twists of plot and all-encompassing, relatively nonthreatening
look at ethnicity, race, religion, and sexual orientation, the film is
guaranteed to hold one's attention and provide plenty of topics for
post-viewing discussion.

About the Filmmakers and Actors of *What's Cooking?*

Of Punjabi Indian descent, director Gurinder Chadha was born in
Kenya and grew up in London. Early in her career, she directed sev-
eral award-winning documentaries about Asian Indians who are
British. She became widely known through her first feature film *Bhaji
on the Beach* (1993), an unusual, touching story of three generations of
Asian Indian women who take a day trip together to the beach at
Blackpool.

When Chadha traveled to Los Angeles to direct *What's Cooking?*,
which she calls her "first American film," she was surprised by many
things. For example, she was unaware of the extent to which the city is
Latino: "When I first went there," she says, "I had no idea what a bur-
rito is" (quotations from the DVD special features). Working together
with her Japanese American husband Paul Mayeda Berges, Chadha
wanted to make a film that "could celebrate the diversity of Americans
today." She explains: "The American films I'd seen that actually dealt

with race were almost always about problems and conflicts. We wanted to move away from that and show how the differences between cultures can actually underscore similarities" (Rich 2000, AR28).

What are these similarities? As you watch the film, you'll see how the families do many of the same things in different ways. For the director herself, "the whole point of the film is that the four families mirror each other . . . they all want the same thing, to keep their families together" (quotation from *www.screenonline.org.uk/people/id/502103/index.html*).

While *What's Cooking?* was quite well received, Chadha's most successful film to date is *Bend It Like Beckham* (2002), in which a young British Indian woman pursues her passion for football (soccer) at the risk of alienating her family. Set in the neighborhood of Southall in West London where Chadha grew up, it "became one of the most popular British films ever and was a far cry from the colonially obsessed images of Asians depicted in mainstream British cinema and television in the 1980s and earlier" (quotation from *www.screenonline. org.uk/film/id/475617/index.html*).

A cast of splendid actors in *What's Cooking?* includes relative newcomers Kristy Wu and Will Lee alongside such veterans as African American Alfre Woodard, who is best known for her award-winning roles in television dramas; Joan Chen, who was born and educated in China, and who, in addition to an acting career that includes roles in *Dim Sum: A Little Bit of Heart* (1985), *The Last Emperor* (1987), and *Heaven and Earth* (1993), has directed *Xiu Xiu: The Sent-Down Girl* (1998) and *Autumn in New York* (2000); Mercedes Ruehl, of Irish and Cuban descent, who won an Oscar for her performance in *The Fisher King* (1991); Lainie Kazan, of Spanish and Jewish heritage, who understudied Barbara Streisand in the original Broadway production of the musical *Funny Girl* and starred in *My Big Fat Greek Wedding* (2002); Khieu Chin, who plays June's mother Suyuan in *The Joy Luck Club* (1993); Julianna Margulies, well known as Nurse Hathaway from the television series *ER*; and Kyra Sedgwick, whose many film credits include *Born on the Fourth of July* (1989) and the television series *The Closer* (2005).

Who's Who in the Film

The Avilas

Elizabeth "Lizzy" Avila (Mercedes Ruehl)—mother

Javier Avila (Victor Rivers)—ex-husband

Anthony "Tony" Avila (Douglas Spain)—son

Sofia Avila (Maria Carmen)—daughter-in-law

Grandma Avila (Elena Lopez)

Daniel "Danny" (A Martinez)—Lizzy's boyfriend

The Nguyens

Trinh Nguyen (Joan Chen)—mother

Duc Nguyen (Francois Chau)—father

Jimmy Nguyen (Will Yun Lee)—oldest brother at college, Sofia's boyfriend

Jenny Nguyen (Kristy Wu)—sister

Joey (Brennan Louie)—brother

Grandma (Kieu Chinh)

Grandpa (Chao Li Chi)

The Seeligs

Ruth "Ruthie" Seelig (Lainie Kazan)—mother

Herb "Herbie" Seelig (Maury Chaykin)—father

Rachel Seelig (Kyra Sedgwick)—daughter

Carla (Julianna Margulies)—Rachel's spouse

The Williamses and friends

Audrey Williams (Alfre Woodard)—mother

Ronald "Ronnie" Williams (Dennis Haysbert)—father

Michael Williams (Eric George)—son

Grandma Grace Williams (Ann Weldon)—grandmother from Chicago

Paula Moore (Shareen Mitchell)—Anglo friend

James Moore (Gregory Itzin)—Anglo friend

Monica Moore (Mariam Parris)—friends' daughter

Director and co-screenwriter—Gurinder Chadha

Co-screenwriter—Paul Mayeda Berges

Spotlight: For Indians No Thanksgiving

To many people living in this country, Thanksgiving is the quintessential American holiday. Regardless of religion, ethnicity, language, or age, everyone can be part of this time to come together with family and friends, enjoy wonderful food, and give thanks for the blessings of life. In this setting, at least, all Americans seem to unite.

But wait. At the Williams's family meal, Monica, when it is her turn to express personal thanks, says: "I'd like to thank our fellow Native Americans who gave us this land in exchange for measles, reservations, and casinos. . . . More like Thanks-taking, don't you think?"

Of course, she is referring to the origins of the holiday, known to every schoolchild in America. Having experienced a very harsh first winter of 1620 in Massachusetts, the surviving colonists (popularly known as Pilgrims) from Plymouth, England, declared a three-day feast in the autumn of 1621. Deeply indebted to local Indians—Samoset (of the Wampanoag Tribe) and Squanto (of the Patuxtet Tribe)—who had taught them to fish, hunt, and plant corn, the Pilgrims invited Massasoit, the local Wampanoag chief, together with approximately 90 Indians from various Eastern Woodlands tribes, to their ceremony, the food for which is thought to have been supplied mostly by the Indians.

So how do Indians today feel about the national holiday Thanksgiving? Of course, there is no single p.o.v., but many Indians have publicly expressed their anti-Thanksgiving sentiments. Native American author Michael Dorris delivers an eloquent, sobering statement in his essay "For Indians, No Thanksgiving" (1994). He writes:

> A majority of reservation Indians reside in the most impoverished counties in the nation. They constitute the ethnic group at the wrong extreme of every scale: most undernourished, most short-lived, least educated, least healthy. For them, Thanksgiving was perhaps their last square meal. (231)

In *A New Religious America* (2001), Diana L. Eck tells of her visit to Plymouth, Massachusetts, on Thanksgiving Day in 1998. While citizens of the town paraded down the street in colonial costume and assembled in the church for a service, local Indians gathered at Plymouth Rock (where the Pilgrims' ship the Mayflower landed almost 400 years ago) for their 29th annual National Day of Mourning. One of the speakers said:

We Indian people do not give thanks just one day a year. Every day we thank the creator for this beautiful earth and for our survival. But we will not give thanks for the invasion of our country; we will not celebrate the theft of our lands and the genocide of our people; we will not sing and dance to please the tourists who came here seeking a Disneyland version of our history. (33)

More information about the United American Indians of New England (UAINE), which organizes the yearly event, is found at *http://home.earthlink.net/~uainendom.*

How should we feel about the Native American p.o.v.s expressed previously? Do they ruin Thanksgiving? Clearly, director Chadha did not want to suggest that we should feel guilty about the holiday, but she didn't want to leave out completely the p.o.v. of non-celebrants, either. What do you think? Perhaps the long-term question is whether there are any ways for those who are wearing the colonial costumes to come together in community with those who are mourning at the rock. Finding new hope and solutions would certainly be cause for meaningful thanksgiving.

Lights! Camera! ACTION!

- Brainstorm ideas with the class about how to build community at your school or on your campus, and design a poster. You might be able to have it printed and hung in public places. Also, check the websites of Northern Sun *(www.northernsun.com)* and Syracuse Cultural Workers *(www.syrculturalworkers.com)* to find issue-oriented posters, T-shirts, buttons, note cards, gifts, and other items.

- Help to organize a potluck that brings together people from different cultural backgrounds. You could organize it in your dorm, in a friendly campus meeting place, or perhaps in a professor's home. Have people label their foods and bring recipes to exchange.

- Help to organize a multicultural or international film festival at your college or university, with opportunities for discussion with knowledgeable people who can express different p.o.v.s. Or simply invite some friends for popcorn and a movie, making sure to leave time to talk.

- Read *Global Uprising: Stories from a New Generation of Activists* by Neva Welton and Linda Wolf (2001) to become inspired about routes to action being taken by young (and some older) people. The new student generation is committed, creative, and energetic. This idealistic book is filled with ideas that are within the reach of people like ourselves.

And Our Final Book Award Goes To . . .

The Middle of Everywhere: The World's Refugees Come to Our Town by Mary Pipher (New York: Harcourt, 2002). A report, not from teeming Los Angeles, but from the unexpectedly multicultural heartland of America—small-town Nebraska. Humane, wise, compassionate Mary Pipher tells one engrossing story after another to illustrate what she says is the "great lesson" of September 11—namely that "we are all connected." She writes: "Either we are all safe or none of us is safe. Either we are all free of fear or none of us is" (xvii). A practicing psychotherapist, Pipher knows how to see things from the p.o.v. of the many refugees—from Russia, Serbia, Croatia, Ethiopia, the Sudan, Liberia, Afghanistan, and more—who live and work in her community. Her book makes us want to open up, to redefine community, and (in the words of writer Gay Talese) to enlarge our capacity to be human.

And Our Final Film Award Goes To. . .

Crash (2005)—A thought-provoking depiction of the state of race and community relations in the United States today. This film follows the intersecting paths of a number of Los Angeles residents from different ethnic backgrounds and walks of life who are all connected to a car accident. The film shows how their lives come together, sometimes harmoniously but at other times with tragic results. *Crash* is an excellent film guaranteed to prompt discussion and debate. Directed by Paul Haggis, it won the 2006 Oscar for Best Motion Picture.

Flashback/ Flashforward

We have now come to the end of our journey through some of America's diverse cultures. We hope you have learned more about yourself and gained a better sense of your own cultural identity. We also hope that you will feel a greater sense of confidence and openness when you encounter new cultures in the future—and that you will explore and enjoy cultural differences. Finally, we hope that you have become more aware of what you personally can do to continue your learning and contribute in positive ways to the cultural settings in which you live and work.

In this final activity, flash back to three times in this course when you felt you learned something important. In your film notebook, describe the flashbacks.

Now flash forward to one time in the future when your thinking or behavior might be affected by what you have learned in this course. Describe the flashforward in your film notebook.

Appendix A

Respect Agreement

- What is needed to create a respectful learning environment?
- What is needed for all students to feel safe and comfortable but also challenged?
- How can we put into practice the theories and ideals we are discussing?

When interacting with others in class, please:

- Maintain confidentiality (of personal or sensitive matters) by not attaching any names to comments when you speak about course discussions with others not in the class.
- Feel free to ask questions.
- Listen considerately and attentively to each other.
- Try not to judge too quickly what others say; instead, ask questions that will help you better understand.
- Speak frankly and honestly, but show sensitivity so as not to hurt others' feelings.
- At all costs, avoid sarcasm and cynicism directed toward others.
- Maintain a sense of humor without trivializing the discussion.
- Take risks by asking questions or expressing yourself on topics about which you may feel anxiety or uncertainty.
- Develop trust by supporting others, especially if they seem to be having difficulty expressing their views, or if they voice ideas that may be unpopular (practice "put ups," not "put downs").
- Try not to be afraid of emotions. The topics you will be examining can be sensitive and upsetting, and emotions may surface. Regard them as a source of learning.

Appendix B

Guidelines for Visits to Religious Services and Places of Worship*

- Please call the place of worship first before you go.
- Introduce yourself as a student who will be visiting this religious service or site as a class assignment. You may want to mention which course you are taking.
- Explain that the purpose of this assignment is to learn more about the particular religion in an attempt to increase mutual respect and understanding. You may or may not wish to announce your own religious background or tradition.
- Ask what day and time services will be held.
- Inquire about appropriate dress. Conservative dress is usually best. Please do not wear jeans.
- If you are going alone, you can ask if you might meet someone at the service who could act as a guide. Alternatively, you might arrive a bit early and ask someone who looks kind or official for assistance.
- Know that you are not expected to participate in rituals; usually you can be seated in an inconspicuous place in the back.
- If donations are collected, or if there is a container for donations, be prepared to contribute a modest amount as a sign of respect. Members will appreciate this.
- Please do not take notes or photographs during the service.
- Express your appreciation verbally as you leave and possibly with a follow-up note.

*Adapted in part from Norine Dresser, *Multicultural Manners: New Rules of Etiquette for a Changing Society* (New York: John Wiley and Sons, 1996). Her chapter "At Places of Worship" is excellent and contains specific advice for observing the worship services of ten religions.

Appendix C

Guidelines for Intercultural Interviews and Chats

Be creative in thinking of people to speak with. Sometimes the best conversations are with people you have known for a long time.

When you request a chat give the person advance notice and try to accommodate to his or her schedule. Explain to the person the purpose of your assignment and give an estimate of how much time you might need.

Choose a quiet place for your meeting. If you choose a campus coffee house, for example, offer to buy something to eat or drink. Phone interviews are also possible if the person lives too far away or is otherwise unavailable.

Prepare by thinking of at least a few questions that will help you understand the other person's perspectives, values, and way of life. Ask if you may take notes.

Clearly, you will need to be sensitive so as not to offend or intrude, but you want to learn, too. Feel your way as to what topics may be too personal or inappropriate. Most people are delighted to be able to share their cultures and perspectives with interested students.

You'll need to practice good listening skills and empathy. If you hear something that seems strange or offensive to you, try, for the time being, to suspend judgment.

Be prepared to share something about yourself if appropriate so as to allow for more of a relaxed chat than a one-way interview.

In your write-up for the class, talk about what you learned—not only about the other person and his or her culture but also about the process itself. How did you feel? How did the conversation go? What was hard? What worked well, and what didn't? How did the other person seem to feel?

Be sure to follow up with a written thank-you note to the person who helped you.

Appendix D

Guidelines for Planning Your Film

This assignment will allow you to familiarize yourself with the topic at hand and also to get a sense of what filmmaking is like so as to gain a new appreciation for movies and view them more critically. Members of the class who are studying filmmaking, film history, or acting—or who have gained cinematic expertise in other ways—can be of special assistance.

Review the two-part article "Film Viewing: How to Watch Movies Intelligently and Critically" at *www.filmsite.org/filmterms.html*. There is also a film glossary on this site and at *www.imdb.com/Glossary*.

Work in small groups of about four to five students. Once you have chosen your topic, decide as a team whether you wish to make a feature film or a documentary (or perhaps an animated film or a biography/biopic). Then decide among yourselves who will take what responsibility: Who will be the director, screenwriter, editor, and cinematographer? Do you need other roles such as costume designer, coordinator of special effects, or dialect coach?

You may vary the assignment in consultation with your instructor. For example, you might wish to: (1) write a portion of the screenplay; (2) film a portion of your movie; (3) map out your plan for part of the film, or for the entire film, including such details as: Which location(s) will you choose? What is the basic plot? Which scenes will you include in what order? Will you work with consultants? If so, what type of experts do you need? What is your p.o.v.? Will you need a narrator, and if so, whom?

You may wish to create a tagline and publicity for your movie.

At the end, write an entry in your film notebook describing the process and explaining what you learned. Your instructor may also ask you to make an oral presentation of your work.

Appendix E

Selected Internet Resources on Films

All-Movie Guide

http://allmovie.com

Directory with reviews and plot summaries

Asian Educational Media Service

www.aems.uiuc.edu

Outstanding site for information on Asian films

CineMedia

www.cinemedia.org

Large film and media directory with 25,000 links

Film Critic

www.filmcritic.com

Excellent site for timely reviews by twenty film critics

The Greatest Films

www.filmsite.org

Detailed information on specific American movies and great links

indieWIRE

www.indiewire.com

Guide to independent films and filmmaking

The Movies, Race, and Ethnicity

www.lib.berkeley.edu/MRC/EthnicImagesVid.html

Excellent videographies and bibliographies

P.O.V. Interactive

www.pbs.org/pov

Site for the independent film series P.O.V.

Rotten Tomatoes

www.rottentomatoes.com

Good reviews

Teach with Movies

http://teachwithmovies.com

Learning guides to more than 250 films for modest yearly fee

Viewing Race

www.viewingrace.org

Excellent guide to documentaries

Appendix F

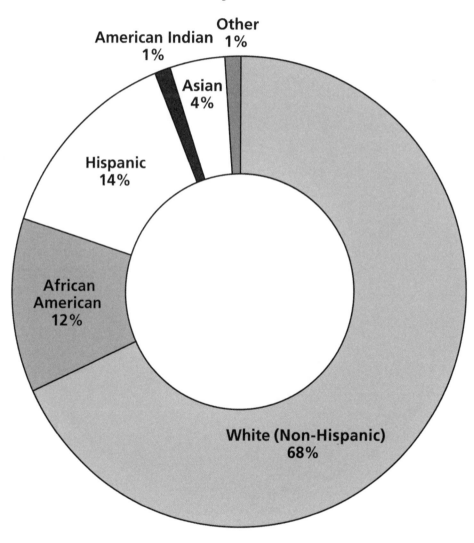

Race and Ethnicity in the United States

Appendix G

Latino Population in the United States by Place of Origin

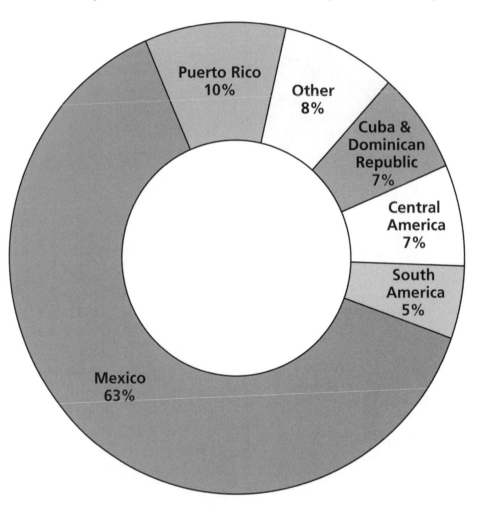

Appendix H

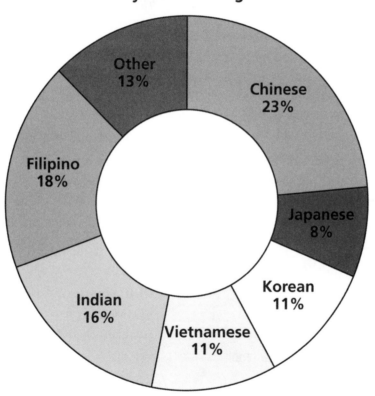

Asian American Population in the United States by Place of Origin

Other 13%

Chinese 23%

Filipino 18%

Japanese 8%

Indian 16%

Korean 11%

Vietnamese 11%

Film Sources

Native American Culture

Powwow Highway (1989)
Handmade Films

Smoke Signals (1998)
Miramax Films

Thunderheart (1992)
TriStar Pictures

Where the Spirit Lives (1989)
Amazing Spirit Productions

African American Culture

Do the Right Thing (1989)
Universal Pictures

Glory (1989)
TriStar Pictures

The Long Walk Home (1990)
New Visions Pictures

Mississippi Burning (1988)
Orion Pictures

Something the Lord Made (2004)
Nina Saxon Film Design

Chinese American Culture

Dragon: The Bruce Lee Story (1993)
Universal Pictures

A Great Wall (1986)
Nanhai

The Joy Luck Club (1993)
Hollywood Pictures

Thousand Pieces of Gold (1999)
American Playhouse

Mexican American Culture

Bread and Roses (2000)
Lions Gate Films, Inc.

El Norte (1983)
Independent Productions

Lone Star (1996)
Castle Rock Entertainment

Real Women Have Curves (2002)
HBO/Newmarket Films

Spanglish (2004)
Columbia Pictures Corporation

Irish American Culture

In America (2003)
Fox Searchlight Pictures

Far and Away (1992)
Imagine Films Entertainment

On the Waterfront (1954)
Columbia Pictures Corporation

This Is My Father (1999)
Father Productions

Muslim American Culture

Aladdin (1992)
Walt Disney Pictures

Ali: Fear Eats the Soul (1974)
Tango Films/Filmverlag der
    Autoren

Bye Bye (1996)
Turbulent Arts

Control Room (2004)
Magnolia Pictures

East Is East (1999)
Alliance Atlantis

Head On (2005)
Strand Releasing

House of Sand and Fog (2003)
DreamWorks

Inside Mecca (2003)
National Geographic Television

Malcolm X (1992)
Warner Brothers

Monsieur Ibrahim (2003)
Sony Pictures Classics

Salut Cousin! (1997)
Seventh Art Releasing

The War Within (2005)
HDNet Films

Gay Culture

Brokeback Mountain (2005)
Alberta Filmworks, Inc.

Philadelphia (1993)
TriStar Pictures

*The Incredibly True Adventure of
    Two Girls in Love* (1995)
Fine Line Features

The Laramie Project (2002)
Good Machine Production

Wedding Banquet (1993)
Samuel Goldwyn Company

Deaf Culture

Beyond Silence (1998)
Miramax Films

Children of a Lesser God (1986)
Paramount Pictures

The Heart Is a Lonely Hunter
    (1968)
Warner Brothers

Mr. Holland's Opus (1995)
Buena Vista Pictures

Creating Community

Crash (2005)
Bull's Eye Entertainment

What's Cooking? (2000)
Flashpoint

Works Cited

To the Students: Developing Your Film Eyes

Bone, Jan, and Ron Johnson. *Understanding the Film: An Introduction to Film Appreciation*. 5th ed. Lincolnwood, IL: NTC Publishing, 1997.

Hilger, Michael. *The American Indian in Film*. Metuchen, NJ: Scarecrow Press, 1986.

To the Instructor: Behind the Scenes

Banks, James. *Teaching Strategies for Ethnic Studies*. 7th ed. Boston: Allyn and Bacon, 2003.

Bean, John. *Engaging Ideas*. San Francisco: Jossey Bass, 1996.

Native American Culture

Alexie, Sherman. *The Business of Fancydancing: Stories and Poems*. Brooklyn, NY: Hanging Loose Press, 1991.

―――. *The Lone Ranger and Tonto Fistfight in Heaven*. New York: HarperCollins, 1993.

Ballantine, Betty, and Ian Ballantine, eds. *The Native Americans: An Illustrated History*. Atlanta: Turner Publishing, 1993.

Blewster, Kelly. "Tribal Visions." *Biblio* 4, no. 3 (March 1999): 22–29.

Cooper, James Fenimore. *The Last of the Mohicans: A Narrative of 1757*. Albany: State University of New York Press, 1982.

Deloria, Vine, Jr. *Custer Died for Your Sins: An Indian Manifesto*. New York: Avon, 1969.

―――. *God Is Red: A Native View of Religion*. Golden, CO: Fulcrum Publishing, 1992.

Gattuso, John, ed. *Insight Guides: Native America*. Boston: Houghton Mifflin, 1993.

Hirschfelder, Arlene, ed. *Native Heritage: Personal Accounts by American Indians 1790 to the Present*. New York: Macmillan, 1995.

Lincoln, Kenneth. *Indi'n Humor: Bicultural Play in Native America*. New York: Oxford University Press, 1993.

Mander, Jerry. *In the Absence of the Sacred: The Failure of Technology and the Survival of the Indian Nations*. San Francisco: Sierra Club Books, 1992.

Mankiller, Wilma. *Every Day Is a Good Day: Reflections by Contemporary Indigenous Women*. Golden, CO: Fulcrum Publishing, 2004.

Peltier, Leonard. *Prison Writings: My Life Is My Sun Dance*. New York: St. Martin's Press, 1999.

Richardson, James D. *Compilation of the Messages and Papers of the Presidents: 1789–1897*. Vol. II. Washington, DC: Government Printing Office, 1896.

Starke, Amy Martinez. "Fry Bread." *The Oregonian* (June 2001): FD1–2.

Summa, Andy. "Writer Aims to Break Stereotypes: Sherman Alexie's 'Smoke Signals' Paints a Different Picture of Native Americans." *The Oregonian* (July 7, 1998): D4.

Wearne, Phillip. *Return of the Indian: Conquest and Revival in the Americas*. Philadelphia: Temple University Press, 1996.

Zinn, Howard. *A People's History of the United States: 1492–Present*. Revised and updated. New York: HarperPerennial Classics, 2005.

African Americans

Appiah, Kwame Anthony, and Henry Louis Gates, Jr., eds. *Africana: The Encyclopedia of the African and African American Experience*. New York: Basic Civitas Books, 1999.

Bennett, Lerone, Jr. *Before the Mayflower: A History of Black America*. 6th ed. New York: Penguin Books, 1993.

Brooks, Roy L. *Integration or Separation: A Strategy for Racial Equality*. Cambridge, MA: Harvard University Press, 1996.

Brown, Dee. *Bury My Heart at Wounded Knee: An Indian History of the American West*. New York: Henry Holt and Company, 1970.

Carnes, Mark C., ed. *Past Imperfect: History According to the Movies*. New York: Henry Holt and Company, 1996.

King, Coretta Scott. "'Long Walk Home' True Look at Past." *The Oregonian* (May 15, 1991): A12.

King, Martin Luther, Jr. *Stride toward Freedom: The Montgomery Story*. New York: Harper & Brothers, 1958.

Lefkowitz, Mary. *Not Out of Africa: How Afrocentrism Became an Excuse to Teach Myth as History*. New York: Basic Books, 1996.

Parks, Rosa. *Quiet Strength*. Grand Rapids, MI: Zondervan, 2000.

Rosen, Jeffrey. "The Lost Promise of School Integration." *New York Times*, April 2, 2000, 4:4–5.

Takaki, Ronald. *A Different Mirror: A History of Multicultural America*. Boston: Little Brown and Company, 1993.

Thoreau, Henry David. *On the Duty of Civil Disobedience*. Chicago: Charles H. Kerr, 1989.

Zinn, Howard. *A People's History of the United States: 1492–Present*. Revised and updated. New York: HarperPerennial Classics, 2005.

Chinese American Culture

Chin, Tsai. *Daughter of Shanghai: The Unforgettable Memoir*. New York: St. Martin's Press, 1994.

Corliss, Richard. "Pacific Overtures." *Time*, September 13, 1993, 68–70.

Hagedorn, Jessica. "Asian Women in Film: No Joy, No Luck." *Ms.* (January–February 1994), 74–79.

———, ed. *Charlie Chan Is Dead 2: At Home in the World—An Anthology of Contemporary Asian American Fiction*. New York: Penguin Books, 2004.

Ling, Huping. *Surviving on the Gold Mountain: A History of Chinese American Women and Their Lives*. Albany, NY: State University of New York Press, 1998.

Liu, Eric. *The Accidental Asian: Notes of a Native Speaker*. New York: Vintage Books, 1998.

Miščević, Dusanka, and Peter Kwong. *Chinese Americans: The Immigrant Experience*. New York: Hugh Lauter Levin Associates, 2000.

Simpson, Blaise. "Stories from the Heart." *Los Angeles Times,* September 5, 1993, 8+.

Takaki, Ronald. *Strangers from a Different Shore: A History of Asian Americans*. Boston: Little, Brown, and Co., 1998.

Tan, Amy. "Joy Luck and Hollywood." In *The Opposite of Fate: A Book of Musings*. New York: G. P. Putnam's Sons, 2003a.

———. "Mother Tongue." In *The Opposite of Fate: A Book of Musings*. New York: G. P. Putnam's Sons, 2003b.

———. *Sagwa, the Chinese Siamese Cat*. New York: Aladdin Paperbacks, 2001.

Xing, Jun. *Asian America through the Lens: History, Representations, and Identity*. Walnut Creek, CA: AltaMira Press, 1998.

Yung, Judy. *Unbound Feet: A Social History of Chinese Women in San Francisco*. Berkeley, CA: University of California Press, 1995.

Mexican American Culture

Anzaldúa, Gloria. *Borderlands/La Frontera: The New Mestiza.* 2nd ed. San Francisco: Aunt Lute Books, 1999.

Barone, Michael. *The New Americans: How the Melting Pot Can Work Again.* Washington, DC: Regnery, 2001.

Campo-Flores, Arian, and Howard Fineman. "A Latino Power Surge." *Newsweek,* May 30, 2005, 24–31.

Farley, Christopher John. "Latin Music Pops." *Time,* May 24, 1999, 74–77.

Fuentes, Carlos. *The Buried Mirror: Reflections on Spain and the New World.* New York: Houghton Mifflin, 1992.

Larmer, Brook. "Latino America." *Newsweek,* July 12, 1999, 48.

Mills, Nicolaus, ed. *Arguing Immigration: The Debate over the Changing Face of America.* New York: Simon and Schuster, 1994.

Sowell, Thomas. *Ethnic America: A History.* New York: Basic Books, 1981.

Irish American Culture

Barone, Michael. *The New Americans: How the Melting Pot Can Work Again.* Washington, DC: Regnery, 2001.

Cahill, Thomas. *How the Irish Saved Civilization: The Untold Story of Ireland's Heroic Role from the Fall of Rome to the Rise of Medieval Europe.* New York: Doubleday, 1995.

Dolman, Bob, and Ron Howard. *Far and Away: The Illustrated Story of a Journey from Ireland to America in the 1890s.* New York: Newmarket Press, 1992.

Graves, Kerry A. *Irish Americans.* Philadelphia: Chelsea House, 2003.

Guglielmo, Jennifer, and Salvatore Salerno, eds. *Are Italians White? How Race Is Made in America.* New York: Routledge, 2003.

Holladay, Valerie. "Easy Steps to Writing Your Family History." *Ancestry* 21, no. 4 (July–August 2003), 14–23.

Ignatiev, Noel. *How the Irish Became White.* New York: Routledge, 1995.

Labaree, Leonard W., ed. *The Papers of Benjamin Franklin.* Vol. 4. New Haven, CT: Yale University Press, 1961.

McCourt, Frank. *Angela's Ashes: A Memoir.* New York: Scribner, 1996.

Sowell, Thomas. *Ethnic America: A History.* New York: Basic Books, 1981.

Muslim American Culture

Abinader, Elmaz. "Profile of an Arab Daughter." In *Open Questions: Readings for Critical Thinking and Writing*, eds. Chris Anderson and Lex Runciman. Boston: Bedford/St. Martin's, 2005.

Abu-Jaber, Diana. *Arabian Jazz: A Novel*. San Diego: Harcourt Brace and Co., 1993.

———. *Crescent: A Novel*. New York: W.W. Norton & Company, 2003.

———. *The Language of Baklava: A Memoir*. New York: Pantheon Books, 2005.

Ahmed, Akbart S. "Introduction." In *Inside Islam: The Faith, the People, and the Conflicts of the World's Fastest-Growing Religion* by John Miller and Aaron Kenedi. New York: Marlow and Company, 2002.

Austin, Allen. *African Muslims in Antebellum America: Transatlantic Stories and Spiritual Struggles*. New York: Routledge, 1997.

Cortés, Carlos E. *The Children Are Watching: How the Media Teach about Diversity*. New York: Teachers College Press, 2000.

Dawood, N. J., trans. *Tales from the Thousand and One Nights*. New York: Penguin, 1973.

Dickerson, Diana. *Scarves of Many Colors: Muslim Women and the Veil*. Joan Hawkinson Bohorfoush Memorial Foundation, Portland, OR, 2000.

Dubus, Andre III. *House of Sand and Fog*. New York: Random House, 1999.

Eck, Diana L. *A New Religious America: How a "Christian Country" Has Become the World's Most Religiously Diverse Nation*. San Francisco: HarperSanFrancisco, 2001.

Goodstein, Laurie. "Hollywood Now Plays Cowboys and Arabs." *New York Times*, November 1, 1998, AR:17+.

Gregorian, Vartan. *Islam: A Mosaic, Not a Monolith*. Washington, DC: Brookings Institution Press, 2003.

Halaby, Laila. *West of the Jordan*. Boston: Beacon Press, 2003.

Miller, John, and Aaron Kenedi. *Inside Islam: The Faith, the People, and the Conflicts of the World's Fastest Growing Religion*. New York: Marlow and Company, 2002.

Nye, Naomi Shihab. "Muchas Gracias por Todo." In *Fuel: Poems by Naomi Shihab Nye*. Rochester, NY: BOA Editions, 1998.

———. *Words under the Words: Selected Poems*. Portland, OR: Eighth Mountain Press, 1995.

Shaheen, Jack G. *Reel Bad Arabs: How Hollywood Vilifies a People*. New York: Olive Branch Press, 2001.

Suleiman, Michael W., ed. "Introduction: The Arab Immigrant Experience." In *Arabs in America: Building a New Future*. Philadelphia: Temple University Press, 1999.

Gay Culture

Berry, Chris. "The New Face of Taiwanese Cinema: An Interview with Ang Lee, Director of *The Wedding Banquet*." *Metro Magazine* 96 (1993a): 40–41.

————. "Taiwanese Melodrama Returns with a Twist in 'The Wedding Banquet.' " *Cinemaya: The Asian Film Magazine* 21 (Autumn 1993b): 52–54.

Cruikshank, Margaret. *The Gay and Lesbian Liberation Movement*. New York: Routledge, 1992.

Halperin, David, M. "Is There a History of Sexuality?" In *The Lesbian and Gay Studies Reader*, eds. Henri Abelove, Michele Aina Barale, and David M. Halperin. New York: Routledge, 1993.

Lustig, Myron W., and Jolene Koester. *Intercultural Competence: Interpersonal Communication across Cultures*. 4th ed. Boston: Allyn and Bacon, 2003.

Newman, Leslea. *Heather Has Two Mommies*. New York: Alyson Books, 1989.

Schamus, James. *Two Films by Ang Lee*. New York: Overlook Press, 1994.

Shapiro, Michele. "Wedding-Bell Blues." *New York* 26, no. 30 (August 2, 1993) 19.

Valentine, Johnny. *The Daddy Machine*. New York: Alyson Books, 2004.

Willhoite, Michael. *Daddy's Roommate*. New York: Alyson Books, 1990.

Deaf Culture

Attanasio, Paul. "Randa Haines' Inner Voice; Overcoming the Obstacles to Direct 'Children of a Lesser God.'" *The Washington Post*, October 12, 1986, F1.

Deaf Culture Lecture #81: Cultural Differences. Perf. Nathie Marbury. Prod. Sign Enhancers Products. Videocassette. ASL Productions, Inc., 1994.

Dolnick, Edward. "Deafness as Culture." *Atlantic Monthly* (September 1993): 37.

Holcomb, Roy, Samuel K. Holcomb, and Thomas K. Holcomb. *Deaf Culture Our Way: Anecdotes from the Deaf Community*. San Diego, CA; DawnSignPress, 1994.

An Introduction to the Deaf Community. Dir. Patrick Graybill. Videocassette. Burtonsville, MD: Sign Media Inc., 1993.

Jepson, Jill. *No Walls of Stone: An Anthology of Literature by Deaf and Hard of Hearing Writers.* Washington, DC: Gallaudet University Press, 1992.

Kehr, Dave. "Director Keeps World of the Deaf at Arm's Length." *Chicago Tribune,* October 3, 1986, 7A.

Knoll, Jack. "Signing: The Language of Love." *Newsweek,* October 20, 1986, 77.

Lane, Harlan, Robert Hoffmeister, and Ben Bahan. *A Journey into the Deaf World.* San Diego, CA: DawnSignPress, 1966.

Matlin, Marlee. *Deaf Child Crossing.* New York: Aladdin Paperbacks, 2002.

Moore, Mathew S., and Linda Levitan. *For Hearing People Only: Answers to Some of the Most Commonly Asked Questions about the Deaf Community, Its Culture, and the 'Deaf Reality.'* 3rd ed. Rochester, NY: Deaf Life Press, 1993.

Noonan, David. "A Little Bit Louder Please." *Newsweek,* June 6, 2005, 42–49.

Shapiro, Joseph P. *No Pity: People with Disabilities Forging a New Civil Rights Movement.* New York: Random House, 1993.

Signing Made Easy!: How to Talk to a Person Who Can't Hear. Dir. Brady Connell. Perf. Anthony Natale. 1996. DVD. C J Productions, 2005.

Solomon, Andrew. "Deaf Is Beautiful." *New York Times Magazine,* August 28, 1994, 44.

Spotnitz, F. "Randa Haines." *American Film* 17, no. 1 (1992): 18–20.

Walker, Lou Ann. "Breaking the Silence." *The Ladies Home Journal,* April 1989, 42+.

———. *A Loss for Words: The Story of Deafness in a Family.* New York: Harper and Row, 1987.

Creating Community

Dorris, Michael. "For Indians No Thanksgiving." In *Paper Trail: Essays.* New York: HarperCollins Publishers, 1994: 228–31.

Eck, Diana L. *A New Religious America: How a "Christian Country" Has Become the World's Most Religiously Diverse Nation.* San Francisco: HarperSanFrancisco, 2001.

Rich, Ruby B. "A Thanksgiving Feast with a Rainbow of Flavors." *New York Times,* November 12, 2000, AR28.

Welton, Neva, and Linda Wolf. *Global Uprising: Stories from a New Generation of Activists*. Gabriola Island, BC: New Society Publishers, 2001.

Appendix B

Dresser, Norine. *Multicultural Manners: New Rules of Etiquette for a Changing Society*. New York: John Wiley and Sons, 1996.